An Introduction to Qu
Text Analysis for Ling

An Introduction to Quantitative Text Analysis for Linguistics: Reproducible Research Using R is a pragmatic textbook that equips students and researchers with the essential concepts and practical programming skills needed to conduct quantitative text analysis in a reproducible manner. Designed for undergraduate students and those new to the field, this book assumes no prior experience with statistics or programming, making it an accessible resource for anyone embarking on their journey into quantitative text analysis.

Through a pedagogical approach which emphasizes intuitive understanding over technical details, readers will gain data literacy by learning to identify, interpret, and evaluate data analysis procedures and results. They will also develop research skills, enabling them to design, implement, and communicate quantitative text analysis projects effectively. The book places a strong emphasis on programming skills, guiding readers through interactive lessons, tutorials, and lab activities using the R programming language and real-world datasets.

This practical textbook is enriched with features that facilitate learning, including thought and practical exercises, a companion website which includes programming demonstrations to develop and augment readers' recognition of how programming strategies are implemented, and a GitHub repository which contains both a set of interactive R programming lessons and lab exercises, which guide readers through practical hands-on programming applications. This textbook is an essential companion to any linguist looking to learn how to incorporate quantitative data analysis into their work.

Jerid Francom is Associate Professor of Spanish and Linguistics at Wake Forest University. His research focuses on the use of language corpora from a variety of sources (news, social media, and other internet sources) to better understand the linguistic and cultural similarities and differences between language varieties for both scholarly and pedagogical projects. He has published on topics including the development, annotation, and evaluation of linguistic corpora and analyzed corpora through corpus, psycholinguistic, and computational methodologies. He also has experience working with and teaching statistical programming with R.

An Introduction to Quantitative Text Analysis for Linguistics

Reproducible Research Using R

Jerid Francom 0000-0001-5972-6330

Routledge
Taylor & Francis Group
LONDON AND NEW YORK

Designed cover image: Getty Images | Man As Thep

First published 2025
by Routledge
4 Park Square, Milton Park, Abingdon, Oxon OX14 4RN

and by Routledge
605 Third Avenue, New York, NY 10158

Routledge is an imprint of the Taylor & Francis Group, an informa business

British Library Cataloguing-in-Publication Data
A catalogue record for this book is available from the British Library

ISBN: 978-1-032-49427-2 (hbk)
ISBN: 978-1-032-49426-5 (pbk)
ISBN: 978-1-003-39376-4 (ebk)

DOI: 10.4324/9781003393764

Typeset in Palatino/ Hack
by Jerid Francom

Publisher's Note
This book has been prepared from camera-ready copy provided by the author.

Visit the web and companion sites at qtalr.com and qtalr.com/resources/.

Contents

Acknowledgments

The journey of creating this textbook has been both challenging and rewarding, and it would not have been possible without the inspiration, support, and invaluable feedback from many individuals. First and foremost, I extend my deepest gratitude to my students at Wake Forest University. Your enthusiasm and curiosity have been a constant source of inspiration, pushing me to address my blind spots and meet your needs more effectively.

I am particularly grateful for the generous feedback from the following individuals, whose insights and suggestions have significantly shaped the development of this book: Laura Aull, Andrea Bowling, Caroline Brady, Declan Golsen, Logan Jacobs, Abby Komiske, Asya Little, Elaine Lu, Jack Nelson, and Sicheng Wang. Your contributions have been instrumental in refining the content and making it more accessible and engaging for future readers.

A special thanks to my colleague and spouse, Dr. Claudia Valdez, for her unwavering support, encouragement, and patience throughout this project. Your feedback and guidance have been invaluable, and I am grateful for your willingness to engage in countless discussions about the content, structure, and pedagogical approach of this book. Most importantly, thank you for your love and understanding, which have sustained me through the ups and downs of this journey.

Finally, I would like to express my appreciation to the R community, especially the developers and contributors of the {tidyverse} and {tidymodels} packages. Your dedication to creating user-friendly and powerful tools for data analysis has revolutionized the field of quantitative text analysis and made it accessible to a broader audience.

Preface

Outcomes

- Comprehend the book's rationale, learning goals, and pedagogical approach.
- Navigate and engage with the book's structure and content effectively.
- Set up the computing environment and utilize textbook and support resources for an optimal learning experience.

The purpose of this preface is to present the rationale behind this textbook, outline the key learning objectives, describe the pedagogical approach, and identify the intended audience. Additionally, this chapter will provide readers with a guide to the book's structure and the scope of its content, as well as a summary of supporting learning and instructor resources. Finally, this chapter will provide readers with information on setting up their computing environment and where to seek support.

Rationale

Data science, an interdisciplinary field that combines knowledge and skills from statistics, computer science, and domain-specific expertise to extract meaningful insight from structured and unstructured data, has emerged as an exciting and rapidly growing field in recent years, driven in large part by the increase in computing power available to the average individual and the abundance of electronic data now available through the internet. These advances have become an integral part of the modern scientific landscape, with data-driven insights now being used to inform decision-making in a wide variety of academic fields, including linguistics and language-related disciplines.

This textbook seeks to meet this growing demand by providing an introduction to the fundamental concepts and practical programming skills from data science applied to the task of quantitative text analysis. It is intended primarily for undergraduate students, but may also be useful for graduates and

10.4324/9781003393764.0

researchers seeking to expand their methodological toolbox. The textbook takes a pedagogical approach which assumes no prior experience with statistics or programming, making it an accessible resource for novices beginning their exploration of quantitative text analysis methods.

Aims

The overarching goal of this textbook is to provide readers with foundational knowledge and practical skills to conduct and evaluate quantitative text analysis using the R programming language and other open source tools and technologies. The specific aims are to develop the reader's proficiency in three main areas:

- **Data literacy**: Identify, interpret and evaluate data analysis procedures and results.
  Throughout this textbook we will explore topics which will help you understand how data analysis methods derive insight from data. In this process you will be encouraged to critically evaluate connections across linguistic and language-related disciplines using data analysis knowledge and skills. Data literacy is an invaluable skillset for academics and professionals but also is indispensable for 21st-century citizens to navigate and actively participate in the "Information Age" in which we live (Carmi, Yates, Lockley, & Pawluczuk, 2020).
- **Research skills**: Design, implement, and communicate quantitative text analysis research.
  This aim does not differ significantly, in spirit, from common learning outcomes in a research methods course. However, working with text will incur a series of key steps in the selection, collection, and preparation of the data that are unique to text analysis projects. In addition, I will stress the importance of research documentation and creating reproducible research as an integral part of modern scientific inquiry (Buckheit & Donoho, 1995).
- **Programming skills**: Develop and apply programming skills to text analysis tasks in a reproducible manner.
  Modern data analysis, and by extension, text analysis is conducted using programming. There are various key reasons for this: a programming approach (1) affords researchers unlimited research freedom —if you can envision it, you can program it, (2) underlies well-documented and reproducible research (Gandrud, 2015), and (3) invites researchers to engage more intimately with the data and the methods for analysis.

These aims are important for linguistics students because they provide a foundation for concepts and in the skills required to succeed in the rapidly evolving landscape of 21st-century research. These abilities enable researchers to evaluate and conduct high-quality empirical investigation across linguistic fields on a wide variety of topics. Moreover, these skills go beyond linguistics research; they are widely applicable across many disciplines where quantitative data analysis and programming are becoming increasingly important. Thus, this textbook provides students with a comprehensive introduction to quantitative text analysis that is relevant to linguistics research and that equips them with valuable skills for their future careers.

Approach

The approach taken in this textbook is designed to accommodate linguistics students and researchers with little to no prior experience with programming or quantitative methods. With this in mind the objective is connect conceptual understanding with practical application. Real-world data and research tasks relevant to linguistics are used throughout the book to provide context and to motivate the learning process[1]. Furthermore, as an introduction to the field, the textbook focuses on the most common and fundamental methods and techniques for quantitative text analysis and prioritizes breadth over depth and intuitive understanding over technical explanations. On the programming side, the **Tidyverse** approach to programming in will be adopted (Wickham, 2014b). This approach provides a consistent syntax across different packages and is known for its legibility, making it easier for readers to understand and write code. Together, these strategies form an approach that is intended to provide readers with an accessible resource to gain a foothold in the field and to equip them with the knowledge and skills to apply quantitative text analysis in their own research.

Structure

The aims and approach described above are reflected in the overall structure of the book and each chapter.

[1]Research data and questions are primarily based on English for wide accessibility as it is the *de facto* language of academics and research. However, the methods and techniques presented in this textbook are applicable to many other languages.

Book level

At the book level, there are five interdependent parts:

Part I "Orientation" provides the necessary background knowledge to situate quantitative text analysis in the wider context of data analysis and linguistic research and to provide a clearer picture of what text analysis entails and its range of applications.

The subsequent parts are directly aligned with the data analysis process. The building blocks of this process are reflected in **'Data to Insight Hierarchy (DIKI)'** visualized in Figure 0.1.

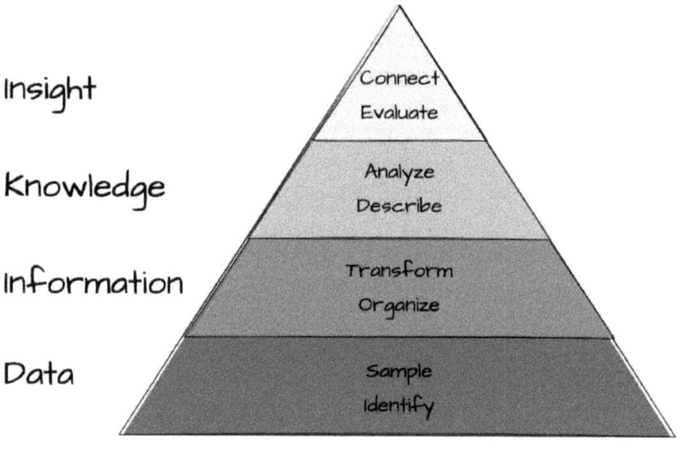

Figure 0.1: Data to Insight Hierarchy (DIKI)[2]

The DIKI Hierarchy highlights the stages and intermediate steps required to derive insight from data. Part II "Foundations" provides a conceptual introduction to the DIKI Hierarchy and establishes foundational knowledge about data, information, knowledge, and insight which is fundamental to developing a viable research plan.

Parts III "Preparation" and IV "Analysis" focus on the implementation process. Part III covers the steps involved in preparing data for analysis, including data acquisition, curation, and transformation. Part IV covers the steps involved in conducting analysis, including exploratory, predictive, and inferential data analysis.

The final part, Part V "Communication", covers the final stage of the data analysis process, which is to communicate the results of the analysis. This includes the structure and content of research reports as well as the process of publishing, sharing, and collaborating on research.

[2]Adapted from Ackoff (1989) and Rowley (2007).

Chapter level

At the chapter level, both conceptual and programming skills are developed in stages[3]. The chapter-level structure is consistent across chapters and can be seen in Table 0.1.

Table 0.1: The general structure and learning progression of a chapter

Component	Purpose	Resource	Stage
Outcomes	Identify the learning objectives for the chapter	Textbook	Indicate
Overview	Provide a brief introduction to the chapter topic	Textbook	Outline
Coding Lessons	Teach programming techniques with hands-on interactive exercises	GitHub	Interact
Content	Combine conceptual discussions and programming skills, incorporating thought-provoking questions, relevant studies, and advanced topic references	Textbook	Explore
Recipes	Offer step-by-step programming examples related to the chapter and relevant for the upcoming lab	Resources Kit website	Examine
Labs	Allow readers to apply chapter-specific concepts and techniques to practical tasks	GitHub	Apply
Summary	Review the key concepts and skills covered in the chapter	Textbook	Review

Each chapter will begin with a list of key learning outcomes followed by a brief introduction to the chapter's content. The goal is to orient the reader to the chapter. Next there will be a prompt to complete the interactive coding lesson(s) to introduce readers to key programming concepts related to the chapter though hands-on experience and then the main content of the chapter will follow. The content will be a combination of conceptual discussions and programming skills, incorporating thought-provoking questions ('Consider this'), relevant studies ('Case study'), and advanced topic references ('Dive deeper'). Together these components form the skills and knowledge phase.

The next phase is the application phase. This phase will include step-by-step programming demonstrations related to the chapter (Recipes) and lab exercises that allow readers to apply their knowledge and skills to chapter-related tasks. Finally, the chapters conclude with a summary of the key concepts and skills covered in the chapter and in the associated activities.

[3]These stages attempt to capture the general progression of learning reflected in Bloom's Taxonomy. See Krathwohl (2002) for a description and revised version.

Resources

The description and location of the available resources to support the aims and approach of this textbook appear in Table 0.2.

Table 0.2: Resources available to support the aims and approach of this textbook

Resource	Description	Location
Textbook	Prose discussion, figures/ tables, R code, case studies, and thought and practical exercises	Physical/ Web[4]
{qtkit}	R package with functions for accessing data and datasets, as well as various useful functions developed specifically for this textbook	CRAN/ GitHub
Resources Kit	Includes Recipes, programming tutorials to enhance the reader's recognition of how programming strategies are implemented, and other supplementary materials including setup Guides, and Instructor materials	GitHub
Lessons	A set of interactive R programming lessons associated with each chapter	GitHub
Labs	A set of lab exercises designed to direct the reader through practical hands-on programming applications	GitHub

All resources are freely available and accessible to readers and are found on the GitHub organization https://github.com/qtalr/. For the textbook and Resources Kit, the code and a link to the website are provided in each respective repository. The development version of the {qtkit} package is available on GitHub and the stable version is available on the Comprehensive R Archive Network (CRAN) (Francom, 2024). The interactive programming lessons and lab exercises are also available on GitHub. Errata should be reported in the respective repository's issue tracker on GitHub.

Getting started

Before jumping in to this and subsequent chapter's textbook activities, it is important to prepare your computing environment and understand how to take advantage of the resources available, both those directly and indirectly associated with the textbook.

[4]https://qtalr.com

R environment

Programming is the backbone for modern quantitative research. Among the many programming languages available, R is a popular open-source language and software environment for statistical computing. R is popular with statisticians and has been adopted as the *de facto* language by many other fields in natural and social sciences, including linguistics. It is freely downloadable from The R Project for Statistical Programming website (The R Foundation, 2024) and is available for macOS, Linux, and Windows operating systems.

Successfully installing R is rarely the last step in setting up your R-enabled computing environment. The majority of R users also install an **integrated development environment** (IDE). An IDE, such as RStudio (Posit, 2024), or a text editor, such as Visual Studio Code (Microsoft, 2024), provide a **graphical user interface** (GUI) for working with R[5]. In effect, these interfaces provide a dashboard for working with R and are designed to make it easier to write and execute R code. IDEs also provide a number of other useful features such as syntax highlighting, code completion, and debugging. IDEs are not required to work with R but they are *highly* recommended.

Choosing to install R and an IDE directly on your personal computer, which is know as your **local environment**, is not the only option to work with R. Other options include working with R in a **remote environment** or a **virtual environment**.

> **Guides** For more information and instructions on setting up an R environment for using this book, consult the Resources Kit "Setting up an R environment" guide.

There are trade-offs in terms of cost, convenience, and flexibility when choosing to work with R in a local, remote, or virtual environment. The choice is yours and you can always change your mind later. The important thing is to get started and begin learning R. Furthermore, any of the approaches described here will be compatible with this textbook.

R packages

As you progress in your R programming experience, you'll find yourself leveraging code from other R users, which is typically provided as packages. Packages are sets of functions and/or datasets that are freely accessible for download, designed to perform a specific set of interrelated tasks. They

[5]For those who prefer a terminal-based text editor, Neovim is a popular choice. Neovim is a text editor that is designed to be extensible and customizable. It is a modern version of the classic Vim text editor.

enhance the capabilities of R. Official R packages can be found in repositories like CRAN (R Community, 2024) or R-universe (ROpenSci, 2024), while other packages can be obtained from code-sharing platforms such as GitHub (GitHub, 2024).

> **Consider this**
> CRAN includes groupings of popular packages related to a given applied programming task called Task Views https://cran.r-project.org/web/views/. Explore the available CRAN Task Views listings. Note the variety of areas (tasks) that are covered in this listing. Now explore in more detail one of the following task views which are directly related to topics covered in this textbook noting the associated packages and their descriptions: (1) Cluster, (2) MachineLearning, (3) NaturalLanguageProcessing, or (4) ReproducibleResearch.

You will download a number of packages at different stages of this textbook, but there is a set of packages that will be key to have from the get go. Once you have access to a working R environment, you can proceed to install the following packages.

> **Guides**
> For instructions on how to install the qtkit package from CRAN or GitHub and download and use the interactive R programming lessons for this textbook, see the Resources Kit "Getting started" guide.

Install the following packages from CRAN.

- tidyverse (Wickham, 2023c)
- tinytex (Xie, 2024)
- swirl (Kross, Carchedi, Bauer, & Grdina, 2020)
- qtkit (Francom, 2024)

You can do this by running Example 0.1 in an R console:

Example 0.1.

```
# install key packages from CRAN
install.packages(c("tidyverse", "tinytex", "swirl", "qtkit"))
```

Git and GitHub

GitHub is a code sharing website. Modern computing is highly collaborative and GitHub is a very popular platform for sharing and collaborating on coding projects. The lab exercises for this textbook are shared on GitHub. To access and complete these exercises you will need to sign up for a (free) account and then set up the version control software Git on your computing environment.

Guides
For more information and instructions on setting up version control and interacting with GitHub consult the Resources Kit "Setting up Git and GitHub" guide.

Getting help

The technologies employed in this approach to text analysis will include a somewhat steep learning curve. And in all honesty, the learning never stops! Both seasoned programmers and beginners alike need assistance. Fortunately, there is a very large community of programmers who have developed many official support resources and who actively contribute to official and unofficial discussion forums. Together these resources provide many avenues for overcoming challenges.

In Table 0.3, I provide a list of steps for seeking help with R.

Table 0.3: Recommended order for seeking help with R

Step	Resource	Description
1	Official R Documentation	Access the official documentation by running `help(package = "package_name")` in an R console. Use the `?` operator followed by the package or function name. Check out available Vignettes by running `browseVignettes("package_name")`.
2	Web Search	Look for package documentation and vignettes on the web. A popular site for this is R-Universe.
3	RStudio Help Toolbar	If you're using RStudio, use the "Help" toolbar menu. It provides links to help resources, guides, and manuals.
4	Online Discussion Forums	Sites like Stack Overflow and RStudio Community are great platforms where the programming community asks and answers questions related to real-world issues.
5	Post Questions with Reprex	When posting a question, especially those involving coding issues or errors, provide enough background and include a reproducible example (reprex) —a minimal piece of code that demonstrates your issue. This helps others understand and answer your question effectively.

Guides
For information on how to create a minimal reproducible example with the {reprex} package (Bryan, Hester, Robinson, Wickham, & Dervieux, 2024), consult the Resources Kit "Creating reproducible examples" guide.

The take-home message here is that you are not alone. There are many people world-wide that are learning to program and/or contribute to the learning of others. The more you engage with these resources and communities the more successful your learning will be. As soon as you are able, pay it forward. Posting questions and offering answers helps the community and engages and refines your skills —a win-win.

Conventions

To facilitate the learning process, this textbook will employ a number of conventions. These conventions are intended to help the reader navigate the text and to signal the reader's attention to important concepts and information.

Prose

The following typographic conventions are used throughout the text:

- *Italics*
  - File names, file extensions, directory paths, and URLs.
- `Fixed-width`
  - Function names, variable and object names, and in-line code including expressions and operators.
- {Curly brackets}
  - R package names
- **Bold**
  - Key concepts when first introduced.
- Linked text[6]
  - Links to internal and external resources and footnotes.

Code blocks

More lengthy code will be presented in code blocks, as seen in Example 0.2.

Example 0.2.

```
# A function that takes a name and returns a greeting
greetings <- function(name) {
  paste("Hello", name)
}

```

[6]https://qtalr.com/resources/

```r
# Apply function to a name
greetings(name = "R user")
```

```
[1] "Hello R user"
```

There are a couple of things to note about the code in Example 0.2. First, it shows the code that is run in R as well as the output that is returned. The code will appear in a box and the output will appear below the box. Both code and output will appear in fixed-width font. Second, the # symbol within a code block is used to signal a **code comment**, a human-facing description. Everything right of a # is not run as code. In this textbook you will see code comments above code on a separate line and/or to the right of code on the same line. It is good practice to comment your code to enhance readability and to help others understand what your code is doing.

All figures, tables, and images in this textbook are generated by code blocks, but only code for those elements that are relevant for discussion will be shown. However, if you wish to see the code for any element in this textbook, you can visit the GitHub repository https://qtalr.github.io/book/.

When referencing a file or portion of a file, it will appear as in Snippet 0.1.

Snippet 0.1. *example.R* file

```r
# Load package
library(tidyverse)

# Add 1 and 1
1 + 1
```

Callouts

Callouts are used to signal the reader's attention to content, activity, and other important sections. The following callouts are used in this textbook:

Content

Outcomes
Learning outcomes for the chapter.

Consider this
Points to consider and questions to explore.

Case study
Case studies which highlight conceptual knowledge and coding skills.

Dive deeper
Additional comments and resources for diving deeper into a topic.

Activities

Lessons
Links to interactive lessons for practicing coding skills.

Recipe
Reading to examine programming concepts.

Lab
Exercises for applying conceptual knowledge and coding skills.

Other

Tip
Tips for using R and related tools.

Warning
Warnings for using R and related tools.

Activities

At this point you should have a working R environment with the core packages including {qtkit} installed. You should also have verified that you have a working Git environment and that you have a GitHub account. If you have not completed these tasks, return to the guides listed above in "Getting started" of this Preface and complete them before proceeding.

The following activities are designed to help you become familiar with the tools and resources that you will be using throughout this textbook. These and subsequent activities are designed to be completed in the order that they are presented in this textbook.

>_ Lessons
What: Intro to Swirl
How: In the R console load {swirl}, run `swirl()`, and follow prompts to select the lesson.
Why: To familiarize you with navigating, selecting, and completing swirl lessons for interactive R programming tutorials.

Recipe
What: Literate Programming and Quarto
How: Read Recipe 0, complete comprehension check, and prepare for Lab 0.
Why: To introduce the concept of Literate Programming and how to create literate documents using R and Quarto.

Lab
What: Writing with code
How: Clone, fork, and complete the steps in Lab 0.
Why: To put literate programming techniques covered in Recipe 0 into practice. Specifically, you will create and edit a Quarto document and render a report in PDF format.

Summary

This preface outlines the textbook's underlying principles, learning goals, teaching methods, and target audience. The chapter also offers advice on how to navigate the book's layout, comprehend its subject matter, and make use of supplementary materials. With this foundation, you're now prepared to dig into quantitative text analysis. I hope you enjoy the journey!

To the instructor

For recommendations on how to use this textbook in your course and to access additional resources, visit the Resources Kit "Instructor Guide". The guide provides information on how to structure your course, how to use the textbook, and how to access additional resources to support your teaching.

Part I

Orientation

In this introductory part, we explore fundamental concepts that are essential for understanding text analysis in its research and methodological context. We start by pointing to the limitations of human cognition in processing vast amounts of information and that underscore the need for scientific methods to objectively analyze data. A brief history of quantitative data analysis highlights the commonalities between text analysis and other quantitative methods. We then discuss the role of quantitative methods in language research, and how text analysis contributes to the field.

1

Text analysis

Outcomes

- Understand the role and goals of data analysis both within and outside of academia.
- Describe the various approaches to quantitative language research.
- Identify the applications of text analysis in different contexts.

In this chapter, I introduce the topic of text analysis and provide the context needed to understand how it fits in a larger universe of science and the ever-ubiquitous methods of data science. Approaches to language analysis, including methodological approaches and the nature of data, are discussed. I then introduce text analysis as a branch of data science and discuss its aims, approaches, implementation, and applications.

>_ Lessons
What: Workspace, Vectors
How: In an R console load {swirl}, run `swirl()`, and follow prompts to select the lesson.
Why: To examine your local workspace in RStudio and understand the relationship between your R workspace and the file system of your computing environment. To explore the key building blocks of the R programming language.

1.1 Enter science

The world around us is full of countless actions and interactions. As individuals, we experience this world, gaining knowledge and building heuristic understanding of how it works. Our minds process countless sensory inputs, which enable skills and abilities that we often take for granted, such as predicting what will happen if someone is about to knock a wine glass off a table and onto a concrete floor. Even if we have never encountered this specific situation before, our minds somehow instinctively make an effort to warn the potential glass-breaker before it is too late.

10.4324/9781003393764.1

You may have attributed this predictive knowledge to 'common sense'. Despite its commonality, it is an incredible display of the brain's capacity to monitor the environment, make connections, and store information without consciously informing us about its processes.

Our brains are efficient but not infallible. They do not store every experience in raw form; we don't have access to records like a computer would. Instead, our brains excel in making associations and predictions that help us navigate the complex world we inhabit. In addition, our brains are prone to biases that can influence our understanding of the world. For example, confirmation bias leads us to seek out information that confirms our beliefs, while the availability heuristic causes us to overestimate the likelihood of easily recalled events.

Our brains are doing some amazing work, but that work can give us the impression that we understand the world better and in more detail than we actually do. In this way, what we think the world is like and what the world is actually like can be two different things. This is problematic for making sense of the world in an objective way. This is where science comes in.

Consider this

How might your own experiences and biases influence your understanding of the world? What are some ways that you can mitigate these biases? Is it ever possible to be completely objective? How might biases influence the way you approach text analysis?

Science starts with a question, identifies and collects data, carefully selected slices of the complex world, submits this data to analysis through clearly defined and reproducible procedures, and reports the results for others to evaluate. This process is repeated, modifying, and manipulating the procedures, asking new questions and positing new explanations, all in an effort to make inroads to bring the complex into tangible view.

In essence what science does is attempt to subvert our inherent limitations by drawing on carefully and purposefully collected samples of observable experience and letting the analysis of these observations speak, even if it goes against our intuitions (those powerful but sometime spurious heuristics that our brains use to make sense of the world).

1.2 Data analysis

1.2.1 Emergence of data science

This science I've described is the one you are likely quite familiar with and, if you are like me, this description of science conjures visions of white coats, labs, and petri dishes. While science's foundation still stands strong in the 21st century, a series of intellectual and technological events mid-20th century set in motion changes that have changed aspects about how science is done, not why it is done. We could call this Science 2.0, but let's use the more popularized term **data science**.

The recognized beginnings of data science are attributed to work in the "Statistics and Data Analysis Research" department at Bell Labs during the 1960s. Although primarily conceptual and theoretic at the time, a framework for quantitative data analysis took shape that would anticipate what would come: sizable datasets which would "[...] require advanced statistical and computational techniques [...] and the software to implement them." (Chambers, 2020) This framework emphasized both the inference-based research of traditional science, but also embraced exploratory research and recognized the need to address practical considerations that would arise when working with and deriving insight from an abundance of machine-readable data.

Fast-forward to the 21st century, a world in which machine-readable data is truly in abundance. With increased computing power, the emergence of the internet, and the wide adoption of mobile devices, electronic communication skyrocketed around the globe. To put this in perspective, in 2019 it was estimated that every minute 511 thousand tweets were posted, 18.1 million text messages were sent, and 188 million emails were sent ("Data never sleeps 7.0," 2019). The data flood has not been limited to language, there are more sensors and recording devices than ever before which capture evermore swaths of the world we live in (Desjardins, 2019).

Where increased computing power gave rise to the influx of data, it is also one of the primary methods for gathering, preparing, transforming, analyzing, and communicating insight derived from this data (Donoho, 2017). The vision laid out in the 1960s at Bell Labs had come to fruition.

1.2.2 Data science toolbelt

Data science is not predicated on data alone. Turning data into insight takes computing skills, statistical knowledge, and domain expertise. This triad has been popularly represented as a Venn diagram such as in Figure 1.1.

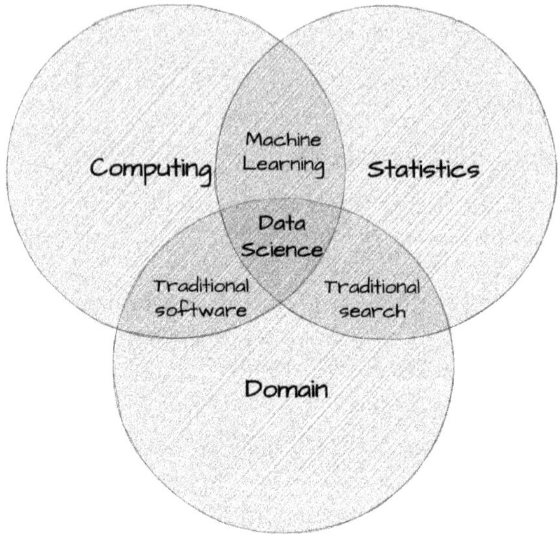

Figure 1.1: Data science Venn diagram adapted from D. Conway (2010).

The **computing skills** component of data science is the ability to write code to perform the data analysis process. This is the primary approach for working with data at scale. The **statistical knowledge** component of data science is the ability to apply statistical methods to data to derive insight by bringing patterns and relationships in the data into view. **Domain expertise** provides researchers insight at key junctures in the development of a research project and aids researchers in evaluating results.

This triad of skills in combination with reproducible research practices is the foundational toolbelt of data science (Hicks & Peng, 2019). **Reproducible research** entails the use of computational tools to automate the process of data analysis. This automation is achieved by writing code that can be executed to replicate the data analysis. This code can then be shared through code sharing repositories, where it can be viewed, downloaded, and executed by others. This adds transparency to the process and allows others to build on previous work enhacing scientific progress along the way (Baker, 2016).

1.2.3 Quant everywhere

Equipped with the data science toolbelt, the interest in deriving insight from data is now almost ubiquitous. The science of data has now reached deep into all aspects of life where making sense of the world is sought. Predicting whether a loan applicant will get a loan (Bao, Lianju, & Yue, 2019), whether a lump is cancerous (Saxena & Gyanchandani, 2020), what films to recommend based on your previous viewing history (Gomez-Uribe & Hunt, 2015), what players a sports team should sign (Lewis, 2004), now all incorporate a common set of data analysis tools.

The data science toolbelt also underlies well-known public-facing language applications. From the language-capable chat applications, plagiarism detection software, machine translation algorithms, and search engines, tangible results of quantitative approaches to language are becoming standard fixtures in our lives.

The spread of quantitative data analysis too has taken root in academia. Even in areas that on first blush don't appear readily approachable in a quantitative manner, such as fields in the social sciences and humanities, data science is making important and sometimes disciplinary changes to the way that academic research is conducted.

This textbook focuses in on a domain that cuts across many of these fields; namely language. At this point let's turn to quantitative approaches to language analysis as we work closer to contextualizing text analysis in the field of linguistics.

1.3 Language analysis

1.3.1 Qualities and quantities

Language is a defining characteristic of our species. Since antiquity, language has attracted interest across disciplines and schools of thought. In the early 20th century, the development of the rigorous approach to study of language as a field in its own right took root (Campbell, 2001), yet a plurality of theoretical views and methodological approaches remained. Contemporary linguistics bares this complex history and even today, it is far from a theoretically and methodologically unified discipline.

Either based on the tenets of theoretical frameworks and/or the objects of study of particular fields, methodological approaches to language research vary. On the one hand, some language research commonly applies qualitative assessment of language structure and/or use. **Qualitative approaches** describe and account for characteristics, or "qualities", that can be observed, but not measured (*e.g.* introspective methods, ethnographic methods, *etc.*)

Case study
Manning (2003) discusses the use of probabilistic models in syntax to account for the variability in language usage and the presence of both hard and soft constraints in grammar. The paper touches on the statistical methods in text analysis, the importance of distinguishing between external and internal language, and the limitations of Generative Grammar. Overall, the paper suggests that usage-based and formal syntax can learn from each other to better understand language variation and change.

On the other hand, other language research programs employ quantitative research methods either out of necessity given the object of study (phonetics, psycholinguistics, *etc.*) or based on theoretical principles (cognitive linguistics, connectionism, *etc.*). **Quantitative approaches** involve "quantities" of properties that can be observed and measured (*e.g.* frequency of use, reaction time, *etc.*).

These latter research areas and theoretical paradigms employ methods that share much of the common data analysis toolbox described in the previous section. In effect, this establishes a common methodological language between other language-based research fields but also with research outside of linguistics.

1.3.2 The nature of data

In quantitative language analysis, there is a key methodological distinction between experimental and observational data, which affects both procedure and interpretation of research.

Experimental approaches start with an intentionally designed hypothesis and lay out a research methodology with appropriate instruments and a plan to collect data that shows promise for shedding light on the likelihood of the hypothesis. Experimental approaches are conducted under controlled contexts, usually a lab environment, in which participants are recruited to perform a task with stimuli that have been carefully curated by researchers to elicit some aspect of language behavior of interest. Experimental approaches to language research are heavily influenced by procedures adapted from psychology.

Observational approaches are a bit more of a mixed bag in terms of the rationale for the study; they may either start with a testable hypothesis or in other cases may start with a more open-ended research question to explore. But a more fundamental distinction between the two approaches is drawn in the amount of control the researcher exerts on the contexts and conditions in which the language behavior data to be collected is produced. Observational approaches seek out records of language behavior that is produced by language speakers for communicative purposes in natural(-istic) contexts. This may take place in labs (language development, language disorders, *etc.*), but more often than not, language is collected from sources where speakers are performing language as part of their daily lives —whether that be posting on social media, speaking on the telephone, making political speeches, writing class essays, reporting the latest news for a newspaper, or crafting the next novel destined to be a New York Times best-seller.

The data acquired from either of these approaches have their trade-offs. The directness and level of control of experimental approaches has the benefit of allowing researchers to precisely track how particular experimental conditions effect language behavior. As these conditions are an explicit part of the design, the resulting language behavior can be more precisely attributed to the experimental manipulation.

The primary shortcoming of experimental approaches is that there is a level of artificialness to this directness and control. Whether it is the language materials used in the task, the task itself, or the fact that the procedure takes place under supervision the language behavior elicited can diverge quite significantly from language behavior performed in natural communicative settings.

Observational approaches show complementary strengths and shortcomings, visualized in Figure 1.2. Whereas experimental approaches may diverge from natural language use, observational approaches strive to identify and collected language behavior data in natural, uncontrolled, and unmonitored contexts. This has the benefit of providing a more ecologically valid representation of language behavior.

However, the contexts in which natural language communication take place are complex relative to experimental contexts. Language collected from natural contexts are nested within the complex workings of a complex world and as such inevitably include a host of factors and conditions which can prove challenging to disentangle from the language phenomenon of interest but must be addressed in order to draw reliable associations and conclusions.

The upshot, then, is two-fold: (1) data collection methods matter for research design and interpretation and (2) there is no single best approach to data collection, each have their strengths and shortcomings.

Ideally, a robust science of language will include insight from both experimental and observational approaches (Gilquin & Gries, 2009). And evermore there is greater appreciation for the complementary nature of experimental and observational approaches and a growing body of research which highlights this recognition.

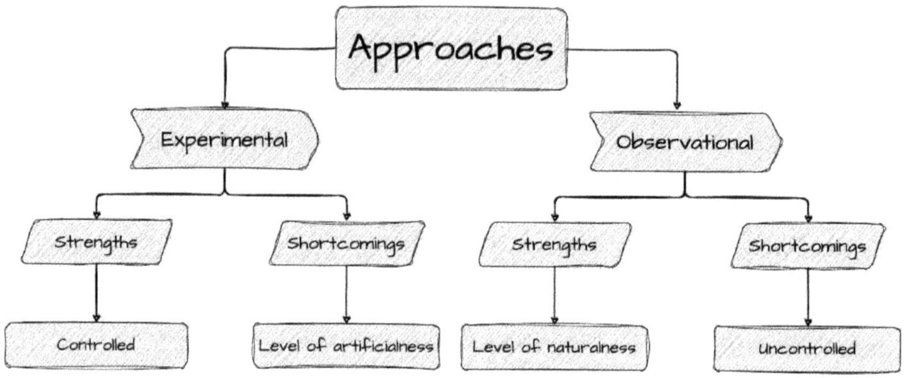

Figure 1.2: Trade-offs between experimental and observational data collection methods

1.4 Text analysis

In a nutshell, **text analysis** is the process of leveraging the data science toolbelt to derive insight from textual data collected via observational methods. In the next subsections, I will unpack this definition and discuss the primary components that make up text analysis including research approaches and technical implementation, as well as practical applications.

1.4.1 Aims

Text analysis is a multifaceted research methodology. It can be used to facilitate the qualitative exploration of smaller, human-digestible textual information, but is more often employed quantitatively to bring to the surface patterns and relationships in large samples of textual data that would be otherwise difficult, if not impossible, to identify manually.

The aims of text analysis are as varied as the research questions that can be asked of language data. Some research questions are data-driven, where the researcher is interested in exploring and uncovering patterns and relationships in the data. Other research questions are theory-driven, where the researcher is interested in testing a hypothesis or evaluating a theory. In either case, the researcher is interested in gaining insight from the data.

The relationship(s) of interest in text analysis may be language internal, where the researcher is interested in the patterns and relationships between linguistic features, or language external, where the researcher is interested in the patterns and relationships between linguistic features and some external variable.

1.4.2 Implementation

Text analysis is a branch of data science. As such, it takes advantage of the data science toolbelt to derive insight from data. It is important to note that, while all of the components of the data science toolbelt are present in text analysis, the relative importance of each varies with the stage research. Computing skills being the most important at the data and information stages, statistical knowledge being the most important to derive knowledge, and domain knowledge leading the way towards insight.

Text is a rather raw form of data. It is more often that not unstructured, meaning that it is not organized in a way such that it can be easily analyzed. The collection, organization, and transformation of text data is a key component of text analysis and computers, are well-suited for this task, as we will see in Chapter 2 and Part III "Preparation".

Once text is transformed to a dataset that can be analyzed, we lean on statistical methods to gain perspective on the relationship(s) of interest. By and large, these methods are the same as those used in other areas of data science. We will provide an overview of these methods in Chapter 3 and do a deeper dive in Part IV "Analysis".

With the results of the analysis in hand, the researcher must interpret the results and evaluate their significance in disciplinary context. This is where domain knowledge comes to the fore. The researcher must be able to interpret the results in light of the research question and the context in which the data was collected and communicate the value of the results to the broader community. Domain knowledge also plays a vital role in framing the research question and designing the research methodology, as we will see in Chapter 4. Then we will return to the role of domain knowledge in interpreting and communicating the results in Part V "Communication".

To ensure that the results of text analysis projects are replicable and transparent, programming strategies and documentation play an integral role at each stage of the implementation of a research project. While there are a number of programming languages that can be used for text analysis, R, widely adopted in linguistics research and is the language of choice for this textbook. R, in combination with literate programming and other tools, provides a robust and reproducible workflow for text analysis projects.

1.4.3 Applications

So what are some applications of text analysis? Most applications stem from Computational Linguistic research, often known as **Natural Language Processing** (NLP) by practitioners. Whether it be using search engines, online translators, submitting your paper to plagiarism detection software, *etc.*, many of the text analysis methods we will cover are at play.

> **Consider this**
> What are some other applications of text analysis that you are aware of? Consider examples from social media, news, entertainment, or other areas of interest. You may also consider how text analysis is used in academia, if you are familiar with any examples.

In academia, the use of quantitative text analysis is even more widespread, despite the lack of public fanfare. In linguistics, text analysis research is often falls under **Corpus Linguistics** (CL). And this approach is applied to a wide range of topics and research questions in both theoretical and applied linguistics fields and subfields, as seen in Examples 1.1 and 1.2.

Example 1.1. Theoretical linguistics

- Hay (2002) use a corpus study to investigate the role of frequency and phonotactics in affix ordering in English.
- Riehemann (2001) explores the extent to which idiomatic expressions (*e.g.* 'raise hell') are lexical or syntactic units.
- Bresnan (2007) investigates the claim that possessed deverbal nouns in English (*e.g.* 'the city's destruction') are subject to a syntactic constraint that requires the possessor to be affected by the action denoted by the deverbal noun.

Example 1.2. Applied linguistics

- Wulff, Stefanowitsch, & Gries (2007) explore differences between British and American English at the lexico-syntactic level in the *into*-causative construction (*e.g.* 'He tricked me into employing him.').
- Eisenstein, O'Connor, Smith, & Xing (2012) track the geographic spread of neologisms (*e.g.* 'bruh', 'af', '-__-') from city to city in the United States using Twitter data collected between 6/2009 and 5/2011.
- Bychkovska & Lee (2017) investigate possible differences between L1-English and L1-Chinese undergraduate students' use of lexical bundles, multiword sequences which are extended collocations (*e.g.* 'as the result of'), in argumentative essays.
- Jaeger & Snider (2007) use a corpus study to investigate the phenomenon of syntactic persistence, the increased tendency for speakers to use a particular syntactic form over an alternate when the syntactic form has been recently processed.

- Voigt et al. (2017) explore potential racial disparities in officer respect in police body camera footage.
- Olohan (2008) investigates the extent to which translated texts imbue more information than source texts through a process known as 'explicitation'.

So too, text analysis is used in a variety of fields outside of linguistics where insight from language is sought, as seen in Example 1.3.

Example 1.3. Language-related fields

- Kloumann, Danforth, Harris, & Bliss (2012) explore the extent to which languages are positively, neutrally, or negatively biased.
- Mosteller & Wallace (1963) provide a method for solving the authorship debate surrounding The Federalist papers.
- L. G. Conway et al. (2012) investigate whether the established drop in language complexity of rhetoric in election seasons is associated with election outcomes.

> **Consider this**
> Language is a key component of human communication and interaction. What are some other areas of research in and outside linguistics that you think could be explored using text analysis methods?

These studies in Examples 1.1, 1.2, and 1.3 are just a few illustrations of the contributions of text analysis used as the primary method to gain a deeper understanding of language structure, function, variation, and acquisition.

As a method, however, text analysis can also be used to support other research methods. For example, text analysis can be used to collect data, generate authentic materials, provide linguistic annotation, and generate hypotheses, for either qualitative or quantitative approaches. Together these efforts contribute to a more robust language science by incorporating externally valid language data and materials and support methodological triangulation in language research (Francom, 2022).

In sum, the applications highlighted in this section underscore the versatility of text analysis as a research method. Whether it be in the public sphere or in academia, text analysis methods furnish a set of powerful tools for gaining insight into the nature of language.

Actitivies

The following activities build on your introduction to R and Quarto in the preface. In these activities you will uncover more features offered by Quarto which will enhance your ability to produce comprehensive reproducible research documents. You will apply the capabilities of Quarto in a practical context conveying the objectives and key discoveries from a primary research article.

Recipe
What: Academic writing with Quarto
How: Read Recipe 1, complete comprehension check, and prepare for Lab 1.
Why: To explore additional functionality in Quarto: numbered sections, table of contents, in-line citations and a document-final references list, and cross-referenced tables and figures.

Lab
What: Crafting scholarly documents
How: Clone, fork, and complete the steps in Lab 1.
Why: To put into practice Quarto functionality to communicate the aim(s) and main finding(s) from a primary research article.

Summary

In this chapter, I started with some general observations about the difficulty of making sense of a complex world. The standard approach to overcoming inherent human limitations in sense making is science. In the 21st century the toolbelt for doing scientific research and exploration has grown in terms of the amount of data available, the statistical methods for analyzing the data, and the computational power to manage, store, and share the data, methods, and results from quantitative research. The methods and tools for deriving insight from data have made significant inroads in and outside academia, and increasingly figure in the quantitative investigation of language. Text analysis is a particular branch of this enterprise based on observational data from real-world language and is used in a wide variety of fields.

Part II

Foundations

Before working on the specifics of a data project, it is important to establish a solid understanding of the characteristics of each of the levels in the "Data, Information, Knowledge, and Insight Hierarchy (DIKI)" and the roles each of these levels have in deriving insight from data. In Chapter 2, we will explore the data and information levels drawing a distinction between two main types of data and then cover how data is structured and transformed to generate information that is fit for statistical analysis. In Chapter 3, I will outline the importance and distinct types of statistical procedures that are commonly used in text analysis. Chapter 4 aims to tie these concepts together and cover the required steps for preparing a research blueprint to guide the implementation of a text analysis project.

2

Data

Outcomes

- Describe the difference between data and information.
- Understand how the tidy approach to data organization can enhance the quality and usability of data.
- Articulate the importance of documentation in promoting reproducible research.

In this chapter, I lay the groundwork for deriving insights from text analysis by focusing on content and structure of data and information. The concepts of populations and samples are introduced, highlighting their similarities and key differences. Connecting these topics to text analysis, language samples, or corpora, are explored, discussing their types, sources, formats, and ethical considerations. Subsequently, I highlight key concepts in creating information from corpus data, such as organization and transformation. Documentation in quantitative research is emphasized addressing the importance of data origin files and data dictionaries.

>_ Lessons

What: Objects, Packages and functions
How: In an R console, load {swirl}, run `swirl()`, and follow prompts to select the lesson.
Why: To introduce you to the main types of objects in R and to understand the role and use of functions and packages in R programming.

10.4324/9781003393764.2

2.1 Data

Data is data, right? The term 'data' is so common in popular vernacular it is easy to assume we know what we mean when we say 'data'. But as in most things in science, where there are common assumptions there are important details that require more careful consideration. Let's turn to the first key distinction that we need to make to start to break down the term 'data': the difference between populations and samples.

2.1.1 Populations and samples

The first thing that comes to many people's mind when the term population is used is human populations (derived from Latin 'populus'). Say for example we pose the question —What's the population of Milwaukee? When we speak of a population in these terms we are talking about the total sum of individuals living within the geographical boundaries of Milwaukee. In concrete terms, a **population** is an idealized set of objects or events in reality which share a common characteristic or belong to a specific category. The term to highlight here is idealized. Although we can look up the US Census report for Milwaukee and retrieve a figure for the population, this cannot truly be the population. Why is that? Well, whatever method that was used to derive this numerical figure was surely incomplete. If not incomplete, by the time someone recorded the figure some number of residents of Milwaukee moved out, moved in, were born, or passed away. In either case, this example serves to point out that populations are not fixed and are subject to change over time.

Likewise when we talk about populations in terms of language we are dealing with an idealized aspect of linguistic reality. Let's take the words of the English language as an analog to our previous example population. In this case the words are the people and English is the grouping characteristic. Just as people, words move out, move in, are born, and pass away. Any compendium of the words of English at any moment is almost instantaneously incomplete. This is true for all populations, save those relatively rare cases in which the grouping characteristics select a narrow slice of reality which is objectively measurable and whose membership is fixed (the complete works of Shakespeare, for example).

Therefore, (most) populations are amorphous moving targets. We subjectively hold them to exist, but in practical terms we often cannot nail down the specifics of populations. So how do researchers go about studying populations if they are theoretically impossible to access directly? The strategy employed is called sampling.

A **sample** is the product of a subjective process of selecting a finite set of observations from an idealized population with the goal of capturing the relevant characteristics of this population. When we talk about data in data science, we are talking about samples.

Whether selecting a sample for your research or evaluating a sample used in someone else's research, there are two key characteristics to consider: the sampling frame and the representativeness. The **sampling frame** is the set of characteristics that define the population of interest. The **representativeness** is the degree to which the sample reflects the characteristics of the population. Both of these concern bias, albeit in different ways. By defining the population, a sampling frame sets the boundaries of the population and therefore the scope of research based on the sample. This bias is not a bad thing, in fact, the more clearly defined the sampling frame the better. Low representativeness, on the other hand, is a type of bias we would like to avoid. Given the nature of samples, perfect representativeness is not achievable. That said, there are a series of sampling strategies that tend to increase the representativeness of a sample, seen in Table 2.1.

Table 2.1: Sampling strategies to increase representativeness

Strategy	Description
Size	Larger samples increase the likelihood of representing the population
Randomized	Avoid invertently including bias in selection
Stratified	Divide the population into sub-populations, 'strata', and sample from each
Balanced	Ensure that the relative size of the strata is reflected in the sample

Together, large randomly selected and balanced stratified samples set the benchmark for sampling. However, hitting this ideal is not always feasible. There are situations where larger samples are not accessible. Alternatively, there may be instances where the population or its strata are not well understood. In such scenarios, researchers have to work with the most suitable sample they can obtain given the limitations of their research project.

2.1.2 Corpora

A sample, as just defined, of a language population is called a **corpus** (*pl.* corpora) . Corpora are often classified into various types. These types reflect general characteristics of the scope of the corpus sampling frame. The most common types of corpora appear in Table 2.2.

Table 2.2: Types of corpora

Type	Sampling scope
Reference	General characteristics of a language population
Specialized	Specific populations, *e.g.* spoken language, academic writing, *etc.*
Parallel	Directly comparable texts in different languages (*i.e.* translations)
Comparable	Indirectly comparable texts in different languages or language varieties (*i.e.* similar sampling frames)

Of the corpus types, **reference corpora** are the least common and most ambitious. These resources aim to model the characteristics of a language population. **Specialized corpora** aim to represent more specific populations. What specialized corpora lack in breadth of coverage, they make up for in depth of coverage by providing a more targeted representation of specific language populations. **Parallel** and **comparable corpora** are both types of specialized corpora which aim to model different languages or different language varieties for direct or indirect comparison, respectively.

Consider this

The 'Standard Sample of Present-Day American English' (known commonly as the Brown Corpus) is widely recognized as one of the first large, machine-readable corpora. Compiled by Kucera & Francis (1967), the corpus is comprised of 1,014,312 words from edited English prose published in the United States in 1961.

Given the sampling frame and the strata and balance for this corpus visualized in this plot, can you determine what language population this corpus aims to represent? What types of research might this corpus support or not support?

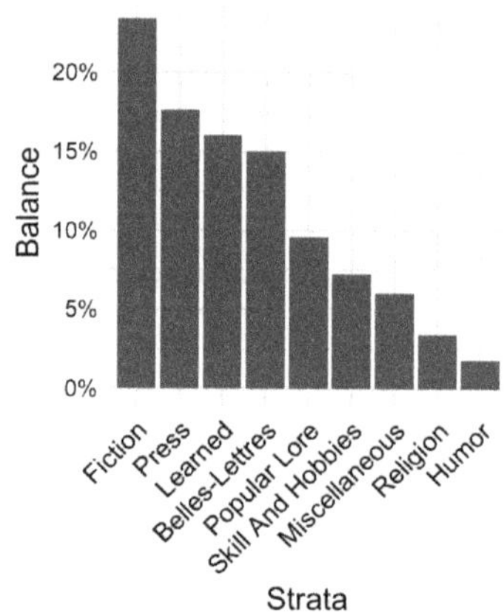

In text analysis, corpora are the raw materials of research. The aim of the quantitative text researcher is to select the corpus, or corpora, which best align with the purpose of the research. For example, a reference corpus such as the American National Corpus (Ide & Macleod, 2001) may be better suited to address a question dealing with the way American English works, but this general resource may lack detail in certain areas, such as medical language, that may be vital for a research project aimed at understanding changes in medical terminology. Furthermore, a researcher studying spoken language might collect a corpus of transcribed conversations from a particular community or region, such as the Santa Barbara Corpus of Spoken American English (Du Bois et al., 2005). While this would not include every possible spoken utterance produced by members of that group, it could be considered a representative sample of the population of speech in that context.

2.1.3 Other considerations

In preparing and conducting research using corpora, the most primary concerns is aligning research goals with the corpus resource. However, there are other, more practical, considerations to keep in mind.

2.1.4 Access

Ensuring access, both in terms of physical access to the data and legal access to the data, should not be overlooked in the design and execution of a project. Simply put, without access to the data, research cannot proceed. It is better to consider access early in the research process to avoid delays and complications later on.

The medium to acquire corpus data most used in contemporary quantitative research is the internet. Although a general search query can lead you to corpus data, there are a few primary sources of corpora you should be aware of, summarized in Table 2.3.

Table 2.3: Sources of corpus data

Source	Description	Examples
Language repositories	Repositories that specialize in language data	Language Data Consortium[1], TalkBank[2]
Data sharing platforms	Platforms that enable researchers to securely store, manage, and share data	GitHub[3], Zenodo[4], Open Science Framework[5]
Developed corpora	Corpora prepared by researchers for research purposes	APIs[6], web scraping

[1]https://www.ldc.upenn.edu/
[2]https://talkbank.org/
[3]https://github.com/
[4]https://zenodo.org/
[5]https://osf.io/
[6]https://ropensci.org/packages/data-access/

It is always advisable to start looking for data in a **language repository**. The advantage of beginning your data search in repositories is that a repository, especially those geared towards the linguistic community, will make identifying language corpora faster than through a general web search . Furthermore, repositories often require certain standards for corpus format and documentation for publication.

> **Consider this**
> Explore some of the resources listed on the Resources Kit "Identifying data and data sources" guide and consider their sampling frames. Can you think of a research question or questions that this resource may be well-suited to support? What types of questions would be less-than-adequate for a given resource?

As part of a general movement towards reproducibility, more corpora are available on **data sharing platforms**. These platforms enable researchers to securely store, manage, and share data with others. Support is provided for various types of data, including documents and code, and as such they are a good place to look as they often include reproducible research projects as well.

Finally, if satisfactory data cannot be found in a repository or data sharing platform, researchers may need to develop their own corpus. There are two primary ways to attain language data from the web. The first is through an **application programming interface** (API). APIs are, as the title suggests, programming interfaces which allow access, under certain conditions, to information that a website or database accessible via the web contains.

> **Dive deeper**
> The process of corpus development is a topic in and of itself. For a more in-depth discussion of the process, see Ädel (2020).

The second, more involved, way to acquire data from the web is is through the process of web scraping. **Web scraping** is the process of harvesting data from the public-facing web. Language texts may be found on sites as uploaded files, such as PDF or DOCX (Word) documents, or found displayed as the primary text of a site. Given the wide variety of documents uploaded and language behavior recorded daily on news sites, blogs and the like, compiling a corpus has never been easier. Having said that, how the data is structured and how much data needs to be retrieved can pose practical obstacles to collecting data from the web, particularly if the approach is to acquire the data by manually instead of automating the task.

Beyond physical access to the data, legal access is also a consideration. Just because data is available on the web does not mean it is free to use. Repositories, APIs, and individual data resources often have **licensing agreements** and **terms of use**, ranging from public domain to proprietary licenses. Respecting intellectual property rights is crucial when working with corpus data. Violating these rights can lead to legal and ethical issues, including lawsuits, fines, and damage to one's professional reputation. To avoid these problems, researchers must ensure they have the necessary permissions to use copyrighted works in their research. Consult the copyright office in your country and/or an academic librarian for guidance on copyright law and fair use as it pertains to your use case.

Formats

Whether you are using a published corpus or developing your own, it is important to understand how the data you want to work with is formatted so you can ensure that you are prepared to conduct the subsequent processing steps. When referring to the format of a corpus, this includes the folder and file structure, the file types, and how file content is encoded electronically. Yet, the most important characteristic, especially for language-based data, is the internal structure of the files themselves. With this in mind let's discuss the difference between unstructured, semi-structured, and structured data.

A corpus may include various types of linguistic (*e.g.* part of speech, syntactic structure, named entities, *etc.*) or non-linguistic (*e.g.* source, dates, speaker information, *etc.*) attributes. These attributes are known as **metadata**, or data about data. As a general rule, files which include more metadata tend to be more internally structured. Internal file structure refers to the degree to which the content has been formatted such that these pieces of information are easy to query and analyze by a computer. Let's review characteristics of the three main types of file structure types and associate common file extensions that files in each have.

Unstructured data is data which does not have a machine-readable internal structure. This is the case for plain text files (*.txt*), which are simply a sequence of characters. For example, in Snippet 2.1 we see a plain text file from the Manually Annotated Sub-Corpus of American English (MASC)(Ide, Baker, Fellbaum, Fillmore, & Passonneau, 2008):

Snippet 2.1. MASC *.txt* file

```
Sound is a vibration. Sound travels as a mechanical wave through a medium,
↪ and in space, there is no medium. So when my shuttle malfunctioned and
↪ the airlocks didn't keep the air in, I heard nothing.
```

Other examples of files which often contain unstructured data include *.pdf* and *.docx* files. While these file types may contain data which appears structured to the human eye, the structure is not designed to be machine-readable. As such the data would typically be read into R as a vector of **character strings**. It is possible to perform only the most rudimentary queries on this type of data, such as string matches. For anything more informative, it is necessary to further process this data, as we will see in Sections 2.2.1 and 2.2.2.

On the other end of the spectrum, **structured data** is data which conforms to a tabular format in which elements in tables and relationships between tables are defined. This makes querying and analyzing easy and efficient. Relational databases (*e.g.* MySQL, PostgreSQL, *etc.*) are designed to store and query structured data. The data frame object in R is also a structured data format. In each case, the data is stored in a tabular format in which each row represents a single observation and each column represents a single attribute whose values are of the same type.

In Snippet 2.2 we see an example of an R data frame object which overlaps with the language in the plain text file in Snippet 2.1:

Snippet 2.2. MASC R data frame

```
   doc_id  date modality token_id word       lemma      pos
    <int> <dbl> <fct>       <int> <chr>      <chr>      <chr>
 1      1  2008 Writing         1 Sound      sound      NNP
 2      1  2008 Writing         2 is         be         VBZ
 3      1  2008 Writing         3 a          a          DT
 4      1  2008 Writing         4 vibration  vibration  NN
 5      1  2008 Writing         5 .          .          .
 6      1  2008 Writing         6 Sound      sound      NNP
 7      1  2008 Writing         7 travels    travel     VBZ
 8      1  2008 Writing         8 as         as         IN
 9      1  2008 Writing         9 a          a          DT
10      1  2008 Writing        10 mechanical mechanical JJ
```

Here we see that the data is stored in a tabular format with each row representing a single observation (`word`) and each column representing a single attribute. This tabular structure supports the increased number of metadata attributes. Internally, R applies a schema to ensure the values in each column are of the same type (*e.g.* `<chr>`, `<dbl>`, `<fct>`, *etc.*). This structured format is designed to be easy to query and analyze and as such is the primary format for data analysis in R.

Semi-structured data data falls between unstructured and structured data. This covers a wide range of file structuring approaches. For example, an otherwise plain text file with part-of-speech tags appended to each word is minimally structured, Snippet 2.3.

Snippet 2.3. MASC *.txt* file with part-of-speech tags

```
Sound/NNP is/VBZ a/DT vibration/NN ./. Sound/NNP travels/VBZ as/IN a/DT
↪  mechanical/JJ wave/NN through/IN a/DT medium/NN ,/, and/CC in/IN
↪  space/NN ,/, there/EX is/VBZ no/DT medium/NN ./. So/RB when/WRB my/PRP$
↪  shuttle/NN malfunctioned/JJ and/CC the/DT airlocks/NNS did/VBD n't/RB
↪  keep/VB the/DT air/NN in/IN ,/, I/PRP heard/VBD nothing/NN ./.
```

Towards the more structured end of semi-structured data, many file formats including *.xml* and *.json* contain hierarchical data. For example, in Snippet 2.4 shows a snippet from a *.xml* file from the MASC corpus.

Snippet 2.4. MASC *.xml* file

```
<a xml:id="penn-N264215" label="tok" ref="penn-n7345" as="anc">
  <fs>
    <f name="base" value="sound"/>
    <f name="msd" value="NNP"/>
    <f name="string" value="Sound"/>
  </fs>
</a>
<node xml:id="penn-n7346">
  <link targets="seg-r13152"/>
</node>
<a xml:id="penn-N264243" label="tok" ref="penn-n7346" as="anc">
  <fs>
    <f name="string" value="is"/>
    <f name="msd" value="VBZ"/>
    <f name="base" value="be"/>
  </fs>
</a>
<node xml:id="penn-n7347">
  <link targets="seg-r13154"/>
</node>
```

The format of semi-structured data is often influenced by characteristics of the data or reflect an author's individual preferences. It is sometimes the case that data will be semi-structured in a less-standard format. For example, the Switchboard Dialog Act Corpus (SWDA) (University of Colorado Boulder, 2008), in Snippet 2.5, includes a *.utt* file extension for files which contain utterances annotated with dialog act tags.

Snippet 2.5. SWDA *.utt* file

```
o       A.1 utt1: Okay. /
qw      A.1 utt2: {D So, }
qy^d    B.2 utt1: [ [ I guess, +
+       A.3 utt1: What kind of experience [ do you, + do you ] have, then with
↪   child care? /
+       B.4 utt1: I think, ] + {F uh, } I wonder ] if that worked. /
qy      A.5 utt1: Does it say something? /
```

Whether standard or not, semi-structured data is often designed to be machine-readable. As with unstructured data, the ultimate goal is to convert the data into a structured format and augment the data where necessary to prepare it for a particular research analysis.

2.2 Information

Identifying an adequate corpus resource, in terms of content, access, and formatting, for the target research question is the first step in moving a quantitative text research project forward. The next step is to select the components or characteristics of this resource that are relevant for the research and then move to organize the attributes of this data into a more informative format. This is the process of converting corpus data into a **dataset** —a tabular representation of particular attributes of the data as the basis for generating information. Once the data is represented as a dataset, it is often manipulated and transformed, adjusting and augmenting the data such that it better aligns with the research question and the target analytical approach.

2.2.1 Organization

Data alone is not informative. Only through explicit organization of the data in a way that makes relationships and meaning explicit does data become information. In this form, our data is called a dataset. This is a particularly salient hurdle in text analysis research. Many textual sources are unstructured or semi-structured. This means relationships that will be used in the analysis have yet to be purposefully drawn and organized as a dataset.

Tidy Data

The selection of the attributes from a corpus and the juxtaposition of these attributes in a relational format, or dataset, that converts data into information is known as **data curation**. The process of data curation minimally involves deriving a base dataset, or *curated dataset*, which establishes the main informational associations according to the philosophical approach outlined by Wickham (2014a).

In this work, a **tidy dataset** refers both to the structural (physical) and informational (semantic) organization of the dataset. Physically, a tidy dataset is a tabular data structure, illustrated in Figure 2.1, where each *row* is an **observation** and each *column* is a **variable** that contains measures of a feature or attribute of each observation. Each *cell* where a given row-column intersect contains a **value** which is a particular attribute of a particular observation for the particular observation-feature pair also known as a *data point*.

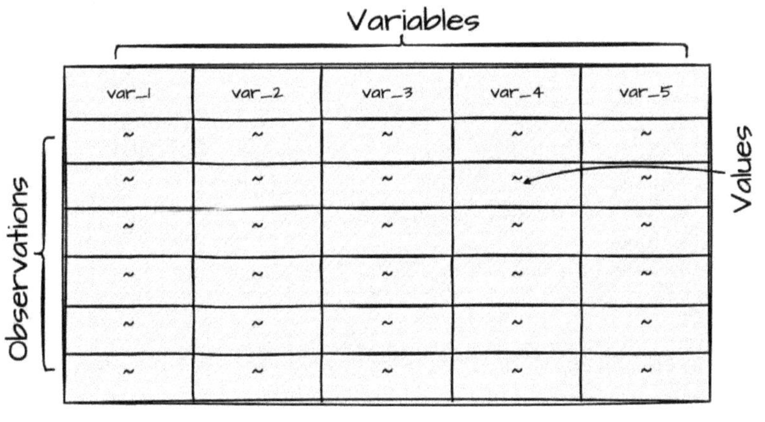

Figure 2.1: Visual summary of the tidy dataset format

In terms of semantics, columns and rows both contribute to the informational value of the dataset. Let's start with columns. In a tidy dataset, each column is a variable, an attribute that can take on a number of values. Although variables vary in terms of values, they do not in type. A variable is of one and only one informational type. Statistically speaking, informational types are defined as **levels of measurement**, a classification system used to semantically distinguish between types of variables. There are four levels (or types) in this system: nominal, ordinal, interval, and ratio.

In practice, however, text analysis researchers often group these levels into three main informational types: categorical, ordinal, and numeric (Gries, 2021). What do these informational types represent? **Categorical data** is for labeled data or classes that answer the question "what?" **Ordinal data** is categorical data with rank order that answers the question "what order?" **Numeric data** is ordinal data with equal intervals between values that answers the question "how much or how many?"

Let's look at an example of a tidy dataset. Using the criteria just described, let's see if we can identify the informational values (categorical, ordinal, or numeric) of the variables that appear in a snippet from the MASC corpus in dataset form in Table 2.4.

Table 2.4: MASC dataset variables

doc_id	modality	date	token_id	word	pos	num_let
1	Writing	2008	1	Sound	NNP	5
1	Writing	2008	2	is	VBZ	2
1	Writing	2008	3	a	DT	1
1	Writing	2008	4	vibration	NN	9
1	Writing	2008	5	.	.	1
1	Writing	2008	6	Sound	NNP	5
1	Writing	2008	7	travels	VBZ	7
1	Writing	2008	8	as	IN	2
1	Writing	2008	9	a	DT	1
1	Writing	2008	10	mechanical	JJ	10

We have seven variables listed as headers for each of the columns. We could go one-by-one left-to-right but let's take another tack. Instead, let's identify all those variables that cannot be numeric —these are all the non-numeral variables: `modality`, `word`, and `pos`. The question to ask of these variables is whether they represent an order or rank. Since modalities, words, and parts of speech are not ordered values, they are all categorical. Now in relation to `doc_id`, `date`, `token_id`, and `num_let`. All four are numerals, so they could be numeric. But they could also be numeral representations of categorical or ordinal data. Before we can move forward, we need to make sure we understand what each variable means and how it is measured, or **operationalized** . The variable name and the values can be helpful in this respect. `doc_id` and `token_id` are unique identifiers for each document and word. `date` is what it sounds like, a date, and is operationalized as a year in the Gregorian calendar. And `num_let` seems quite descriptive as well, number of letters, appearing as a letter count.

With this in mind, let's return to the question of whether these variables are numeric, ordinal, or categorical. Starting with the trickiest one, `date`, we can ask the question to identify numeric data: "how much or how many?". In the case of `date`, the answer is neither. A date is a point in time, not a quantity.

So `date` is not numeric. But it does provide information about order. Hence, `date` is ordinal. Next, `num_let` is numeric because it answers the question "how many?". Now, `doc_id` and `token_id` are both identifiers, so they are not numeric, but the question is whether they encode order as well. In this case, it depends. If the identifiers are assigned in a way that reflects the order of the documents or tokens, then they are ordinal. It is more likely the case that the `doc_id` is not ordinal, but the `token_id` is. This is because the `token_id` is likely assigned in the order the words appear in the document.

Let's turn to the second semantic value of a tidy dataset. In a tidy dataset, each row is an observation. But an observation of what? This depends on what the unit of observation is. That sounds circular, but its not. The **unit of observation** is simply the primary entity that is being observed or measured (Sedgwick, 2015). Even without context, it can often be identified in a dataset by looking at the level of specificity of the variable values and asking what each variable describes. When one variable appears to be the most individualized and other variables appear to describe that variable, then the most individualized variable is likely the unit of observation of the dataset, *i.e.* the meaning of each observation.

> **Consider this**
> Data can be organized in many ways. It is important to make clear that data in tabular format in itself does not constitute a dataset, in the tidy sense we will be using. Can you think of examples of tabular information that would not be in a tidy format? What would be the implications of this for data analysis?

Applying these strategies to Table 2.4, we can see that each observation at its core is a word. We see that the values of each observation are the attributes of each word. `word` is the most individualized variable and the `pos`, `num_let`, and `token_id` all describe the word.

The other variables `doc_id`, `modality`, and `date` are not direct attributes of the word. Instead, they are attributes of the document in which the word appears. Together, however, they all provide information about the word.

As we round out this section on data organization, it is important to stress that the purpose of curation is to represent the corpus data in an informative, tidy format. A curated dataset serves as a reference point making relationships explicit, enabling more efficient querying, and paving the way for further processing before analysis.

2.2.2 Transformation

At this point, have introduced the first step towards creating a dataset ready for analysis, data curation. However, a curated dataset is rarely the final organizational step before proceeding to statistical analysis. Many times, if not always, the curated dataset requires **transformation** to derive or generate new data for the dataset. This process may incur row-wise (observation) or column-wise (variable) level changes, as illustrated in Figure 2.2.

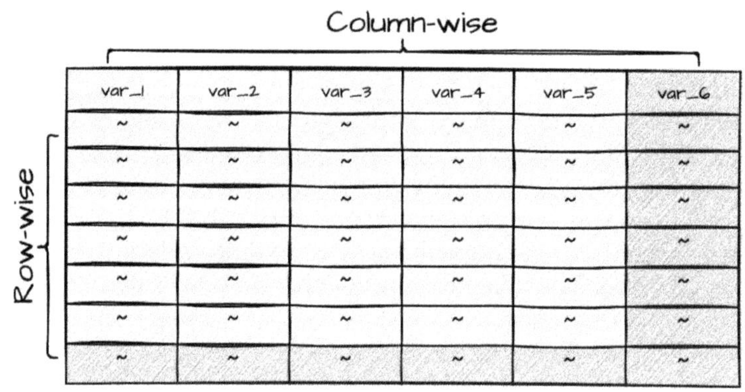

Figure 2.2: Visualization of row-wise and column-wise transformation operations on a dataset

The results build on and manipulate the curated dataset to produce a *transformed dataset*. While there is typically one curated dataset that serves as the base organizational dataset, there may be multiple transformed datasets, each aligning with the informational needs of specific analyses in the research project.

In what follows, we will group common transformation processes into two purpose-based groupings: preparation and enrichment. The process may include one or more of the subsequent transformations but is rarely linear and is most often iterative. The bottom line is, however, to make the dataset more informative and more amenable to the particular aims of a given analysis.

Preparation

The purpose of preparation transformations is to clean, standardize, and derive the key attributes of the dataset on which further processing will depend. Common preparation transformations include text normalization and text tokenization.

Let's take a toy dataset, in Table 2.5, as a starting point for exploring various transformations. In this dataset, we have three variables, `text_id`, `sent_id`, and `sentence`. It has five observations.

Table 2.5: A toy dataset with three variables, `text_id`, `sent_id`, and `sentence`

text_id	sent_id	sentence
1	1	It's a beautiful day in the US, and our group decided to visit the famous Grand Canyon.
1	2	As we reached the destination, Jane said, "I can't believe we're finally here!"
1	3	The breathtaking view left us speechless; indeed, it was a sight to behold.
1	4	During our trip, we encountered tourists from different countries, sharing stories and laughter.
1	5	For all of us, this experience will be cherished forever.

Text normalization is the process of standardizing text to convert the text into a uniform format and reduce unwanted variation and noise. It is often a preliminary step in data transformation processes which include variables with text.

The normalization we apply will depend on the specific needs of the project, but can include operations such as eliminating missing, redundant, or anomalous observations, changing the case of the text, removing punctuation, standardizing forms, *etc.* The goal is to reduce the noise in the text and make it more amenable to analysis.

Normalization should be applied with an understanding of how the changes will impact the analysis. For example, looking at Table 2.5, lowercasing can be useful for reducing differences between words that are otherwise identical, yet differ in case due to word position in a sentence ("The" versus "the"). However, lowercasing can also be problematic if the case of the word carries semantic value, such as in the case of "US" (United States) and "us" (first-person plural pronoun). In this case, lowercasing would conflate the two words. Other normalization tasks, and their implications, should be considered in a similar manner.

Text tokenization involves adapting the text such that it reflects the target linguistic unit that will be used in the analysis. This is a row-wise operation expanding the number of rows, if the linguistic unit is smaller than the original variable, or reducing the number of rows, if the linguistic unit is larger than the original variable.

Text variables can be tokenized at any linguistic level, to the extent we can operationalize the linguistic unit. The operationalized linguistic unit is known as a **term**. For example, terms can be characters, words, sentences, *etc.* When we refer to the individual units of term, we use the expression **tokens**. Another key term to introduce is **types**, which refers to the unique tokens in a

Table 2.6: Word and character tokenization examples

(a) Character trigram tokenization

text_id	sent_id	trigram
1	1	its
1	1	tsa
1	1	sab
1	1	abe
1	1	bea
1	1	eau
1	1	aut
1	1	uti
1	1	tif
1	1	ifu

(b) Word bigram tokenization

text_id	sent_id	bigram
1	1	it's a
1	1	a beautiful
1	1	beautiful day
1	1	day in
1	1	in the
1	1	the us
1	1	us and
1	1	and our
1	1	our group
1	1	group decided

term variable. For example, in sentence 1 in Table 2.5, there are 16 types and 17 tokens—as 'the' is repeated. Note that there will always be at least as many tokens as types, but there can be many more tokens than types for any given term variable.

Sequential groupings of characters and words, ngrams, are also common terms used in text analysis. For example, a word bigram is a sequence of two words, and a character trigram is a sequence of three characters.

Case study
Serigos (2020) explores the social stratification of anglicisms in Argentine media. The author presents a method for automatically detecting anglicisms in Spanish texts. In combination with other methods, character ngrams are used to determine the language of a word. The method is based on the observation that the distribution of character ngrams is different between languages.

In Table 2.6, we see examples of tokenization at word and character levels. At its core, tokenization is the process which enables the quantitative analysis of text. Choosing the right tokenization level is crucial for the success of the analysis.

Enrichment

Enrichment transformations are designed to add new attributes to the dataset. These attributes may be derived from the existing attributes or may be integrated from other datasets. Common enrichment transformations include generation, recoding, and integration of observations and/or variables.

Generation is the process of creating new variables based on implicit information within existing variables. It is a row- and column-wise operation which in text analysis often includes linguistic annotation such as part-of-speech tagging, morphological features, syntactic constituents, *etc.* These annotations can be used to generate new variables that capture linguistic information that is not explicitly present in the text.

Linguistic annotation can be done manually by linguist coders and/or done automatically using natural language processing (NLP) tools. To illustrate the process of automatic linguistic annotation, we will start with the dataset from Table 2.5. Applying a pre-trained English model (Silveira et al., 2014) from the Universal Dependencies (UD) project (de Marneffe, Manning, Nivre, & Zeman, 2021), we can generate linguistic annotation for each word in the `sentence` variable.

Table 2.7: Automatic linguistic annotation example

id	token	pos	feats	relation
1	As	IN	NA	mark
2	we	PRP	Case=Nom|Number=Plur|Person=1|PronType=Prs	nsubj
3	reached	VBD	Mood=Ind|Tense=Past|VerbForm=Fin	advcl
4	the	DT	Definite=Def|PronType=Art	det
5	destination	NN	Number=Sing	obj
6	,	,	NA	punct
7	Jane	NNP	Number=Sing	nsubj
8	said	VBD	Mood=Ind|Tense=Past|VerbForm=Fin	root
9	,	,	NA	punct
10	"	``	NA	punct
11	I	PRP	Case=Nom|Number=Sing|Person=1|PronType=Prs	nsubj
12	ca	MD	VerbForm=Fin	aux
13	n't	RB	NA	advmod
14	believe	VB	VerbForm=Inf	ccomp
15	we	PRP	Case=Nom|Number=Plur|Person=1|PronType=Prs	nsubj
16	're	VBP	Mood=Ind|Tense=Pres|VerbForm=Fin	cop
17	finally	RB	NA	advmod
18	here	RB	PronType=Dem	ccomp
19	!	.	NA	punct
20	"	''	NA	punct

The annotated dataset in Table 2.7 is now tokenized by word and includes the key variables `pos` (Penn treebank tagset[7]), `feats` (morphological features), and `relation` (dependency relations). These variables provide information about the grammatical category and syntactic structure of each word in the sentence. The results of this process enables more direct access during analysis to features that were hidden or otherwise difficult to access.

[7] https://www.ling.upenn.edu/courses/Fall_2003/ling001/penn_treebank_pos.html

⚠ Warning
Automated linguistic annotation can offer rapid access to abundant and highly dependable linguistic data for numerous languages. However, linguistic annotation tools are not infallible. They are tools developed by training computational algorithms to identify patterns in previously annotated and verified datasets, resulting in a language model. This model is then employed to predict linguistic annotations for new language data. The accuracy of the linguistic annotation heavily relies on the congruence between the language sampling frame of the trained data and that of the dataset to be automatically annotated.

Recoding is the process of transforming the values of one or more variables into new values which are more amenable to analysis. This is a column-wise operation which is used to make explicit information more accessible. Typical operations include extraction, reclassification, and calculation.

In terms of **extraction**, the goal is to distill relevant information from existing variables. For example, extracting the year from a date variable, or extracting the first name from a full name variable. In text analysis, extraction is often used to extract information from text variables. Say we have a dataset with a variable containing conversation utterances. We may want to extract some characteristic from those utterances and capture their occurrence in a new variable.

Reclassification aims to simplify complex variables, making it easier to identify patterns and trends relevant for the research question. For example, the surface forms of words can be reduced to their stemmed or lemmatized forms. **Stemming** is the process of reducing inflected words to their word stem, base, or root form. **Lemmatization** is the process of reducing inflected words to their dictionary form, or lemma.

In Table 2.8, we see an example of recoding surface forms of words to their stemmed and lemmatized forms.

Table 2.8: Reclassification of surface forms of words to their stemmed and lemmatized forms

text_id	sent_id	word	stem	lemma
1	2	as	a	as
1	2	we	we	we
1	2	reached	reach	reach
1	2	the	the	the
1	2	destination	destin	destination
1	2	jane	jane	jane
1	2	said	said	say
1	2	i	i	i
1	2	can	can	can
1	2	not	not	not

Table 2.8: Reclassification of surface forms of words to their stemmed and lemmatized forms

text_id	sent_id	word	stem	lemma
1	2	believe	believ	believe
1	2	we	we	we
1	2	are	are	be
1	2	finally	final	finally
1	2	here	here	here

Case study
Inflectional family size is the number of inflectional forms for a given word and can be calculated from a corpus by counting the number of surface forms for each lemma in the corpus (Kostić, Marković, & Baucal, 2003). Baayen, Feldman, & Schreuder (2006) found that words with larger inflectional family size are associated with faster word recognition times in lexical processing tasks.

Reclassification transformations can be useful for simplifying complex variables, making it easier to identify patterns, as we see in Table 2.8. However, it is important to consider the trade-offs of reclassification and to ensure that the result aligns with the research question. For example, reclassifying a numeric variable to a categorical variable or a categorical variable into a variable with fewer levels variable can lead to loss of information about the original levels (Baayen, 2010).

Calculations of measures can also be seen as a recoding operation. In text analysis, measures are often used to describe the properties of a document or linguistic unit. For example, the number of words in a corpus document, the lengths of sentences, the number of clauses in a sentence, *etc.* In turn, these measures can be used to calculate other measures, such as lexical diversity or syntactic complexity measures. The end result makes the dataset more informative and amenable to analysis.

Integration is a transformation step which can be row-wise or column-wise. Row-wise integration is the process of combining datasets by appending observations from one dataset to another. Column-wise integration is the process of combining datasets by appending variables from one dataset to another.

To integrate in row-wise manner, the datasets involved in the process must have the same variables and variable types. This process is often referred to as **concatenating datasets**, and is visualized in Figure 2.3a. It can be thought of as stacking datasets on top of each other to create a larger dataset. Remember, having the same variables and variable types is not the same has having the same values.

Take, for example, a case when a corpus resource contains data for two populations. In the course of curating and transforming the datasets, it may make more sense to work with the datasets separately. However, when it comes time to analyze the data, it may be more convenient to work with the datasets as a single dataset. In this case, the datasets can be concatenated to create a single dataset.

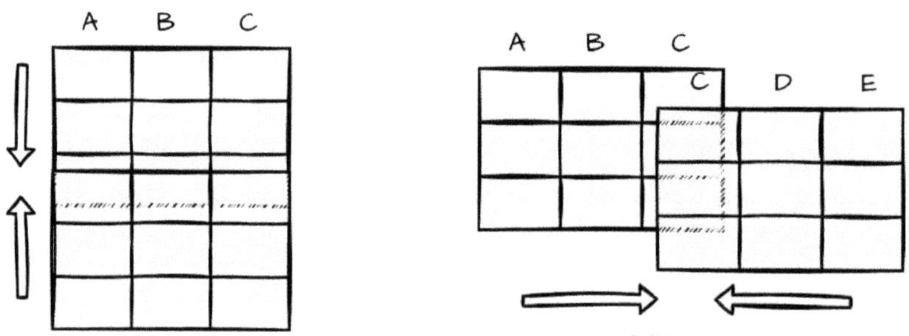

(a) Concatenating (b) Joining

Figure 2.3: Visual summary of row-wise and column-wise integration operations on datasets

Integrating datasets can be performed in a column-wise manner as well. In this process, the datasets need not have the exact same variables and variable types, rather it is required that the datasets share a common variable of the same informational type that can be used to index the datasets. This process is often referred to as **joining datasets** and is visualized in Figure 2.3b.

Corpus resources often include metadata in stand-off annotation format. That is, the metadata is not embedded in the corpus files, but rather is stored in a separate file. The metadata and corpus files will share a common variable which can be used to join the metadata with the corpus files, in turn creating a more informative dataset.

2.3 Documentation

As we have seen in this chapter, acquiring corpus data and converting that data into information involves a number of conscious decisions and implementation steps. As a favor to ourselves, as researchers, and to the research community, it is crucial to document these decisions and steps. Documentation includes a data origin file for the acquired corpus data, data dictionaries for the curated and transformed datasets, and well-documented code for the processing steps.

2.3.1 Data origin

Data acquired from corpus resources should be accompanied by information about the **data origin**. Table 2.9 provides the types of information that should be included in the data origin file.

Table 2.9: Data origin information

Information	Description
Resource name	Name of the corpus resource.
Data source	URL, DOI, *etc.*
Data sampling frame	Language, language variety, modality, genre, *etc.*
Data collection date(s)	The date or date range of the data collection.
Data format	Plain text, XML, HTML, *etc.*
Data schema	Relationships between data elements: files, folders, *etc.*
License	CC BY, CC BY-NC, *etc.*
Attribution	Citation information for the data source.

For many corpus resources, the corpus documentation will include all or most of this information as part of the resource download or documented online. If this information is not present in the corpus resource or you compile your own, it is important to document this information yourself. This information can be documented in a file, usually in a tabular plain text file, such as a comma-separated values (CSV) or spreadsheet file , for example an Microsoft Excel *.xlsx* file, that is included with the corpus resource.

2.3.2 Data dictionaries

The process of organizing the data into a dataset, curation, and modifications to the dataset in preparation for analysis, transformation, each include a number of project-specific decisions. These decisions should be documented.

On the one hand, each dataset that is created should have a **data dictionary** file. A data dictionary is a document that describes the variables in a dataset including the information in Table 2.10. Organizing this information in a tabular format, such as a CSV file or spreadsheet, can make it easy for others to read and understand your data dictionary.

On the other hand, the data curation and transformation steps should be documented in the code that is used to create the dataset. This is one of the valuable features of a programmatic approach to quantitative research. The transparency of this documentation is enhanced by using **literate programming** strategies to intermingling prose descriptions and code the steps in the same, reproducible document.

Table 2.10: Data dictionary information

Information	Description
Variable name	The name of the variable as it appears in the dataset, *e.g.* `participant_id`, `modality`, *etc.*
Readable name	A human-readable name for the variable, *e.g.* 'Participant ID', 'Language modality', *etc.*
Variable type	The type of information that the variable contains, *e.g.* 'categorical', 'ordinal', *etc.*
Variable description	A prose description expanding on the readable name and can include measurement units, allowed values, *etc.*

By providing a comprehensive data dictionary and using a programmatic approach to data curation and transformation, you ensure that you can retrace your own steps and others can easily understand and work with your dataset.

> **Tip**
> It is conventional to work with variable names for datasets in R using the same conventions that are used for naming objects. It is a matter of taste which convention is used. I have adopted 'snake_case' as my personal preference (*e.g* `token_id`). There are also alternatives such as 'camelCase' (*e.g.* `tokenId`) and 'PascalCase' (*e.g.* `TokenId`). Regardless of the convention you choose, it is good practice to be consistent.
> It is also of note that the variable names should be balanced for meaningfulness and brevity. This brevity is of practical concern but can lead to somewhat opaque variable names. Ensure you provide a description of your variables in a data dictionary.

Activities

In the following activities, we will be tackle a common scenario in data analysis: to read, to inspect, and to write datasets. The recipe will discuss the necessary packages and functions to accomplish these tasks including {readr} and {dplyr}. The recipe will also refresh and expand on the elements of code blocks in Quarto documents such as the `label`, `echo`, `message`, and `include` options.

Recipe
What: Reading, inspecting, and writing datasets
How: Read Recipe 2, complete comprehension check, and prepare for Lab 2.
Why: To use literate programming in Quarto to work with R coding strategies for reading, inspecting, and writing datasets.

Lab
What: Dive into datasets
How: Clone, fork, and complete the steps in Lab 2.
Why: To read datasets from packages and from plain-text files, inspect and report characteristics of datasets, and write datasets to plain-text files.

Summary

In this chapter we have focused on data and information —the first two components of DIKI Hierarchy. First, a distinction is made between populations and samples, the latter being a intentional and subjective selection of observations from the world which attempt to represent the population of interest. The result of this process is known as a corpus. Whether developing a corpus or selecting an existing corpus, it is important to vet the sampling frame for its applicability and viability as a resource for a given research project.

Once a viable corpus is identified, then that corpus is converted into a curated dataset which adopts the tidy dataset format where each column is a variable, each row is an observation, and the intersection of columns and rows contain values. This curated dataset serves to establish the base informational relationships from which your research will stem.

The curated dataset will most likely require transformations which may include normalization, tokenization, recoding, generation, and/or integration to enhance the usefulness of the information to analysis. A transformed dataset or set of datasets will the result from this process.

Finally, documentation should be implemented at the acquisition, curation, and transformation stages of the analysis project process. The combination of data origin, data dictionary, and literate programming files establishes documentation of the data and implementation steps to ensure transparent and reproducible research.

3

Analysis

Outcomes

- Recall the fundamental concepts and principles of statistics in data analysis.
- Articulate the roles of diagnostic, analytic, and interpretive statistics in quantitative analysis.
- Compare the similarities and differences between analytic approaches to data analysis.

The goal of an analysis is to break down complex information into simpler components which are more readily interpretable. In what follows, we will cover the main steps in this process. The first is to inspect the data to ensure its quality and understand its characteristics. The second is to interrogate the data to uncover patterns and relationships and interpret the findings. To conclude this chapter, I will outline methods for and the importance of communicating the analysis results and procedure in a transparent and reproducible manner.

>_ Lessons
What: Summarizing data, Visual summaries
How: In an R console, load {swirl}, run `swirl()`, and follow prompts to select the lesson.
Why: To showcase methods for statistical summaries of vectors and data frames and to create informative graphics that enhance data interpretation and analysis.

3.1 Describe

The goal of descriptive statistics is to summarize the data in order to understand and prepare the data for the analysis approach to be performed. This is accomplished through a combination of statistic measures and/or tabular or graphic summaries. The choice of descriptive statistics is guided by the type of data, as well as the question(s) being asked of the data.

10.4324/9781003393764.3

In descriptive statistics, there are four basic questions that are asked of each of the variables in the dataset. Each correspond to a different type of descriptive measure.

1. **Central tendency**: Where do the data points tend to be located?
2. **Dispersion**: How spread out are the data points?
3. **Distribution**: What is the overall shape of of the data points?
4. **Association**: How are these data points related to other data points?

To ground this discussion I will introduce a new dataset. This dataset is drawn from the Barcelona English Language Corpus (BELC) (Muñoz, 2006), which is found in the TalkBank repository. I've selected the "Written composition" task from this corpus which contains 80 writing samples from 36 second language learners of English at different ages. Participants were given the task of writing for 15 minutes on the topic of "Me: my past, present and future". Data was collected for participants from one to three times over the course of seven years (at 10, 12, 16, and 17 years of age).

In Table 3.1 we see the data dictionary for the BELC dataset which reflects structural and transformational steps I've done so we start with a tidy dataset with `essay_id` as the unit of observation.

Table 3.1: Data dictionary for the BELC dataset

variable	name	type	description
essay_id	Essay ID	categorical	Unique identifier for each essay
part_id	Participant ID	categorical	Identifier for each participant learner
sex	Sex	categorical	Sex of the participant
group	Group	ordinal	Time group of the essay, ordered from T1 to T4 (10, 12, 16, and 17 years old)
tokens	Tokens	numeric	Number of word tokens in the essay
types	Types	numeric	Number of unique word types in the essay
ttr	TTR	numeric	Type-Token Ratio (TTR) of the essay
prop_l2	Proportion of L2	numeric	Proportion of words in the essay identified as second (target) language (L2)

Now, let's take a look at the first few observations of the BELC dataset to get another perspective on the dataset as we view the values of the dataset.

Table 3.2: First 5 observations of the BELC dataset

essay_id	part_id	sex	group	tokens	types	ttr	prop_l2
E1	L01	female	T2	79	46	0.582	0.987
E2	L02	female	T1	18	18	1.000	0.667
E3	L02	female	T3	101	53	0.525	1.000
E4	L05	female	T1	20	17	0.850	0.900
E5	L05	female	T3	158	80	0.506	0.987

Case study
Type-token ratio (TTR) is a standard metric for measuring lexical diversity, but it is not without its flaws. Most importantly, TTR is highly sensitive to the word length of the text. Duran (2004) discusses this limitation, and the limitations of other lexical diversity measures and proposes a new measure D which shows a stronger correlation with language proficiency in their comparative studies.j

In Table 3.2, each of the variables is an attribute or measure of the `essay_id` variable. `tokens` is the number of total words, `types` is the number of unique words, `ttr` is the ratio of unique words to total words. This is known as the Type-Token Ratio and it is a standard metric for measuring lexical diversity. Finally, the proportion of L2 words (English) to the total words (tokens) is provided in `prop_l2`.

Let's now turn our attention to exploring descriptive measures using the BELC dataset.

3.1.1 Central tendency

The central tendency is a measure which aims to summarize the data points in a variable as the most representative, middle, or most typical value. There are three common measures of central tendency: the mode, mean and median. Each differ in how they summarize the data points.

The **mode** is the value that appears most frequently in a set of values. If there are multiple values with the highest frequency, then the variable is said to be multimodal. A versatile central tendency measure, the mode can be applied all levels of measurement. However, in practice is almost exclusively used to summarize categorical variables.

The most common central tendency measures for numeric variables are the mean and the median. The **mean** is a summary statistic calculated by summing all the values and dividing by the number of values. The **median** is calculated by sorting all the values in the variable and then selecting the middle value.

Table 3.3: Central tendency measures for the BELC dataset

(a) Categorical variables

Variable	Top Counts
essay_id	E1: 1, E10: 1, E11: 1, E12: 1
part_id	L05: 3, L10: 3, L11: 3, L12: 3
sex	fem: 48, mal: 32
group	T1: 25, T3: 24, T2: 16, T4: 15

(b) Numeric variables

Variable	Mean	Median
tokens	67.62	56.5
types	41.85	38.5
ttr	0.68	0.66
prop_l2	0.96	0.99

Consider this

Grieve, Nini, & Guo (2018) compiled an 8.9 billion-word corpus of geo-tagged posts from Twitter 2013-2014 in the United States. The authors provide a search interface[a] to explore the relationship between lexical usage and geographic location. Explore this corpus searching for terms related to slang ("hella", "wicked"), geographical ("mountain", "river"), meteorological ("snow", "rain"), and/or any other terms. What types of patterns do you find? What are the benefits and/or limitations of this type of data, data summarization, and/or interface?

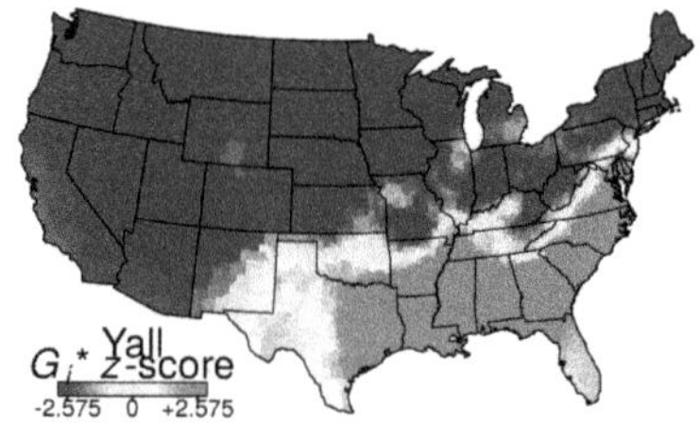

[a]https://isogloss.shinyapps.io/isogloss/

As the mode is the most frequent value, the `top_counts` measure in Table 3.3 provides the most frequent value for the categorical variables. Mean and median appear but we notice that the mean and median are not the same for the numeric variables. Differences that appear between the mean and median will be of interest to us later in this chapter.

3.1.2 Dispersion

To understand how representative a central tendency measure is we use a calculation of the spread of the values around the central tendency, or **dispersion**. Dispersion is a measure of how spread out the values are around the central tendency. The more spread out the values, the less representative the central tendency measure is.

Table 3.4: Dispersion measures for the BELC dataset

(a) Categorical variables

Variable	Norm Entropy
essay_id	1
part_id	0.98
sex	0.97
group	0.98

(b) Numeric variables

Variable	SD	IQR
tokens	44.2	61.25
types	23.03	31.5
ttr	0.13	0.149
prop_l2	0.1	0.027

For categorical variables, the spread is framed in terms of how balanced the values are across the levels. One way to do this is to use proportions. The **proportion** of each level is the frequency of the level divided by the total number of values. Another way is to calculate the (normalized) entropy. **Entropy** is a single measure of uncertainty. The more balanced the values are across the levels, the closer entropy is 1. In practice, however, proportions are often used to assess the balance of the values across the levels.

The most common measure of dispersion for numeric variables is the **standard deviation**. The standard deviation is calculated by taking the square root of the variance. The **variance** is the average of the squared differences from the mean. So, more succinctly, the standard deviation is a measure of the spread of the values around the mean. Where the standard deviation is anchored to the mean, the **interquartile range** (IQR) is tied to the median. The median represents the sorted middle of the values, in other words the 50th percentile. The IQR is the difference between the 75th percentile and the 25th percentile.

Dive deeper

The inability to compare summary statistics across variables is a key reason why **standardization** is often applied before submitting a dataset for analysis (Baayen, 2008; Johnson, 2008).

Standardization is a scale-based transformation that changes the scale of the values to a common scale, or *z-scores* . The result of this transformation puts data points of each variable on the same scale and allows for direct comparison. Furthermore, standardization also mitigates the influence of variables with large values relative to other variables. This is particularly important in multivariate (*i.e.* multiple variable) analysis where the influence of variables with large values can be magnified.

The caveat is that standardization masks the original meaning of the data. That is, if we consider token frequency, before standardization, we can say that a value of 1000 tokens is 1000 tokens. After standardization, we can only say that a value of 1 is 1 standard deviation from the mean. This is why standardization is often applied after the descriptive phase of analysis.

Table 3.5: Frequency table for variables sex and group.

(a) Sex

sex	Frequency	Proportion
female	48	0.6
male	32	0.4

(b) Time group

group	Frequency	Proportion
T1	25	0.312
T2	16	0.200
T3	24	0.300
T4	15	0.188

In Table 3.4a, the entropy helps us understand the balance of the values across the levels of the categorical variables. In Table 3.4b, the standard deviation and IQR provide a sense of the spread of the values around the mean and median, respectively, for the numeric variables.

When interpreting numeric central tendency and dispersion values, it is important to only directly compare column-wise. That is, focusing only on a single variable, not across variables. Each variable, as is, is measured on a different scale and only relative to itself can we make sense of the values.

3.1.3 Distributions

Summary statistics of the central tendency and dispersion of a variable provide a sense of the most representative value and how spread out the data is around this value. However, to gain a more comprehensive understanding of the variable, it is key to consider the frequencies of all the data points. The **distribution** of a variable is the pattern or shape of the data that emerges when the frequencies of all data points are considered. This can reveal patterns that might not be immediately apparent from summary statistics alone.

When assessing the distribution of categorical variables, we can use a frequency table or bar plot. **Frequency tables** display the frequency and / or proportion each level in a categorical variable in a clear and concise manner. In Table 3.5 we see the frequency table for the variable sex and group.

A **bar plot** is a type of plot where the x-axis is a categorical variable and the y-axis is the frequency of the values. The frequency is represented by the height of the bar. The variables can be ordered by frequency, alphabetically, or some other order. Figure 3.1 is a bar chart for the variables sex and group ordered alphabetically.

(a) Bar plot for `sex`

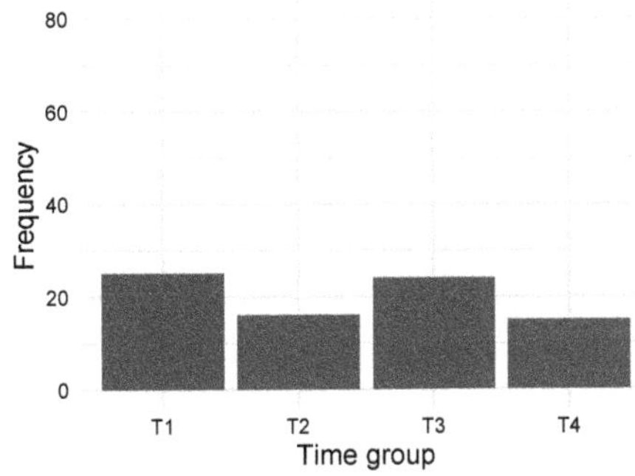

(b) Bar plot for `group`

Figure 3.1: Bar plots for categorical variables `sex` and `group`

So for a frequency table or bar plot, we can see the frequency of each level of a categorical variable. This gives us some knowledge about the BELC dataset: there are more girls in the dataset and more essays appear in first and third time groups. If we were to see any clearly lopsided categories, this would be a sign of imbalance in the data and we would need to consider how this might impact our analysis.

> **Consider this**
> The goal of descriptive statistics is to summarize the data in a way that is meaningful and interpretable. With this in mind, compare the frequency tables and bar plots in Table 3.5 and Figure 3.1. Does one provide a more interpretable summary of the data? Why or why not? Are there any other ways you might communicate this distribution more effectively?

Numeric variables are best understood visually. The most common visualizations of the distribution of a numeric variable are histograms and density plots. **Histograms** are a type of bar plot where the x-axis is a numeric variable and the y-axis is the frequency of the values falling within a determined range of values, or bins. The frequency of values within each bin is represented by the height of the bars.

Density plots are a smoothed version of histograms. The y-axis of a density plot is the probability of the values. When frequent values appear closely together, the plot line is higher. When the frequency of values is lower or more spread out, the plot line is lower.

Both the histogram in Figure 3.2a and the density plot in Figure 3.2b show the distribution of the variable `tokens` in slightly different ways which translate into trade-offs in terms of interpretability.

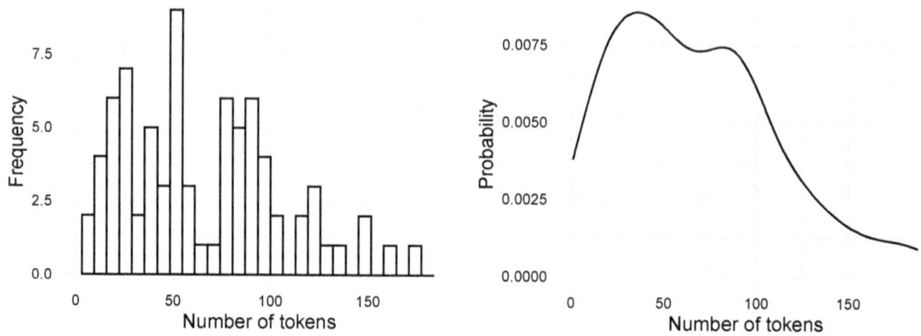

(a) Histogram (b) Density plot

Figure 3.2: Distribution plots for the variable `tokens`.

The histogram shows the frequency of the values in bins. The number of bins and/or bin width can be changed for more or less granularity. A rough grain histogram shows the general shape of the distribution, but it is difficult to see the details of the distribution. A fine grain histogram shows the details of the distribution, but it is difficult to see the general shape of the distribution. The density plot shows the general shape of the distribution, but it hides the details of the distribution. Given this trade-off, it is often useful explore outliers with histograms and the overall shape of the distribution with density plots.

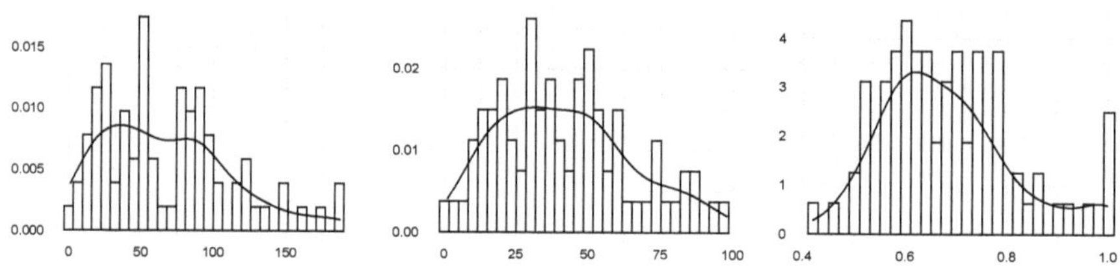

(a) Number of tokens (b) Number of types (c) Type-token ratio score

Figure 3.3: Histograms for numeric variables `tokens`, `types`, and `ttr`.

In Figure 3.3 we see both histograms and density plots combined for the variables `tokens`, `types`, and `ttr`. Focusing on the details captured in the histogram we are better able to detect potential outliers. Outliers can reflect valid values that are simply extreme or they can reflect something erroneous in the data. To distinguish between these two possibilities, it is important to know the context of the data.

Take, for example, Figure 3.3c. We see that there is a bin near the value 1.0. Given that the type-token ratio is a ratio of the number of types to the number of tokens, it is unlikely that the type-token ratio would be exactly 1.0 as this would mean that every word in an essay is unique. Another, less dramatic, example is the bin to the far right of Figure 3.3a. In this case, the bin represents the number of tokens in an essay. An uptick in the number of essays with a large number of tokens is not surprising and would not typically be considered an outlier. On the other hand, consider the bin near the value 0 in the same plot. It is unlikely that a true essay would have 0, or near 0, words and therefore a closer look at the data is warranted.

It is important to recognize that outliers contribute undue influence to overall measures of central tendency and dispersion. To appreciate this, let's consider another helpful visualization called a **boxplot**. A boxplot is a visual representation which aims to represent the central tendency, dispersion, and distribution of a numeric variable in one plot.

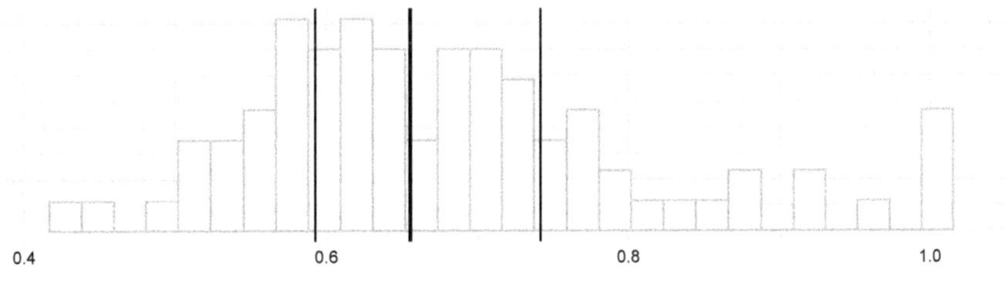

(a) Histogram

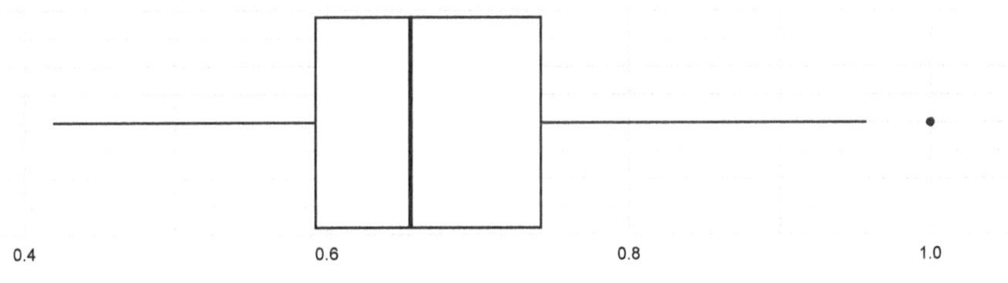

(b) Boxplot

Figure 3.4: Understanding the similarities between boxplots and histograms

In Figure 3.4b we see a boxplot for `ttr` variable. The box in the middle of the plot represents the interquartile range (IQR) which is the range of values between the first quartile and the third quartile. The solid line in the middle of the box represents the median. The lines extending from the box are called 'whiskers' and provide the range of values which are within 1.5 times the IQR. Values outside of this range are plotted as individual points.

Now let's consider boxplots from another angle. Just above in Figure 3.4a I've plotted a histogram. In this view, we can see that a boxplot is a simplified histogram augmented with central tendency and dispersion statistics. While histograms focus on the frequency distribution of data points, boxplots focus on the data's quartiles and potential outliers.

Concerning outliers, it is important to address them to safeguard the accuracy of the analysis. There are two main ways to address outliers: eliminate observations with outliers or transform the data. The elimination, or **trimming**, of outliers is more extreme as it removes data but can be the best approach for true outliers. Transforming the data is an approach to mitigating the influence of extreme but valid values. **Transformation** involves applying a mathematical function to the data which changes the scale and/or shape of the distribution, but does not remove data nor does it change the relative order of the values.

The exploration of the data points with histograms and boxplots has helped us to identify outliers. Now we turn to the question of the overall shape of the distribution.

When values are symmetrically dispersed around the central tendency, the distribution is said to be normal. The **normal distribution** is characterized by a distribution where the mean and median are the same. The normal distribution has a key role in theoretical inference and is the foundation for many statistical tests. This distribution is also known as the Gaussian distribution or a bell curve for the hallmark bell shape of the distribution. In a normal distribution, extreme values are less likely than values near the center.

When values are not symmetrically dispersed around the central tendency, the distribution is said to be skewed. A distribution in which values tend to disperse to the left of the central tendency is **left skewed** and a distribution in which values tend to disperse to the right of the central tendency is **right skewed**.

Simulations of these distributions appear in Figure 3.5.

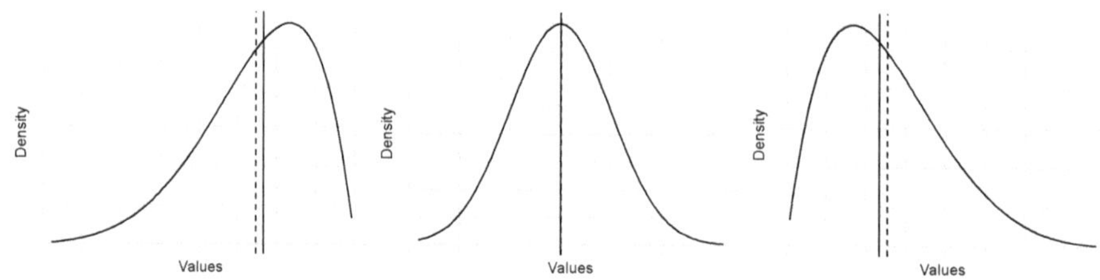

(a) Left-skewed (b) Normal (c) Right-skewed

Figure 3.5: Mean and median for normal and skewed distributions

Assessing the distribution of a variable is important for two reasons. First, the distribution of a variable can inform the choice of statistical test in theory-based hypothesis testing. Data that are normally, or near-normally distributed are often analyzed using parametric tests while data that exhibit a skewed distributed are often analyzed using non-parametric tests. Second, highly skewed distributions have the effect of compressing the range of values. This can lead to a loss of information and can make it difficult to detect patterns in the data.

Skewed frequency distributions are commonly found for linguistic units (*e.g.* phonemes, morphemes, words, *etc.*). However, these distributions tend to a follow a particular type of skew known as a Zipf distribution. According to **Zipf's law** (Zipf, 1949), the frequency of a linguistic unit is inversely proportional to its rank. In other words, the most frequent units will appear twice as often as the second most frequent unit, three times as often as the third most frequent unit, and so on.

The plot in Figure 3.6a is simulated data that fits a Zipfian distribution.

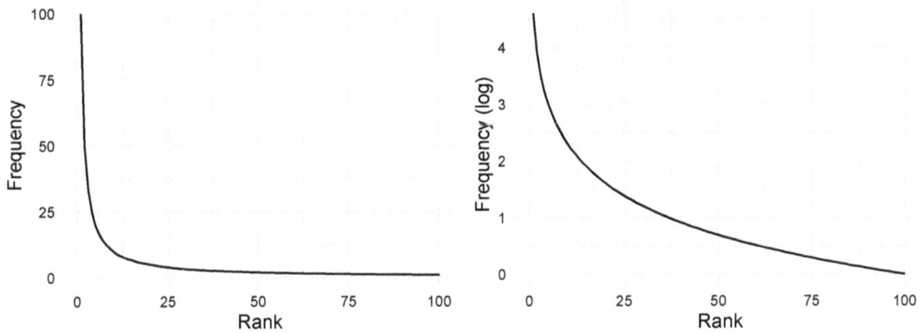

(a) Zipfian distribution

(b) Log-transformed Zipfian distribution

Figure 3.6: Zipfian distribution

Zipf's law describes a theoretical distribution, and the actual distribution of units in a corpus is affected by various sampling factors, including the size of the corpus. The larger the corpus, the closer the distribution will be to the Zipf distribution.

Dive deeper

As stated above, Zipfian distributions are typical of natural language and are observed at various linguistic levels. This is because natural language is a complex system, and complex systems tend to exhibit Zipfian distributions. Other examples of complex systems that exhibit Zipfian distributions include the size of cities, the frequency of species in ecological communities, the frequency of links in the World Wide Web, *etc.*

In the case that a variable is highly skewed (such as in linguistic frequency distributions), it is often useful to attempt to transform the variable to reduce the skewness. In contrast to scale-based transformations (*e.g.* centering and scaling), shape-based transformations change the scale and the shape of the distribution. The most common shape-based transformation is the logarithmic transformation. The **logarithmic transformation** (log transformation) takes the log (typically base 10) of each value in a variable. The log transformation is useful for reducing the skewness of a variable as it compresses large values and expands small values. If the skewness is due to these factors, the log transformation can help, as in the case of the Zipfian distribution in Figure 3.6b.

It is important to note, however, that if scale-based transformations are to be applied to a variable, they should be applied after the log transformation as the log of negative values is undefined.

3.1.4 Association

We have covered the first three of the four questions we are interested in asking in a descriptive assessment. The fourth, and last, question is whether there is an association between variables. If so, what is the directionality and what is the apparent magnitude of the dependence? Knowing the answers to these questions will help frame our approach to analysis.

To assess association, the number and information types of the variables under consideration are important. Let's start by considering two variables. If we are working with two variables, we are dealing with a **bivariate** relationship. Given there are three informational types (categorical, ordinal, and numeric), there are six logical bivariate combinations: categorical-categorical, categorical-ordinal, categorical-numeric, ordinal-ordinal, ordinal-numeric, and numeric-numeric.

The directionality of a relationship will take the form of a tabular or graphic summary depending on the informational value of the variables involved. In Table 3.6, we see the appropriate summary types for each of the six bivariate combinations.

Table 3.6: Summaries for different combinations of variable types

	Categorical	Ordinal	Numeric
Categorical	Contingency table	Contingency table/ Bar plot	Pivot table/ boxplot
Ordinal	-	Contingency table/ Bar plot	Pivot table/ boxplot
Numeric	-	-	scatterplot

Table 3.7: Contingency tables for categorical variable `sex` and ordinal variable `group`

(a) Counts

group	female	male	Total
T1	14	11	25
T2	11	5	16
T3	13	11	24
T4	10	5	15
Total	48	32	80

(b) Percentages

group	female	male	Total
T1	56.00%	44.00%	100.00%
T2	68.75%	31.25%	100.00%
T3	54.17%	45.83%	100.00%
T4	66.67%	33.33%	100.00%
Total	60.00%	40.00%	100.00%

Let's first start with the combinations that include a categorical or ordinal variable. Categorical and ordinal variables reflect measures of class-type information. To assess a relationship with these variable types, a table is always a good place to start. When combined together, a contingency table is the appropriate table. A **contingency table** is a cross-tabulation of two class-type variables, basically a two-way frequency table. This means that three of the six bivariate combinations are assessed with a contingency table: categorical-categorical, categorical-ordinal, and ordinal-ordinal.

In Table 3.7 we see contingency tables for the categorical variable `sex` and ordinal variable `group` in the BELC dataset. A contingency table may include only counts, as in Table 3.7a, or may include proportions or percentages in an effort to normalize the counts and make them more comparable, as in Table 3.7b.

It is sometimes helpful to visualize a contingency table as a bar plot when there are a larger number of levels in either or both of the variables. Again, looking at the relationship between `sex` and `group`, we see that we can plot the counts or the proportions. In Figure 3.7, we see both.

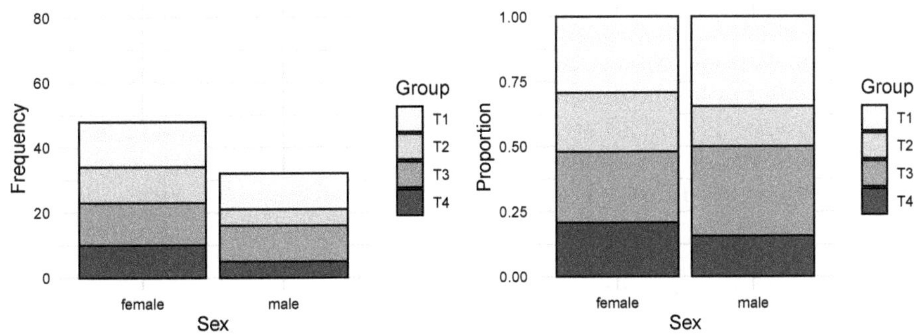

(a) Counts (b) Proportions

Figure 3.7: Bar plots for the relationship between `sex` and `group`

To summarize and assess the relationship between a categorical or an ordinal variable and a numeric variable , we cannot use a contingency table. Instead, this type of relationship is best summarized in a table using a summary statistic in a **pivot table**. A pivot table is a table in which a class-type variable is used to group a numeric variable by some summary statistic appropriate for numeric variables, *e.g.* mean, median, standard deviation, *etc.*

In Table 3.8, we see a pivot table for the relationship between `group` and `tokens` in the BELC dataset. Specifically, we see the mean number of tokens by group. We see the mean number of tokens increases from Group T1 to T4, which is consistent with the idea that the students in the higher groups are writing longer essays.

Table 3.8: Pivot table for the mean `tokens` by `group`

group	mean_tokens
T1	29.6
T2	58.7
T3	83.9
T4	114.5

Although a pivot table may be appropriate for targeted numeric summaries, a visualization is often more informative for assessing the dispersion and distribution of a numeric variable by a categorical or ordinal variable. There are two main types of visualizations for this type of relationship: a boxplot and a **violin plot**. A violin plot is a visualization that summarizes the distribution of a numeric variable by a categorical or ordinal variable, adding the overall shape of the distribution, much as a density plot does for histograms..

In Figure 3.8, we see both a boxplot and a violin plot for the relationship between `group` and `tokens` in the BELC dataset. From the boxplot in Figure 3.8a, we see a general trend towards more tokens used by students in higher groups. But we can also appreciate the dispersion of the data within each group looking at the boxes and whiskers. On the surface it appears that the data for groups T1 and T3 are closer to each other than groups T2 and T4, in which there is more variability within these groups. Furthermore, we can see outliers in groups T1 and T3, but not in groups T2 and T4. From the violin plot in Figure 3.8b, we can see the same information, but we can also see the overall shape of the distribution of tokens within each group. In this plot, it is very clear that group T4 includes a wide range of token counts.

The last bivariate combination is numeric-numeric. To summarize this type of relationship a scatterplot is used. A **scatterplot** is a visualization that plots each data point as a point in a two-dimensional space, with one numeric variable on the x-axis and the other numeric variable on the y-axis. Depending on the type of relationship you are trying to assess, you may want to add a trend

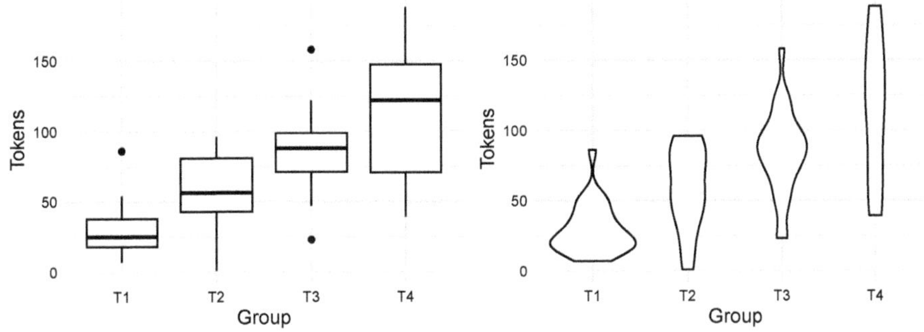

(a) Boxplot (b) Violin plot

Figure 3.8: Boxplot and violin plot for the relationship between `group` and `tokens`

line to the scatterplot. A trend line is a line that summarizes the overall trend in the relationship between the two numeric variables. To assess the extent to which the relationship is linear, a straight line is drawn which minimizes the distance between the line and the points.

In Figure 3.9, we see a scatterplot and a scatterplot with a trend line for the relationship between `ttr` and `types` in the BELC dataset. We see there is an apparent positive relationship between these two variables, which is consistent with the idea that as the number of types increases, the type-token ratio increases. In other words, as the number of unique words increases, so does the lexical diversity of the text. Since we are evaluating a linear relationship, we are assessing the extent to which there is a **correlation** between `ttr` and `types`. A correlation simply means that as the values of one variable change, the values of the other variable change in a consistent manner.

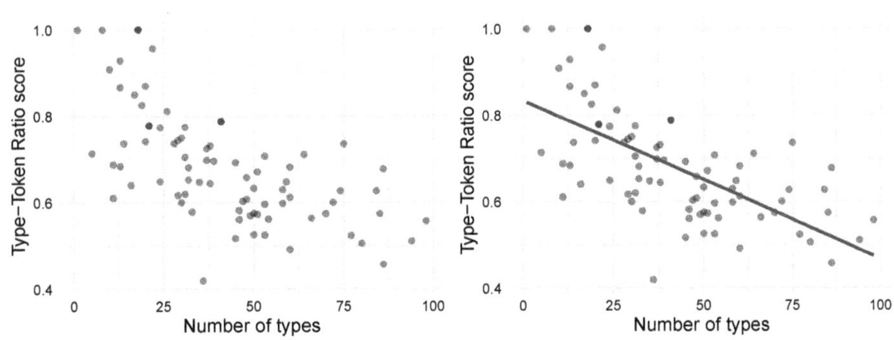

(a) Points (b) Points with a linear trend line

Figure 3.9: Scatterplot for the relationship between `ttr` and `types`

3.2 Analyze

The goal of analysis, generally, is to generate knowledge from information. The type of knowledge generated and the process by which it is generated, however, differ and can be broadly grouped into three analysis types: exploratory, predictive, and inferential.

In this section, I will elaborate briefly on the distinctions between analysis types seen in Table 3.9. I will structure the discussion moving from the least structured (inductive) to most structured (deductive) approach to deriving knowledge from information with the aim to provide enough information for you to identify these research approaches in the literature and to make appropriate decisions as to which approach your research should adopt.

Table 3.9: Overview of analysis types

Type	Aims	Approach	Methods	Evaluation
Exploratory	Explore: gain insight	Inductive, data-driven, and iterative	Descriptive, pattern detection with machine learning (unsupervised)	Associative
Predictive	Predict: validate associations	Semi-deductive, data-/ theory-driven, and iterative	Predictive modeling with machine learning (supervised)	Model performance, feature importance, and associative
Inferential	Explain: test hypotheses	Deductive, theory-driven, and non-iterative	Hypothesis testing with statistical tests	Causal

3.2.1 Explore

In **exploratory data analysis (EDA)**, we use a variety of methods to identify patterns, trends, and relations within and between variables. The goal of EDA is uncover insights in an inductive, data-driven manner. That is to say, that we do not enter into EDA with a fixed hypothesis in mind, but rather we explore intuition, probe anecdote, and follow hunches to identify patterns and relationships and to evaluate whether and why they are meaningful. We are admittedly treading new or unfamiliar terrain letting the data guide our analysis. This means that we can use and reuse the same data to explore different angles and approaches, adjusting our methods and measures as we go. In this way, EDA is an iterative, meaning generating process.

In line with the investigative nature of EDA, the identification of variables of interest is a discovery process. We most likely have an intuition about the variables we would like to explore, but we are able to adjust our variables as need be to suit our research aims. When the identification and selection of variables is open, the process is known as **feature engineering**. A process that is as much an art as a science, feature engineering leverages a mixture of relevant domain knowledge, intuition, and trial and error to identify features that serve to best represent the data and to best serve the research aims. Furthermore, the roles of features in EDA are fluid —no variable has a special status, as seen in Figure 3.10. We will see that in other types of analysis, some or all the roles of the variables are fixed.

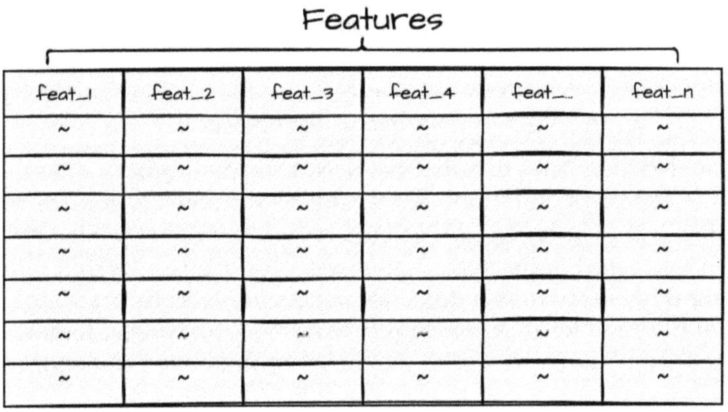

Figure 3.10: Roles of variables in exploratory data analysis

Any given dataset could serve as a starting point to explore many different types of research questions. In order to maintain research coherence so our efforts to not careen into a free-for-all, we need to tether our feature engineering to a unit of analysis that is relevant to the research question. A **unit of analysis** is the entity that we are interested in studying. Not to be confused with the unit of observation, which is the entity that we are able to observe and measure (Sedgwick, 2015). Depending on the perspective we are interested in investigating, the choice of how to approach engineering features to gain insight will vary.

By the same token, approaches for interrogating the dataset can differ significantly, between research projects and within the same project, but for instructive purposes, let's draw a distinction between descriptive methods and unsupervised learning methods, as seen in Table 3.10.

Table 3.10: Some common exploratory data analysis methods

Descriptive Methods	Unsupervised Learning Methods
Frequency analysis	Cluster analysis
Co-occurence analysis	Principal component analysis
Keyness analysis	Topic Modeling
	Vector space models

The first group, **descriptive methods** can be seen as an extension of the descriptive statistics covered earlier in this chapter including statistic, tabular, and visual techniques. The second group, **unsupervised learning**, is a subtype of machine learning in which an algorithm is used to find patterns within and between variables in the data without any guidance (supervision). In this way, the algorithm, or machine learner, is left to make connections and associations wherever they may appear in the input data.

Either through descriptive, unsupervised learning methods, or a combination of both, EDA employs quantitative methods to summarize, reduce, and sort complex datasets in order to provide the researcher novel perspective to be qualitatively assessed. Exploratory methods produce results that require associative thinking and pattern detection. Speculative as they are, the results from exploratory methods can be highly informative and lead to new insight and inspire further study in directions that may not have been expected.

3.2.2 Predict

Predictive data analysis (PDA) employs a variety of techniques to examine and evaluate the association strength between a variable or set of variables, with a specific focus on predicting a target variable. The aim of PDA is to construct models that can accurately forecast future outcomes, using either data-driven or theory-driven approaches. In this process, **supervised learning** methods, where the machine learning algorithm is guided (supervised) by a target outcome variable, are used. This means we don't begin PDA with a completely open-ended exploration, but rather with an objective —accurate predictions. However, the path to achieving this objective can be flexible, allowing us freedom to adjust our models and methods. Unlike EDA, where the entire dataset can be reused for different approaches, PDA requires a portion of the data to be reserved for evaluation, enhancing the validity of our predictive models. Thus, PDA is an iterative process that combines the flexibility of exploratory analysis with the rigor of confirmatory analysis.

There are two types of variables in PDA: the outcome variable and the predictor variables, or features. The **outcome variable** is the variable that the researcher is trying to predict. It is the only variable that is necessarily fixed as part of the research question. The features are the variables that are used to predict the outcome variable. An overview of the roles of these variables in PDA is shown in Figure 3.11.

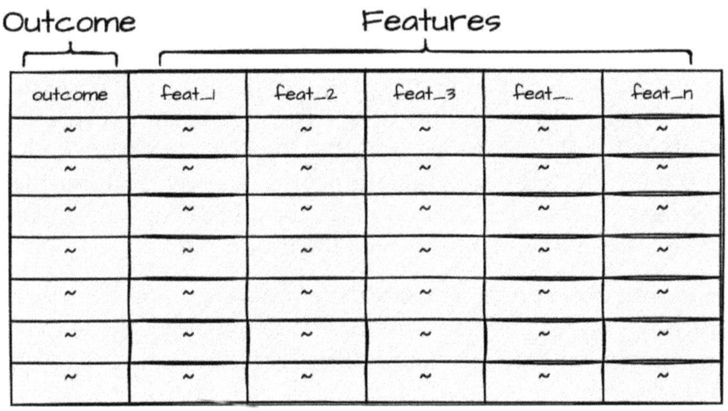

Figure 3.11: Roles of variables in predictive data analysis

Feature selection can be either data-driven or theory-driven. Data-driven features are those that are engineered to enhance predictive power, while theory-driven features are those that are selected based on theoretical relevance.

The approach to interrogating the dataset includes three main steps: feature engineering, model selection, and model evaluation. We've discussed feature engineering, so what is model selection and model evaluation?

Model selection is the process of choosing a machine learning algorithm and set of features that produces the best prediction accuracy for the outcome variable. To refine our approach such that we arrive at the best combination of algorithm and features, we need to train our machine learner on a variety of combinations and evaluate the accuracy of each.

There are many different types of machine learning algorithms, each with their own strengths and weaknesses. The first rough cut is to decide what type of outcome variable we are predicting: categorical or numeric. If the outcome variable is categorical, we are performing a **classification** task, and if the outcome variable is numeric, we are performing a **regression** task. As we see in Table 3.11, there are various algorithms that can be used for each task.

Table 3.11: Some common supervised learning algorithms used in PDA

Classification	Regression
Logistic Regression	Linear Regression
Random Forest Classifier	Random Forest Regressor
Support Vector Machine	Support Vector Regression
Neural Network Classifier	Neural Network Regressor

There are a number of algorithm-specific strengths and weaknesses to be considered in the process of model selection. These hinge on characteristics of the data, such as the size of the dataset, the number of features, the type of features, and the expected type of relationships between features or on computing resources, such as the amount of time available to train the model or the amount of memory available to store the model.

Model evaluation is the process of assessing the accuracy of the model on the test set, which is a proxy for how well the model will generalize to new data. Model evaluation is performed quantitatively by calculating the accuracy of the model. It is important to note that whether the accuracy metrics are good is to some degree qualitative judgment.

3.2.3 Infer

The most commonly recognized of the three data analysis approaches, **inferential data analysis (IDA)** is the bread-and-butter of science. IDA is a deductive, theory-driven approach in which all aspects of analysis stem from a premise, or hypothesis, about the nature of a relationship in the world and then aims to test whether this relationship is statistically supported given the evidence. Since the goal is to infer conclusions about a certain relationship in the population based on a statistical evaluation of a (corpus) sample, the representativeness of the sample is of utmost importance. Furthermore, the use of the data is limited to the scope of the hypothesis —that is, the data cannot be used iteratively for exploratory purposes.

The selection of variables and the roles they play in the analysis are determined by the hypothesis. In a nutshell, a **hypothesis** is a formal statement about the state of the world. This statement is theory-driven, meaning that it is predicated on previous research. We are not exploring or examining relationships, rather we are testing a specific relationship. In practice, however, we are in fact proposing two mutually exclusive hypotheses. The first is the **alternative hypothesis**, or H_1. This is the hypothesis I just described —the statement grounded in the previous literature outlining a predicted relationship. The second is the **null hypothesis**, or H_0. This is the flip-side of the hypothesis testing coin and states that there is no difference or relationship. Together H_1 and H_0 cover all logical outcomes.

Now, in standard IDA one variable is the response variable and one or more variables are explanatory variables. The **response variable**, sometimes referred to as the outcome or dependent variable, is the variable which contains the information which is hypothesized to depend on the information in the explanatory variable(s). It is the variable whose variation a research study seeks to explain. An **explanatory variable**, sometimes referred to as an independent or predictor variable, is a variable whose variation is hypothesized to explain the variation in the response variable.

Explanatory variables add to the complexity of a study because they are part of our research focus, specifically our hypothesis. It is, however, common to include other variables which are not of central focus, but are commonly assumed to contribute to the explanation of the variation of the response variable. These are known as **control variables**. Control variables are included in the analysis to account for the influence of other variables on the relationship between the response and explanatory variables, but will not be included in the hypothesis nor interpreted in our results.

We can now see in Figure 3.12 the variables roles assigned to variables in a hypothesis-driven study.

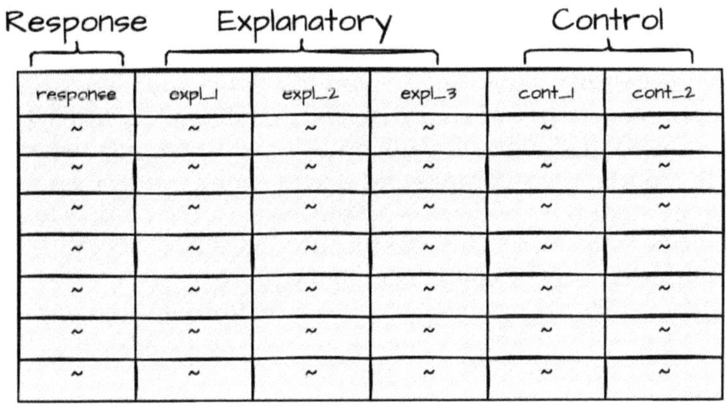

Figure 3.12: Roles of variables in inferential data analysis

The type of statistical test that one chooses is based on (1) the informational value of the dependent variable and (2) the number of predictor variables included in the analysis. Together these two characteristics go a long way in determining the appropriate class of statistical test (see Gries (2013) and Paquot & Gries (2020) for a more exhaustive description).

IDA relies heavily on quantitative evaluation methods to draw conclusions that can be generalized to the target population. It is key to understand that our goal in hypothesis testing is not to find evidence in support of H_1, but rather to assess the likelihood that we can reliably reject H_0.

Traditionally, p-values have been used to determine the likelihood of rejecting H_0. A **p-value** is the probability of observing a test statistic as extreme as the one observed, given that H_0 is true. However, p-values are not the only metric used to evaluate the likelihood of rejecting H_0. Other metrics, such as effect size and confidence intervals, are also used to interpret the results of hypothesis tests.

3.3 Communicate

Conducting research should be enjoyable and personally rewarding but the effort you have invested and knowledge you have generated should be shared with others. Whether part of a blog, presentation, journal article, or for your own purposes it is important to document your analysis results and process in a way that is informative and interpretable. This enhances the value of your work, allowing others to learn from your experience and build on your findings.

3.3.1 Report

The most widely recognized form of communicating research is through a report. A report is a narrative of your analysis, including the research question, the data you used, the methods you applied, and the results you obtained. We are both reporting our findings and documenting our process to inform others of what we did and why we did it but also to invite readers to evaluate our findings for themselves. The scientific process is a collaborative one and evaluation by peers is a key component of the process.

3.3.2 Document

While a good report will include the most vital information to understand the procedures, results, and findings of an analysis, there is much more information generated in the course of an analysis which does not traditionally appear in prose. If a research project is conducted programmatically, however, data, code, and documentation can be made available to others as part of the communication process. Increasingly, researchers are sharing their data and code as part of the publication process. This allows others to reproduce the analysis and verify the results contributing to the collaborative nature of the scientific process.

Together, data, code, and documentation form a **research compendium**. As you can imagine, the research process can quickly become complex and unwieldy as the number of files and folders grows. If not organized properly, it can be difficult to find the information you need. Furthermore, if not documented, decisions made in the course of the analysis can be difficult or impossible to trace. For this reason, it is recommendable to follow a set of best practices for organizing and documenting your research compendium. We will cover this in more detail in subsequent chapters.

Activities

In the following activities, we will build on our understanding of how to summarize data using statistics, tables, and plots. We will dive deeper into the use of {skimr} (Waring et al., 2022) to summarize data and the {ggplot2} (Wickham, Chang, et al., 2024) to create plots. We also introduce producing Quarto tables and figures with appropriate code block options. We will reinforce our understanding of {readr} (Wickham, Hester, & Bryan, 2024) to read in data and {dplyr} (Wickham, François, Henry, Müller, & Vaughan, 2023) to manipulate data.

> **Recipe**
> **What**: Descriptive assessment of datasets
> **How**: Read Recipe 3, complete comprehension check, and prepare for Lab 3.
> **Why**: To explore appropriate methods for summarizing variables in datasets given the number and informational values of the variable(s).

> **Lab**
> **What**: Trace the datascape
> **How**: Clone, fork, and complete the steps in Lab 3.
> **Why**: To identify and apply the appropriate descriptive methods for a vector's informational value and to assess both single variables and multiple variables with the appropriate statistical, tabular, and/or graphical summaries.

Summary

In this chapter we have focused on description and analysis —the third component of the DIKI Hierarchy. This is the stage where we begin to derive knowledge from the data which includes first performing a descriptive assessment of the individual variables and relationships between variables. Only after we have a better understanding of our data, we move to the analysis stage. We outlined three data analysis types in this chapter: exploratory, predictive, and inferential. Each of these embodies distinct approaches to deriving knowledge from data. Ultimately the choice of analysis type is highly dependent on the goals of the research.

I rounded out this chapter with a short description of the importance of communicating the analysis process and results. Reporting, in its traditional form, is documented in prose in an article. Yet even the most detailed reporting in a write-up still leaves many practical, but key, points of the analysis obscured. A programming approach provides the procedural steps taken that when shared provide the exact methods applied. Together with the write-up, a research compendium which provides the scripts to run the analysis and documentation on how to run the analysis forms an integral part of creating reproducible research.

4

Research

Outcomes

- Identify a research area and problem by listing key strategies and describing their contribution towards research identification.
- Explain the significance of a well-framed research question in guiding the overall research project.
- Comprehend how the conceptual and practical steps involved in developing a research blueprint aid not only the researcher but also the broader scientific community.

In this chapter, we discuss how to frame research —that is, how to position your research project's findings to contribute insight to understanding of the world. We will cover how to connect with the literature, selecting a research area and identifying a research problem, and how to design research best positioned to return relevant findings that will connect with this literature, establishing a research aim and research question. We will round out this chapter with a guide on developing a research blueprint—a working plan to organize the conceptual and practical steps to implement the research effectively and in a way that supports communicating the research findings and the process by which the findings were obtained.

>_ Lessons
What: Project Environment
How: In an R console, load {swirl}, run `swirl()`, and follow prompts to select the lesson.
Why: To highlight the importance of the computing environment in R for project management and reproducibility.

10.4324/9781003393764.4

4.1 Frame

Together, a research area, problem, aim and question, and the research blueprint that forms the conceptual and practical scaffolding of the project ensure from the outset that the project is solidly grounded in the main characteristics of good research. These characteristics, summarized by Cross (2006), are found in Table 4.1.

Table 4.1: Characteristics of good research (Cross, 2006)

Characteristic	Description
Purposive	Based on identification of an issue or problem worthy and capable of investigation
Inquisitive	Seeking to acquire new knowledge
Informed	Conducted from an awareness of previous, related research
Methodical	Planned and carried out in a disciplined manner
Communicable	Generating and reporting results which are feasible and accessible by others

With these characteristics in mind, let's get started with the first component to address —connecting with the literature.

4.2 Connect

4.2.1 Research area

The first decision to make in the research process is to identify a research area. A **research area** is a general area of interest where a researcher wants to derive insight and make a contribution to understanding. For those with an established research trajectory in language, the area of research to address through text analysis will likely be an extension of their prior work. For others, which include new researchers or researchers that want to explore new areas of language research or approach an area through a language-based lens, the choice of area may be less obvious. In either case, the choice of a research area should be guided by a desire to contribute something relevant to a theoretical, applied, and/ or practical matter of personal interest. Personal relevance goes a long way to developing and carrying out *purposive* and *inquisitive* research.

So how do we get started? Consider your interests in a language or set of languages, a discipline, a methodology, or some applied area. Language is at the heart of the human experience and therefore found in some fashion anywhere one seeks to find it. But it is a big world and more often than not the general question about what area to select is sometimes the most difficult. To get the ball rolling, it is helpful to peruse disciplinary encyclopedias or handbooks of linguistics and language-related academic fields (*e.g.* Encyclopedia of Language and Linguistics (Brown, 2005), A Practical Guide to Electronic Resources in the Humanities (Dubnjakovic & Tomlin, 2010), Routledge Encyclopedia of Translation Technology (Chan, 2014))

A more personal, less academic, approach is to consult online forums, blogs, *etc* that one already frequents or can be accessed via an online search. Through social media you may find particular people that maintain a blog worth browsing. Perusing these resources can help spark ideas and highlight the kinds of questions that interest you.

Regardless of whether your inquiry stems from academic, professional, or personal interest, try to connect these findings to academic areas of research. Academic research is highly structured and well-documented, and making associations with this network will aid in subsequent steps in developing a research project.

4.2.2 Research problem

Once you've made a rough-cut decision about the area of research, it is now time to take a deeper dive into the subject area and jump into the literature. This is where the rich structure of disciplinary research will provide aid to traverse the vast world of academic knowledge and identify a research problem. A **research problem** highlights a particular topic of debate or uncertainty in existing knowledge which is worthy of study.

Surveying the relevant literature is key to ensuring that your research is *informed*, that is, connected to previous work. Identifying relevant research to consult can be a bit of a 'chicken or the egg' problem —some knowledge of the area is necessary to find relevant topics, some knowledge of the topics is necessary to narrow the area of research. Many times the only way forward is to jump into conducting searches. These can be world-accessible resources (*e.g.* Google Scholar) or limited-access resources that are provided through an academic institution (*e.g.* Linguistics and Language Behavior Abstracts, ERIC, PsycINFO, *etc.*). Some organizations and academic institutions provide research guides to help researcher's access the primary literature. There are even a new breed of search engines that are designed to help researchers aggregate and search academic literature (*e.g.* Scite, Elicit, *etc.*). Another avenue to explore are journals and conference proceedings dedicated to linguistics and language-related research. Text analysis is a rapidly expanding methodology, which is being applied to a wide range of research areas.

To explore research related to text analysis it is helpful to start with the (sub)discipline name(s) you identified when selecting your research area, more specific terms that occur to you or key terms from the literature, and terms such as 'corpus study' or 'corpus-based'. The results from first searches may not turn out to be sources that end up figuring explicitly in your research, but it is important to skim these results and the publications themselves to mine information that can be useful to formulate better and more targeted searches.

Relevant information for honing your searches can be found throughout an academic publication. However, pay particular attention to the abstract, in articles, and the table of contents, in books, and the cited references. Abstracts and tables of contents often include discipline-specific jargon that is commonly used in the field. In some articles, there is even a short list of key terms listed below the abstract which can be extremely useful to seed better and more precise search results. The references section will contain relevant and influential research. Scan these references for publications which appear to narrow in on your topic of interest and treat it like a search in its own right.

Once your searches begin to show promising results it is time to keep track and organize these references. Whether you plan to collect thousands of references over a lifetime of academic research or your aim is centered around one project, software such as Zotero[1], Mendeley[2], or BibDesk[3] provide powerful, flexible, and easy-to-use tools to collect, organize, annotate, search, and export references. Citation management software is indispensable for modern research —and often free!

As your list of relevant references grows, you will want to start the investigation process in earnest. Begin skimming (not reading) the contents of each of these publications, starting with what appears to be the most relevant first. Annotate these publications using highlighting features of the citation management software to identify: (1) the stated goal(s) of the research, (2) the data source(s) used, (3) the information drawn from the data source(s), (4) the analysis approach employed, and (5) the main finding(s) of the research as they pertain to the stated goal(s).

[1]https://www.zotero.org/
[2]https://www.mendeley.com/
[3]https://bibdesk.sourceforge.io/

Next, in your own words, summarize these five key areas in prose adding your summary to the notes feature of the citation management software. This process will allow you to efficiently gather and document references with the relevant information to guide the identification of a research problem, to guide the formation of your problem statement, and ultimately, to support the literature review that will figure in your project write-up.

From your preliminary annotated summaries you will undoubtedly start to recognize overlapping and contrasting aspects in the research literature. These aspects may be topical, theoretical, methodological, or appear along other lines. Note these aspects and continue to conduct more refine searches, annotate new references, and monitor for any emerging uncertainties, limitations, debates, and/ or contradictions which align with your research interest(s). When a promising pattern takes shape, it is time to engage with a more detailed reading of those references which appear most relevant highlighting the potential gap(s) in the literature.

At this point you can focus energy on more nuanced aspects of a particular gap in the literature with the goal to formulate a problem statement. A **problem statement** directly acknowledges a gap in the literature and puts a finer point on the nature and relevance of this gap for understanding. This statement reflects your first deliberate attempt to establish a line of inquiry. It will be a targeted, but still somewhat general, statement framing the gap in the literature that will guide subsequent research design decisions.

4.3 Define

4.3.1 Research aim

With a problem statement in hand, it is now time to consider the goal(s) of the research. A **research aim** frames the type of inquiry to be conducted. Will the research aim to explore, predict, or explain? As you can appreciate, the research aim is directly related to the analysis methods we touched upon in Chapter 3.

To gauge how to frame your research aim, reflect on the literature that led you to your problem statement and the nature of the problem statement itself. If the gap at the center of the problem statement is a lack of knowledge, your research aim may be exploratory. If the gap concerns a conjecture about a relationship, then your research may take a predictive approach. When the gap points to the validation of a relationship, then your research will likely be inferential in nature. Before selecting your research aim it is also helpful to consult the research aims of the primary literature that led you to your research statement.

Typically, a problem statement addressing a subtle, specific issue tends to adopt research objectives similar to prior studies. In contrast, a statement focusing on a broader, more distinct issue is likely to have unique research goals. Yet, this is more of a guideline than a strict rule.

It's crucial to understand both the existing literature and the nature of various types of analyses. Being clear about your research goals is important to ensure that your study is well-placed to produce results that add value to the current understanding in an informed manner.

4.3.2 Research question

The next step in research design is to craft the research question. A **research question** is a clearly defined statement which identifies an aspect of uncertainty and the particular relationships that this uncertainty concerns. The research question extends and narrows the line of inquiry established in the research statement and research aim. To craft a research question, we can use the research statement for the content and the research aim for the form.

Form

The form of a research question will vary based on the research aim, which as I mentioned, is intimately connected to the analysis approach. For inferential-based research, the research question will actually be a statement, not a question. This statement makes a testable claim about the nature of a particular relationship —*i.e.* asserts a hypothesis.

For illustration, let's posit a hypothesis (H_1), leaving aside the implicit null hypothesis (H_0), seen in Example 4.1.

Example 4.1. *Women use more questions than men in spontaneous conversations.*

For predictive- and exploratory-based research, the research question is in fact a question. A reframing of the example hypothesis for a predictive-based research question might take the form seen in Example 4.2.

Example 4.2. *Can the number of questions used in spontaneous conversations predict if a speaker is male or female?*

And a similar exploratory-based research question might take the form seen in Example 4.3.

Example 4.3. *Do men and women differ in terms of the number of questions they use in spontaneous conversations?*

The central research interest behind these hypothetical research questions is, admittedly, quite basic. But from these simplified examples, we are able to appreciate the similarities and differences between the forms of research statements that correspond to distinct research aims.

Content

In terms of content, the research question will make reference to two key components: unit of analysis and unit of observation. As seen in previous chapters, together the unit of analysis and unit of observation form the semantic and structural backbone of the research design. The unit of analysis is the primary element on which the insight into the research question is derived and the unit of observation is the primary element which provides the organizational structure of the dataset to be analyzed.

In our examples, the unit of analysis is *speakers*. Note, however, that the current unit of analysis is somewhat vague in the example research questions. A more precise unit of analysis would include more information about the population from which the speakers are drawn (*i.e.* English speakers, American English speakers, American English speakers of the Southeast, *etc.*). The unit of observation is *spontaneous conversations*. This will be reflected in our dataset as the meaning of each row in the dataset.

In examples 4.1, 4.2, and 4.3, we identified the number of conversations as part of the research question. Later in the research process it will be key to operationalize this variable. For example, will the number of conversations be the total number of conversations in the dataset or will it be the average number of conversations per speaker? These are important questions to consider as they will influence variable selection, statistical choices, and ultimately the interpretation of the results. Operationalizing the variables is a key part of the research design. Without inclusion and exclusion criteria, the research question is not well-defined and the meaningfulness of the results will be obscured (Larsson & Biber, 2024).

4.4 Blueprint

The efforts to develop a research question will produce a clear and focused line of inquiry with the necessary background literature and a well-defined problem statement that forms the basis of *purposeful*, *inquisitive*, and *informed* research (returning to Cross's characteristics of research in Table 4.1).

Moving beyond the research question in the project means developing and laying out the research design in a way such that the research is *methodical* and *communicable*. In this textbook, the method to achieve these goals is through the development of a research blueprint. The blueprint includes two components: (1) the conceptual plan and (2) the organizational scaffolding that will support the implementation of the research (Ignatow & Mihalcea, 2017).

In what follows, I will cover the main aspects of developing a research blueprint. I will start with the conceptual plan and then move on to the organizational scaffolding.

4.4.1 Plan

Importance of establishing a feasible research design from the outset and documenting the key aspects required to conduct the research cannot be understated. On the one hand, this process links a conceptual plan to a tangible implementation. In doing so, a researcher is better-positioned to conduct research with a clear view of what will be entailed. On the other hand, a promising research question may present unexpected challenges once a researcher sets about to implement the research. This is not uncommon to encounter issues that require modification or reevaluation of the viability of the project. However, a well-documented research plan will help a researcher to identify and address many of these challenges at the conceptual level before expending unnecessary effort during implementation.

Let's now consider the subsequent steps to develop a research plan, outlined in Table 4.2.

Table 4.2: Research plan checklist

Step	Stage	Activity
1	Research Question or Hypothesis	Formulate a research question or hypothesis based on a thorough review of existing literature including references. This will guide every subsequent step from data selection to interpretation of results.
2	Data Source(s)	Identify viable data source(s) and vet the sample data in light of the research question. Consider to what extent the goal is to generalize findings to a target population, and ensure that the corpus aligns as much as feasible with this target.
3	Key Variables	Determine the key variables needed for the research, define how they will be operationalized, and ensure they can be derived from the corpus data. Additionally, identify any features that need to be extracted, recoded, generated, or integrated from other data sources.
4	Analysis Method	Choose an appropriate method of analysis to interrogate the dataset. This choice should be in line with your research aim (*e.g.*, exploratory, predictive, or inferential). Be aware of what each method can offer and how it addresses your research question.
5	Interpretation & Evaluation	Establish criteria to interpret and evaluate the results. This will be a function of the relationship between the research question and the analysis method.

First, identify a viable data source. Viability includes the accessibility of the data, availability of the data, and the content of the data. If a purported data source is not accessible and/ or it has stringent restrictions on its use, then it is not a viable data source. If a data source is accessible and available, but does not contain the building blocks needed to address the research question, then it is not a viable data source. A corpus resource's sampling frame should align, to the extent feasible, with the target population(s).

The second step is to identify the key variables needed to conduct the research and then ensure that this information can be derived from the corpus data. The research question will reference the unit of analysis and the unit of observation, but it is important to pinpoint what the key variables will be. We want to envision what needs to be done to derive these variables. There may be features that need to be extracted, recoded, generated, and/ or integrated from other sources to address the research question, as discussed in Chapter 2.

The third step is to identify a method of analysis to interrogate the dataset. The selection of the analysis approach that was part of the research aim (*i.e.* explore, predict, or explain) and then the research question goes a long way to narrowing the methods that a researcher must consider. But there are a number of factors which will make some methods more appropriate than others.

Exploratory research is the least restricted of the three types of analysis approaches. Although it may be the case that a research will not be able to specify from the outset of a project what the exact analysis methods will be, an attempt to consider what types of analysis methods will be most promising to provide results to address the research question goes a long way to steering a project in the right direction and grounding the research. As with the other analysis approaches, it is important to be aware of what analysis methods are available and what type of information they produce in light of the research question.

For predictive-based research, the informational value of the outcome variable is key to deciding whether the prediction will be a classification task or a regression task. This has downstream effects when it comes time to evaluate and interpret the results. Although the feature engineering process in predictive analyses means that the features do not need to be specified from the outset and can be tweaked and changed as needed during an analysis, it is a good idea to start with a basic sense of what features most likely will be helpful in developing a robust predictive model.

In inferential research, the number and information values of the variables to be analyzed will be of key importance (Gries, 2013). The informational value of the response variable will again narrow the search for the appropriate method and statistical test to employ. The number of explanatory variables also plays an important role. All details need not be nailed down at this point, but it is helpful to have them on your radar to ensure that when the time comes to analyze the data, the appropriate steps are followed.

The last of the main components of the research plan concerns the interpretation and evaluation of the results. This step brings the research plan full circle, connecting the research question to the methods employed. It is important to establish from the outset what the criteria will be to evaluate the results. This is in large part a function of the relationship between the research question and the analysis method. For example, in exploratory research, the results will be evaluated qualitatively in terms of the associative patterns that emerge. Predictive and inferential research leans more heavily on quantitative metrics, in particular the accuracy of the prediction or the strength of the relationship between the response and explanatory variable(s), respectively. However, these quantitative metrics require qualitative interpretation to determine whether the results are meaningful in light of the research question.

In addition to addressing the steps outlined in Table 4.2, it is also important to document the strengths and shortcomings of the research plan including the data source(s), the information to be extracted from the data, and the analysis methods. If there are potential shortcomings, which there most often are, sketch out contingency plans to address these shortcomings. This will help buttress your research and ensure that your time and effort is well-spent.

Dive deeper

You may consider pre-registering your prospectus to ensure that your plans are well-documented and to provide a timestamp for your research. Pre-registration can also be a helpful way to get feedback on your research from colleagues and experts in the field. Popular pre-registration platforms include Open Science Framework[a] and Center for Open Science[b].

[a] https://osf.io/

[b] https://www.cos.io/initiatives/prereg/

The research plan together with the information collected to develop the research question is known as a prospectus. A **prospectus** is a document that outlines the key aspects of the research plan and is used to guide the research process. It is a living document that will be updated as the research progresses and as new information is collected.

4.4.2 Scaffold

The next step in developing a research blueprint is to consider how to physically implement your project. This includes how to organize files and directories in a fashion that provides the researcher a logical and predictable structure to work with. As the research progresses, the structure will house the data, code, and output of the research as well as the documentation of the research process —together known as a **research compendium**. In addition to a strong write-up of the research, a research compendium ensures that the research is *communicable*.

Communicable research is reproducible research. Reproducibility strategies are a benefit to the researcher (in the moment and in the future) as it leads to better work habits and to better teamwork and it makes changes to the project easier. Reproducibility is also of benefit to the scientific community as shared reproducible research enhances replicability and encourages cumulative knowledge development (Gandrud, 2015).

In Table 4.3, I outline a set of guiding principles that characterize reproducible research (Gentleman & Temple Lang, 2007; Marwick, Boettiger, & Mullen, 2018).

Table 4.3: Reproducible research principles

No.	Principle	Description
1	Plain text	All files should be plain text which means they contain no formatting information other than whitespace.
2	Clear separation	There should be a clear separation between the inputs, process steps, and outputs of research. This should be apparent from the directory structure.
3	Original data	A separation between original data and data created as part of the research process should be made. Original data should be treated as 'read-only'. Any changes to the original data should be justified, generated by the code, and documented (see point 7).
4	Modular scripts	Each computing file (script) should represent a particular, well-defined step in the research process.
5	Modular files	Each script should be modular —that is, each file should correspond to a specific goal in the analysis procedure with input and output only corresponding to this step.
6	Main script	The project should be tied together by a 'main' script that is used to coordinate the execution of all the project steps.
7	Document everything	Everything should be documented. This includes data collection, data preprocessing, processing steps, script code comments, data description in data dictionaries, information about the computing environment and packages used to conduct the analysis, and detailed instructions on how to reproduce the research.

These seven principles in Table 4.3 can be physically implemented in numerous ways. In recent years, there has been a growing number of efforts to create R packages and templates to quickly generate the scaffolding and tools to facilitate reproducible research. Some notable R packages include {workflowr} (Blischak, Carbonetto, & Stephens, 2019), {ProjectTemplate} (White, 2023), and {targets} (Landau, 2021), but there are many other resources for R included on the CRAN Task View for Reproducible Research[4].

There are many advantages to working with pre-existing frameworks for the savvy R programmer including the ability to quickly generate a project scaffold, to efficiently manage changes to the project, and to buy in to a common framework that is supported by a community of developers.

On the other hand, these frameworks can be a bit daunting for the novice R programmer. At the most basic level, a project can implement the seven principles outlined above with a directory structure and a set of key files seen in Snippet 4.1.

Snippet 4.1. Minimal Project Framework

```
project/
├── input/
│   └── ...
├── code/
│   └── ...
├── output/
│   └── ...
├── DESCRIPTION
├── Makefile
└── README
```

The *project/* directory is composed of three main sections: *input/*, *code/*, and *output/* making the distinction between each transparent in the directory structure. The *input/* will house the data used and created in the project, ensuring that the original data is kept separate from the data created in the research process. The *code/* section will house the scripts that will conduct the project steps including acquiring, curating, transforming, and analyzing the data. These scripts will read and write data and generate output including figures, reports, results, and tables. Lastly, the *output/* section will house the resulting output from the project steps.

At the root of the project directory are three files which describe, document, and execute the project. The *Makefile* is used to automate the execution of the project steps. In effect, it is a script that runs scripts. In addition to coordinating the execution of the project steps, a Makefile will often include commands to set up the computing environment and packages. The *README*

[4]https://cran.r-project.org/web/views/ReproducibleResearch.html

and *DESCRIPTION* files provide on overview of the project from both a conceptual and technical perspective. The *README* file includes a description of the project rationale, aims, and findings and instructions on how to reproduce the research. The *DESCRIPTION* file includes technical information about the computing environment and packages used to conduct the analysis.

The project structure in Snippet 4.1 meets the minimal structural requirements for reproducible research and is a good starting point for a project scaffold. However, aspects of this structure can be adjusted in minimal or more sophisticated ways to meet the needs of a particular project while still conforming to the principles outlined in Table 4.3, as we will see when we return to this topic in Chapter 11.

Activities

The following activities will build on your experience with R and cloning a GitHub repository, and recent experience with understanding the computing environment. The goal will be to bring you up to speed such that you can begin to work on your own research projects and understand how to use the tools and resources available to you to manage your project.

Recipe
What: Understanding the computing environment
How: Read Recipe 4, complete comprehension check, and prepare for Lab 4.
Why: To introduce components of the computing environment and how to manage a reproducible research project structure.

Lab
What: Scaffolding reproducible research
How: Clone, fork, and complete the steps in Lab 4.
Why: To establish a repository and project structure for reproducible research and apply new Git and Github skills to fork, clone, commit, and push changes.

Summary

The aim of this chapter is to provide the key conceptual and practical points to guide the development of a viable research project. Good research is purposive, inquisitive, informed, methodological, and communicable. It is not, however, always a linear process. Exploring your area(s) of interest and connecting with existing work will help couch and refine your research. But practical considerations, such as the existence of viable data, technical skills, and/ or time constrains, sometimes pose challenges and require a researcher to rethink and/ or redirect the research in sometimes small and other times more significant ways. The process of formulating a research question and developing a viable research plan is key to supporting viable, successful, and insightful research. To ensure that the effort to derive insight from data is of most value to the researcher and the research community, the research should strive to be methodological and communicable, adopting best practices for reproducible research.

Part III

Preparation

This part, Preparation, will address data acquistion, curation, and transformation steps and present strategies to implement them. The goal of data preparation is to create a dataset which is ready for analysis. In each of these three upcoming chapters, I will outline some of the main characteristics to consider in each of these research steps and provide authentic examples of working with R to implement these steps. In Chapter 5, this includes the most common strategies for acquiring data: downloads and APIs. In Chapter 6, we turn to organize data into rectangular, or 'tidy', format. Depending on the data or dataset acquired for the research project, the steps necessary to shape our data into a base dataset will vary, as we will see. In Chapter 7, we will work to manipulate curated datasets to create datasets which are aligned with the research aim and research question. This often includes normalizing values, recoding variables, and generating new variables as well as sourcing and integrating information from other datasets with the dataset to be submitted for analysis.

Each of these chapters will cover the necessary documentation to trace our steps and provide a record of the data preparation process. Documentation serves to inform the analysis and interpretation of the results and also forms the cornerstone of reproducible research.

5

Acquire

Outcomes

- Identify common strategies for acquiring corpus data.
- Describe how to organize and document data acquisition to support reproducibility.
- Recall R programming concepts and strategies relevant to acquiring data.

As we start down the path to executing our research blueprint, our first step is to acquire the primary data that will be employed in the project. This chapter covers two strategies for acquiring corpus data: downloads and APIs. We will encounter various file formats and folder structures in the process and we will address how to effectively organize our data for subsequent processing. Crucial to our efforts is the process of documenting our data. We will learn to provide data origin information to ensure key characteristics of the data and its source are documented. Along the way, we will explore R coding concepts including control statements and custom functions relevant to the task of acquiring data. By the end of this chapter, you will not only be adept at acquiring data from diverse sources but also capable of documenting it comprehensively, enabling you to replicate the process in the future.

>_ Lessons
What: Control Statements, Custom Functions
How: In an R console, load {swirl}, run `swirl()`, and follow prompts to select the lesson.
Why: To recognize the logic behind code that can make dynamic choices and to recall how functions serve to produce efficient, reusable, and more legible code.

10.4324/9781003393764.5

5.1 Downloads

The most common and straightforward method for acquiring corpus data is through direct downloads. In a nutshell, this method involves navigating to a website, locating the data, and downloading it to your computing environment. In some cases access to the data requires manual intervention and in others the process can be implemented programmatically. The data may be contained in a single file or multiple files. The files may be archived or unarchived. The data may be hierarchically organized or not. Each resource will have its own unique characteristics that will influence the process of acquiring the data. In this section, we will work through examples to demonstrate the general process of acquiring data through downloads.

5.1.1 Manual

In contrast to the other data acquisition methods we will cover in this chapter, **manual downloads** require human intervention. This means that manual downloads are non-reproducible in a strict sense and require that we keep track of and document our procedure. It is a very common for research projects to acquire data through manual downloads as many data resources require some legwork before they are accessible for downloading. These can be resources that require institutional or private licensing and fees, require authorization/ registration, and/ or are only accessible via resource search interfaces.

The resource we will use for this demonstration is the Corpus Escrito del Español como L2 (CEDEL2)[1] (Lozano, 2022), a corpus of Spanish learner writing. It includes L2 writing from students with a variety of L1 backgrounds. For comparative purposes it also includes native writing for Spanish, English, and several other languages.

The CEDEL2 corpus is a freely available resource, but to access the data you must first use a search interface to select the relevant characteristics of the data of interest. Following the search/download link you can find a search interface that allows the user to select the sub-corpus and filter the results by a set of attributes.

For this example let's assume that we want to acquire data to use in a study comparing the use of the Spanish preterit and imperfect past tense aspect in written texts by English L1 learners of Spanish to native Spanish speakers. To acquire data for such a project, we will first select the sub-corpus "Learners of

[1]http://cedel2.learnercorpora.com/

L2 Spanish". We will set the results to provide full texts and filter the results to "L1 English - L2 Spanish". Additionally, we will set the medium to "Written". This will provide us with a set of texts for the L2 learners that we can use for our study. The search parameters and results are shown in Figure 5.1.

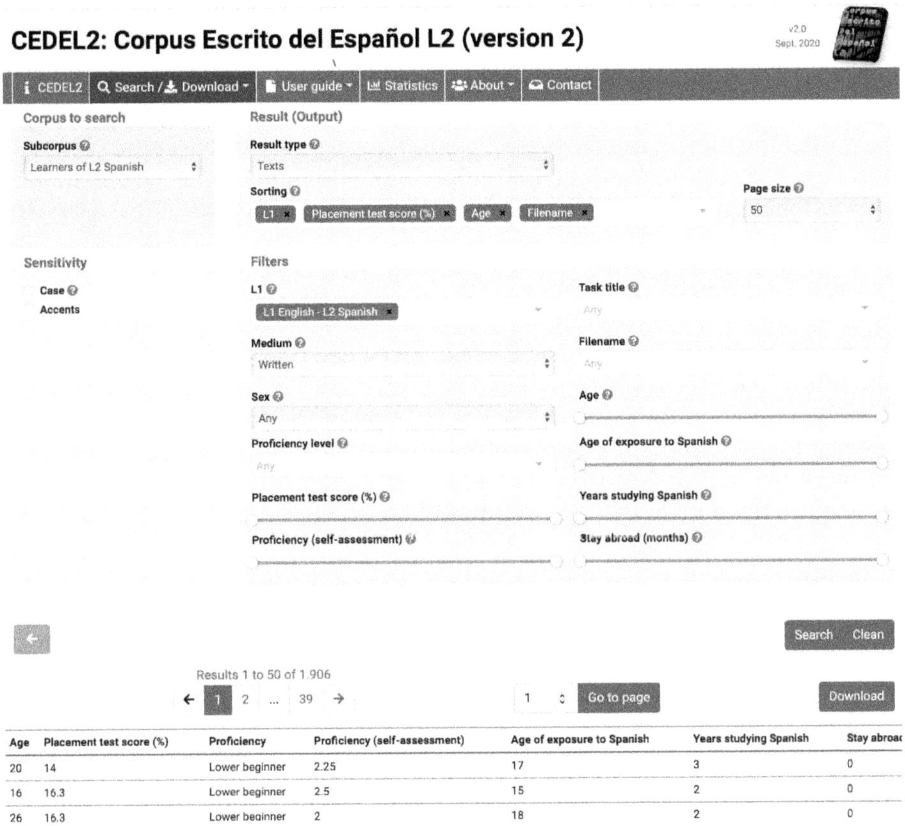

Figure 5.1: Search results for the CEDEL2 Corpus

The 'Download' link now appears for this search criteria. Following this link will provide the user a form to fill out. This particular resource allows for access to different formats to download (Texts only, Texts with metadata, CSV (Excel), CSV (Others)). I will select the 'CSV (Others)' option so that the data is structured for easier processing downstream in subsequent processing steps. Then I save the CSV in the *data/original/* directory of my project and create a sub-directory named *cedel2/*, as seen in Snippet 5.1.

Snippet 5.1. Project structure for the CEDEL2 corpus learner data download

```
data/
├── analysis/
├── derived/
└── original/
    └── cedel2/
        └── cedel2-l1-english-learners.csv
```

Note that the file is named *cedel2-l1-english-learners.csv* to reflect the search criteria used to acquire the data. In combination with other data documentation, this will help us to maintain transparency.

Now, after downloading the L2 learner and the native speaker data into the appropriate directory, we move on to the next processing step, right? Not so fast! Imagine we are working on a project with a collaborator. How will they know where the data came from? What if we need to come back to this data in the future? How will we know what characteristics we used to filter the data? The directory and file names may not be enough. To address these questions we need to document the origin of the data, and in the case of data acquired through manual downloads, we need to document the procedures we took to acquire the data to the best of our ability.

Tip

There are many ways to create and edit CSV files. You can use a spreadsheet program like MS Excel or Google Sheets, a text editor like Notepad or TextEdit, or an IDE like RStudio. {qtkit} provides a convenient function, `create_data_origin()` to create a CSV file with the data origin boilerplate structure. This CSV file then can be edited to add the relevant information in any of the programs.

Using a spreadsheet program is the easiest method for editing tabular data. The key is to save the file as a CSV file, and not as an Excel file, to maintain our adherence to the principle of using open formats for reproducible research.

As discussed in Section 2.3.1, all acquired data should be accompanied by a data origin file. The majority of this information can typically be identified on the resource's website and/ or the resource's documentation. In the case of the CEDEL2 corpus, the corpus homepage provides most of the information we need. The data origin file for the CEDEL2 corpus is seen in Table 5.1.

Structurally, data documentation files should be stored close to the data they describe. So for our data origin file this means adding it to the *data/original/* directory. Naming the file in a transparent way is also important. I've named the file *cedel2_do.csv* to reflect the name of the corpus, the meaning of the file as data origin with a suffixed *_do, *and the file extension* .csv* to reflect the file format. CSV files reflect tabular content. It is not required that data origin files are tabular, but it makes it easier to read and display them in literate programming documents.

Table 5.1: Data origin file for the CEDEL2 corpus

attribute	description
Resource name	CEDEL2: Corpus Escrito del Español como L2.
Data source	http://cedel2.learnercorpora.com/, https://doi.org/10.1177/02676583211050522
Data sampling frame	Corpus that contains samples of the language produced from learners of Spanish as a second language. For comparative purposes, it also contains a native control subcorpus of the language produced by native speakers of Spanish from different varieties (peninsular Spanish and all varieties of Latin American Spanish), so it can be used as a native corpus in its own right.
Data collection date(s)	2006-2020.
Data format	CSV file. Each row corresponds to a writing sample. Each column is an attribute of the writing sample.
Data schema	A CSV file for L2 learners and a CSV file for native speakers.
License	CC BY-NC-ND 3.0 ES
Attribution	Lozano, C. (2022). CEDEL2: Design, compilation and web interface of an online corpus for L2 Spanish acquisition research. *Second Language Research*, *38*(4), 965–983. https://doi.org/10.1177/02676583211050522.

Given this is a manual download we also need to document the procedure used to retrieve the data in prose. The script in the *process/* directory that is typically used to acquire the data is not used to programmatically retrieve data in this case. However, to keep things predictable we will use this file to document the download procedure. I've created a Quarto file named *1_acquire_data.qmd* in the *process/* directory of my project. A glimpse at the directory structure of the project at this point is seen in Snippet 5.2.

Even though the *1_acquire_data.qmd* file is not used to programmatically retrieve the data, it is still a useful place to document the download procedure. This includes the **uniform resource locator** (URL) of the resource, the search criteria used to filter the data, and the file format and location of the data. It is also good to include and display your data origin file in this file as a formatted table.

Snippet 5.2. Project structure for the CEDEL2 corpus data acquisition

```
project/
├── process/
│   ├── 1_acquire_data.qmd
│   └── ...
├── data/
│   ├── analysis/
│   ├── derived/
│   └── original/
│       ├── cedel2_do.csv
│       └── cedel2/
│           ├── cedel2-l1-english-learners.csv
│           └── cedel2-native-spanish-speakers.csv
├── reports/
├── DESCRIPTION
├── Makefile
└── README
```

Manually downloading other resources will inevitably include unique processes for obtaining the data, but in the end the data should be archived in the project structure in the *data/original/* directory and documented in the appropriate places. Note that acquired data is always treated as 'read-only', meaning it is not modified in any way. This gives us a fixed starting point for subsequent steps in the data preparation process.

5.1.2 Programmatic

There are many resources that provide corpus data that is directly accessible for which programmatic downloads can be applied. A **programmatic download** is a download in which the process can be automated through code. Thus, this is a reproducible process. The data can be acquired by anyone with access to the necessary code.

In this case, and subsequent data acquisition procedures in this chapter, we use the *1_acquire_data.qmd* Quarto file to its full potential intermingling prose, code, and code comments to execute and document the download procedure.

To illustrate how this works to conduct a programmatic download, we will work with the Switchboard Dialog Act Corpus (SWDA) (University of Colorado Boulder, 2008). The version that we will use is found on the Linguistic Data Consortium under the Switchboard-1 Release 2 Corpus. The corpus and related documentation are linked on the catalog page https://catalog.ldc.upenn.edu/docs/LDC97S62/.

From the documentation we learn that the corpus contains transcripts for 1155 5-minute two-way telephone conversations among English speakers for all areas of the United States. The speakers were given a topic to discuss and the conversations were recorded. The corpus metadata and annotations for sociolinguistic and discourse features.

This corpus, as you can image, could support a wide range of interesting research questions. Let's assume we are following research conducted by Tottie (2011) to explore the use of filled pauses such as "um" and "uh" and traditional sociolinguistic variables such as sex, age, and education in spontaneous speech by American English speakers.

> **Dive deeper**
> You may be wondering what the difference between *.zip*, *.tar*, and *.tar.gz* files are. The *.zip* file format is the most common. It groups file and directories into one file (an archive) and compresses it to reduce the size of the file in one step when the file is created.
> The *.tar* file format is used archive files and folders, it does not perform compression. Gzipping performs the compression to the *.tar* file resulting in a file with the *.tar.gz* extension. Notably the *.gz* compression is highly efficient for large files. Take the *swda.tar.gz* file for example. It has a compressed file size of 4.6 MB, but when uncompressed it is 16.9 MB. This is a 73% reduction in file size.

With this goal in mind, let's get started writing the code to download and organize the data in our project directory. First, we need to identify the URL for the data that we want to download. More often than not this file will be some type of **archive file** with an extension such as *.zip* (Zipped file), *.tar* (Tarball file), or *tar.gz* (Gzipped tarball file), which is the case for the SWDA corpus. Archive files make downloading multiple files easy by grouping files and directories into one file.

Example 5.1.

```r
# URL to SWDA corpus archive file
file_url <-
  "https://catalog.ldc.upenn.edu/docs/LDC97S62/swb1_dialogact_annot.tar.gz"

# Relative path to project/data/original directory
file_path <- "../data/original/swda.tar.gz"

# Download SWDA corpus archive file
download.file(url = file_url, destfile = file_path)
```

In R, we can use the `download.file()` function from base R, as seen in Example 5.1. The `download.file()` function minimally requires two arguments: `url` and `destfile`. These correspond to the file to download and the location where it is to be saved to disk. To break out the process a bit, I will assign the URL and destination file path to variables and then use the `download.file()` function to download the file.

> **Warning**
> Note that the `file_path` variable in Example 5.1 is a **relative path** to the *data/original/* directory. A relative path specifies the location of a file or directory relative to the current working directory. The `../` at the beginning of the path indicates that the file is located in the parent directory of the current working directory. It is also possible to use a full or **absolute path** to specify the location of a file or directory. An absolute path specifies the location of a file or directory from the root directory of the file system. For example, on a Unix-like system (*e.g.* Linux, macOS, *etc.*) the root directory is `/` and on a Windows system it is `C:\`. An absolute path also includes the intermediate directories between the root directory and the file or directory. As an absolute path reflects both operating system and unique file system structure not related to the project, it is not recommended for use in a reproducible research project.

As we can see looking at the directory structure, in Snippet 5.3, the *swda.tar.zip* file has been added to the *data/original/* directory.

Snippet 5.3. Project structure for the SWDA archive file download

```
data/
├── analysis/
├── derived/
└── original/
    └── swda.tar.zip
```

Once an archive file is downloaded, however, the file needs to be 'unarchived' to reveal the directory structure and files. To unarchive this *.tar.gz* file we use the `untar()` function with the arguments `tarfile` pointing to the *.tar.gz* file and `exdir` specifying the directory where we want the files to be extracted to. Again, I will assign the arguments to variables. Then we can unarchive the file using the `untar()` function.

Example 5.2.

```
# Relative path to the archive file
tar_file <- "../data/original/swda.tar.gz"

# Relative path to the directory to extract to
extract_to_dir <- "../data/original/swda/"
```

```

# Unarchive/ decompress .zip file and extract to our target directory
untar(tar_file, extract_to_dir)
```

The directory structure of *data/* in Snippet 5.4 now shows the *swda.tar.gz* file and the *swda* directory that contains the unarchived directories and files.

Snippet 5.4. Project structure for the SWDA files unarchived

```
data/
├── analysis/
├── derived/
└── original/
    ├── swda/
    │   ├── README
    │   ├── doc/
    │   ├── sw00utt/
    │   ├── sw01utt/
    │   ├── sw02utt/
    │   ├── sw03utt/
    │   ├── sw04utt/
    │   ├── sw05utt/
    │   │   sw06utt/
    │   ├── sw07utt/
    │   ├── sw08utt/
    │   ├── sw09utt/
    │   ├── sw10utt/
    │   ├── sw11utt/
    │   ├── sw12utt/
    │   └── sw13utt/
    └── swda.tar.gz
```

At this point we have acquired the data programmatically and with this code as part of our workflow anyone could run this code and reproduce the same results.

The code as it is, however, is not ideally efficient. First, the *swda.tar.gz* file is not strictly needed after we unarchive it, and it occupies disk space if we keep it. And second, each time we run this code the file will be downloaded from the remote server and overwrite the existing data. This leads to unnecessary data transfer and server traffic and will overwrite the data if it already exists in our project directory, which could be problematic if the data changes on the remote server. Let's tackle each of these issues in turn.

To avoid writing the *swda.tar.gz* file to disk (long-term) we can use the `tempfile()` function to open a temporary holding space for the file in the computing environment. This space can then be used to store the file, unarchive it, and then the temporary file will automatically be deleted. We assign the temporary space to an R object we will name `temp_file` with the `tempfile()` function. This object can now be used as the value of the argument `destfile` in the `download.file()` function.

Example 5.3.

```
# URL to SWDA corpus archive file
file_url <-
  "https://catalog.ldc.upenn.edu/docs/LDC97S62/swb1_dialogact_annot.tar.gz"

# Create a temporary file space for our .tar.gz file
temp_file <- tempfile()

# Download SWDA corpus archive file
download.file(file_url, temp_file)
```

> **Tip**
> In Example 5.3, I've used the values stored in the objects `file_url` and `temp_file` in the `download.file()` function without specifying the argument names —only providing the names of the objects. R will assume that values of a function map to the ordering of the arguments. If your values do not map to ordering of the arguments you are required to specify the argument name and the value. To view the ordering of objects hit `tab` after entering the function name or consult the function documentation by prefixing the function name with `?` and hitting `enter`.

At this point our downloaded file is stored temporarily on disk and can be accessed and unarchived to our target directory using *temp_file* as the value for the argument `tarfile` from the `untar()` function. I've assigned our target directory path to `extract_to_dir` and used it as the value for the argument `exdir`.

Example 5.4.

```
# Assign our target directory to `extract_to_dir`
extract_to_dir <- "../data/original/swda/"

# Unarchive/ decompress .tar.gz file and extract to our target directory
untar(tarfile = temp_file, exdir = target_dir)
```

Our directory structure in Example 5.4 is the same as in Snippet 5.4, minus the *swda.tar.gz* file.

The second issue I raised concerns the fact that running this code as part of our project will repeat the download each time our script is run. Since we would like to be good citizens and avoid unnecessary traffic on the web and avoid potential issues in overwriting data, it would be nice if our code checked to see if we already have the data on disk and if it exists, then skip the download, if not then download it.

The desired functionality we've described can be implemented using the `if()` function. The `if()` function is one of a class of functions known as control statements. **Control statements** allow us to control the flow of our code by evaluating logical statements and processing subsequent code based on the logical value it is passed as an argument.

So in this case we want to evaluate whether the data directory exists on disk. If it does, then skip the download, if not, proceed with the download. In combination with `else` which provides the 'if not' part of the statement, we have the following logical flow in Example 5.5.

Example 5.5.

```
if (DIRECTORY_EXISTS) {
  # Do nothing
} else {
  # Download data
}
```

We can simplify this statement by using the `!` operator which negates the logical value of the statement it precedes. So if the directory exists, `!DIRECTORY_EXISTS` will return `FALSE` and if not, `!DIRECTORY_EXISTS` will return `TRUE`. In other words, if the directory does not exist, download the data. This is shown in Example 5.6.

Example 5.6.

```
if (!DIRECTORY_EXISTS) {
  # Download data
}
```

Now, to determine if a directory exists in our project directory we will turn to {fs} (Hester, Wickham, & Csárdi, 2024). {fs} provides a set of functions for interacting with the file system, including `dir_exists()`. `dir_exists()` takes a path to a directory as an argument and returns the logical value, `TRUE`, if that directory exists, and `FALSE` if it does not.

We can use this function to evaluate whether the directory exists and then use the `if()` function to process the subsequent code based on the logical flow we set out in Example 5.6. Applied to our project, the code will look like Example 5.7.

Example 5.7.

```
# Load the {fs} package
library(fs)

# URL to SWDA corpus archive file
file_url <-
  "https://catalog.ldc.upenn.edu/docs/LDC97S62/swb1_dialogact_annot.tar.gz"

# Create a temporary file space for our .tar.gz file
temp_file <- tempfile()

# Assign our target directory to `extract_to_dir`
extract_to_dir <- "../data/original/swda/"

# Check if our target directory exists
# If it does not exist, download the file and extract it
if (!dir_exists(extract_to_dir)) {
  # Download SWDA corpus archive file
  download.file(file_url, temp_file)

  # Unarchive/ decompress .tar.gz file and extract to our target directory
  untar(tarfile = temp_file, exdir = extract_to_dir)
}
```

The code in Example 5.7 is added to the *1_acquire_data.qmd* file. When this file is run, the SWDA corpus data will be downloaded and extracted to our project directory. If the data already exists, the download will be skipped, just as we wanted.

Now, before we move on, we need to make sure to document the process. Now that our Quarto document includes code, add code comments to explain the processing logic. And, as always, create a data origin file as with the relevant information. The data origin file will be stored in the *data/original/* directory and the Quarto file will be stored in the *process/* directory.

We've leveraged R to automate the download and extraction of the data, depending on the existence of the data in our project directory. But you may be asking yourself, "Can't I just navigate to the corpus page and download the data manually myself?" The simple answer is, "Yes, you can." The more nuanced answer is, "Yes, but consider the trade-offs."

The following scenarios highlight some advantages to automating the process. If you are acquiring data from multiple files, it can become tedious to document the manual process for each file such that it is reproducible. It's possible, but it's error prone.

Now, if you are collaborating with others, you will want to share this data with them. It is very common to find data that has limited restrictions for use in academic projects, but the most common limitation is redistribution. This means that you can use the data for your own research, but you cannot share it with others. If you plan on publishing your project to a code repository to share the data as part of your reproducible project, you would be violating the terms of use for the data. By including the programmatic download in your project, you can ensure that your collaborators can easily and effectively acquire the data themselves and that you are not violating the terms of use.

5.2 APIs

A convenient alternative method for acquiring data in R is through package interfaces to web services. These interfaces are built using R code to make connections with resources on the web through **application programming interfaces** (APIs). Websites such as Project Gutenberg, Twitter, Reddit, and many others provide APIs to allow access to their data under certain conditions, some more limiting for data collection than others. Programmers (like you!) in the R community take up the task of wrapping calls to an API with R code to make accessing that data from R convenient, and of course reproducible.

Dive deeper

Many, many web services provide API access. These APIs span all kinds of data, from text to images to video to audio. Visit the Public APIs website[a] to explore the diversity of APIs available.

ROpenSci maintains a curated list of R packages that provide access to data from web services. Visit the ROpenSci website[b] to explore the packages available.

[a] https://publicapis.io/

[b] https://ropensci.org/packages/data-access/

In addition to popular public APIs, there are also APIs that provide access to repositories and databases which are of particular interest to linguists. For example, Wordbank[2] provides access to a large collection of child language corpora through {wordbankr} (Braginsky, 2024), and Glottolog[3], World Atlas of Language Structures[4] (WALS), and PHOIBLE[5] provide access to large collections of language metadata that can be accessed through {lingtypology} (Moroz, 2017).

Let's work with an R package that provides access to the TalkBank[6] database. The TalkBank project (Macwhinney, 2024) contains a large collection of spoken language corpora from various contexts: conversation, child language, multilinguals, *etc.* Resource information, web interfaces, and links to download data in various formats can be found by perusing individual resources linked from the main page. However, {TBDBr} (Kowalski & Cavanaugh, 2024) provides convenient access to corpora using R once a corpus resource is identified.

The CABNC (Albert, de Ruiter, & de Ruiter, 2015) contains the demographically sampled portion[7] of the spoken portion of the British National Corpus (BNC) (Leech, 1992).

Useful for a study aiming to research spoken British English, either in isolation or in comparison to American English (SWDA)..

First, we need to install and load {TBDBr}, as in Example 5.8.

Example 5.8.

```
# Load the TBDBr package
library(TBDBr)
```

{TBDBr} provides a set of common `get*()` functions for acquiring data from the TalkBank corpus resources. These include: `getParticipants()`, `getTranscripts()`, `getTokens()`, `getTokenTypes()`, and `getUtterances()`.

For each of these functions, the first argument is `corpusName`, which is the name of the corpus resource as it appears in the TalkBank database. The second argument is `corpora`, which takes a character vector describing the path to the data. For the CABNC, these arguments are `"ca"` and `c("ca", "CABNC")` respectively. To determine these values, TBDBr provides the `getLegalValues()` interactive function which allows you to interactively select the repository name, corpus name, and transcript name, if necessary.

[2] http://wordbank.stanford.edu/
[3] https://glottolog.org/
[4] https://wals.info/
[5] https://phoible.org/
[6] https://talkbank.org/
[7] http://www.natcorp.ox.ac.uk/docs/URG/BNCdes.html

Tip
For any package loaded in your R session, you can list all of its functions and datasets using the `ls()` function. For example, `ls("package:TBDBr")` will list all of the functions and datasets in {TBDBr}.
To view all of the arguments for a function, use the `args()` function. For example, `args(getUtterances)` will list all of the arguments for the `getUtterances()` function.

Another important aspect of these functions is that they return data frame objects. Since we are accessing data that is in a structured database, this makes sense. However, we should always check the documentation for the object type that is returned by function to be aware of how to work with the data.

Let's start by retrieving the utterance data for the CABNC and preview the data frame it returns using `glimpse()`.

Example 5.9.

```
# Set corpus_name and corpus_path
corpus_name <- "ca"
corpus_path <- c("ca", "CABNC")

# Get utterance data
utterances <-
  getUtterances(
    corpusName = corpus_name,
    corpora = corpus_path
    )

# Preview the data
glimpse(utterances)
```

```
Rows: 235,901
Columns: 10
$ filename  <list> "KB0RE000", "KB0RE000", "KB0RE000", "KB0RE000", "KB0RE000",~
$ path      <list> "ca/CABNC/KB0/KB0RE000", "ca/CABNC/KB0/KB0RE000", "ca/CABNC~
$ utt_num   <list> 0, 1, 2, 3, 4, 5, 6, 7, 8, 9, 10, 11, 12, 13, 14, 15, 16, 1~
$ who       <list> "PS002", "PS006", "PS002", "PS006", "PS002", "PS006", "PS00~
$ role      <list> "Unidentified", "Unidentified", "Unidentified", "Unidentifi~
$ postcodes <list> <NULL>, <NULL>, <NULL>, <NULL>, <NULL>, <NULL>, <NULL>, <NU~
$ gems      <list> <NULL>, <NULL>, <NULL>, <NULL>, <NULL>, <NULL>, <NULL>, <NU~
$ utterance <list> "You enjoyed yourself in America", "Eh", "did you", "Oh I c~
$ startTime <list> "0.208", "2.656", "2.896", "3.328", "5.088", "6.208", "8.32~
$ endTime   <list> "2.672", "2.896", "3.328", "5.264", "6.016", "8.496", "9.31~
```

Inspecting the output from Example 5.9, we see that the data frame contains 235,901 observations and 10 variables.

The summary provided by `glimpse()` also provides other useful information. First, we see the data type of each variable. Interestingly, the data type for each variable in the data frame is a list object. Being that a list is two-dimensional data type, like a data frame, we have two-dimensional data inside two-dimensional data. This is known as a **nested structure**. We will work with nested structures in more depth later, but for now it will suffice to say that we would like to 'unnest' these lists and reveal the list-contained vector types at the data frame level.

To do this we will pass the `utterances` data frame to the, appropriately named, `unnest()` function from {tidyr} (Wickham, Vaughan, & Girlich, 2024). `unnest()` takes a data frame and a vector of variable names to unnest, `cols = c()`. To unnest all variables, we will use the `everything()` function from {dplyr} to select all variables at once. We will use the result to overwrite the `utterances` object with the unnested data frame.

Example 5.10.

```
# Unnest the data frame
utterances <-
  utterances |>
  unnest(cols = everything())

# Preview the data
glimpse(utterances)
```

```
Rows: 235,901
Columns: 10
$ filename  <chr> "KB0RE000", "KB0RE000", "KB0RE000", "KB0RE000", "KB0RE000", ~
$ path      <chr> "ca/CABNC/KB0/KB0RE000", "ca/CABNC/KB0/KB0RE000", "ca/CABNC/~
$ utt_num   <dbl> 0, 1, 2, 3, 4, 5, 6, 7, 8, 9, 10, 11, 12, 13, 14, 15, 16, 17~
$ who       <chr> "PS002", "PS006", "PS002", "PS006", "PS002", "PS006", "PS002~
$ role      <chr> "Unidentified", "Unidentified", "Unidentified", "Unidentifie~
$ postcodes <lgl> NA, NA, NA, NA, NA, NA, NA, NA, NA, NA, NA, NA, NA, NA, NA, ~
$ gems      <lgl> NA, NA, NA, NA, NA, NA, NA, NA, NA, NA, NA, NA, NA, NA, NA, ~
$ utterance <chr> "You enjoyed yourself in America", "Eh", "did you", "Oh I co~
$ startTime <chr> "0.208", "2.656", "2.896", "3.328", "5.088", "6.208", "8.32"~
$ endTime   <chr> "2.672", "2.896", "3.328", "5.264", "6.016", "8.496", "9.312~
```

The output from Example 5.10 shows that the variables are now one-dimensional vector types.

Returning to the information about our data frame from `glimpse()`, the second thing to notice is we get a short preview of the values for each variable. There are a couple of things we can glean from this. One is that we can confirm or clarify the meaning of the variable names by looking at the values. The other thing to consider is whether the values show any patterns that may be worthy of more scrutiny. For example, various variables appear to contain the same values for each observation. For a variable like `filename`, this is expected as the first values likely correspond to the same file. However, for the variables `postcodes` and `gems` the values are 'NA'. This suggests that these variables may not contain any useful information and we may want to remove them later.

For now, however, we want to acquire and store the data in its original form (or as closely as possible). So now, we have acquired the utterances data and have it in our R session as a data frame. To store this data in a file, we will first need to consider the file format. Data frames are tabular, so that gives us a few options.

Since we are working in R, we could store this data as an R object, in the form of an R data serialization (RDS) file. An RDS file is a binary file. Binary files cannot be viewed in plain text format. However, these files can be read back into R as an R object exactly as there were (including factors, sorting, *etc.*). This is a good option if we want to store the data for use in R, but not if we want to share the data with others or use it in other software.

Another option is to store the data as a spreadsheet file, such as XSLX (MS Excel). This may make viewing and editing the contents more convenient, but it depends on the software available to you and others. A third, more viable option, is to store the data as a CSV file. CSV files are plain text files that can be read and written by most software. This makes CSV files one of the most popular for sharing tabular data. For this reason, we will store the data as a CSV file.

{readr} provides the `write_csv()` function for writing data frames to CSV files. The first argument is the data frame to write, and the second argument is the path to the file to write. Note, however, that the directories in the path we specify need to exist. If they do not, we will get an error.

In this case, I would like to write the file *utterances.csv* to the *../data/original/cabnc/* directory. The original project structure does not contain a *cabnc/* directory, so I need to create one. To do this, I will use `dir_create()` from {fs}.

Example 5.11.

```
# Create the target directory
dir_create("../data/original/cabnc/")

# Write the data frame to a CSV file
write_csv(utterances, "../data/original/cabnc/utterances.csv")
```

Chaining the steps covered in Examples 5.9, 5.10, and 5.11, we have a succinct and legible code to acquire, adjust, and write utterances from the CABNC in Example 5.12.

Example 5.12.

```r
# Set corpus_name and corpus_path
corpus_name <- "ca"
corpus_path <- c("ca", "CABNC")

# Create the target directory
dir_create("../data/original/cabnc/")

# Get utterance data
getUtterances(
  corpusName = corpus_name,
  corpora = corpus_path
) |>
  unnest(cols = everything()) |>
  write_csv("../data/original/cabnc/utterances.csv")
```

If our goal is just to acquire utterances, then we are done acquiring data and we move on to the next step. However, if we want to acquire other datasets from the CABNC, say participants, tokens, *etc.*, then we can either repeat the steps in Example 5.12 for each data type, or we can write a function to do this for us!

A function serves us to make our code more legible and reusable for the CABNC, and since the TalkBank data is structured similarly across corpora, we can also use the function to acquire data from other corpora, if need be.

To write a function, we need to consider the following:

1. What is the name of the function?
2. What arguments does the function take?
3. What functionality does the function provide?
4. Does the function have optional arguments?
5. How does the function return the results?

Taking each in turn, the name of the function should be descriptive of what the function does. In this case, we are acquiring and writing data from Talkbank corpora. A possible name is `get_talkbank_data()`. The required arguments of the `get*()` functions will definitely figure in our function. In addition, we will need to specify the path to the directory to write the data. With these considerations, we can write the function signature in Example 5.13.

Example 5.13.

```
get_talkbank_data <- function(corpus_name, corpus_path, target_dir) {
  # ...
}
```

The next thing to consider is what functionality the function provides. In this case, we want to acquire and write data from Talkbank corpora. We can start by leveraging the code steps in Example 5.12, making some adjustments to the code replacing the hard-coded values with the function arguments and adding code to create the target file name based on the `target_dir` argument.

Example 5.14.

```
get_talkbank_data <- function(corpus_name, corpus_path, target_dir) {

  # Create the target directory
  dir_create(target_dir)

  # Set up file path name
  utterances_file  <- path(target_dir, "utterances.csv")

  # Acquire data and write to file
  getUtterances(corpusName = corpus_name, corpora = corpus_path) |>
    unnest(cols = everything()) |>
    write_csv(utterances_file)
}
```

Before we address the obvious feature missing, which is the fact that this function in Example 5.14 only acquires and writes data for utterances, let's consider some functionality which would make this function more user-friendly.

What if the data is already acquired? Do we want to overwrite it, or should the function skip the process for files that already exist? By skipping the process, we can save time and computing resources. If the files are periodically updated, then we might want to overwrite existing files.

To achieve this functionality we will use an `if()` statement to check if the file exists. If it does, then we will skip the process. If it does not, then we will acquire and write the data.

Example 5.15.

```
get_talkbank_data <- function(corpus_name, corpus_path, target_dir) {

  # Create the target directory
  dir_create(target_dir)

  # Set up file path name
  utterances_file  <- path(target_dir, "utterances.csv")

  # If the file does not exist, then...
  # Acquire data and write to file
  if(!file_exists(utterances_file)) {
    getUtterances(corpusName = corpus_name, corpora = corpus_path) |>
      unnest(cols = everything()) |>
      write_csv(utterances_file)
  }
}
```

We can also add functionality to Example 5.15 to force overwrite existing files, if need be. To do this, we will add an optional argument to the function, `force`, which will be a logical value. We will set the default to `force = FALSE` to preserve the existing functionality. If `force = TRUE`, then we will overwrite existing files. Then we add another condition to the `if()` statement to check if `force = TRUE`. If it is, then we will overwrite existing files.

Example 5.16.

```
get_talkbank_data <- function(corpus_name, corpus_path, target_dir, force =
  ↪ FALSE) {

  # Create the target directory
  dir_create(target_dir)

  # Set up file path name
  utterances_file  <- path(target_dir, "utterances.csv")

  # If the file does not exist, then...
  # Acquire data and write to file
  if(!file_exists(utterances_file) | force) {
    getUtterances(corpusName = corpus_name, corpora = corpus_path) |>
      unnest(cols = everything()) |>
      write_csv(utterances_file)
  }
}
```

From this point, we add the functionality to acquire and write the other data available from Talkbank corpora, such as participants, tokens, *etc.* This involves adding additional file path names and `if()` statements to check if the files exist surrounding the processing steps to Example 5.16. It may be helpful to perform other input checks, print messages, *etc.* for functions that we plan to share with others. I will leave these enhancements as an exercise for the reader.

Dive deeper

If you are interested in learning more about writing functions, check out the Writing Functions chapter[a] in the R for Data Science[b] book.

If you find yourself writing functions that are useful for multiple projects, you may want to consider creating an R package. R packages are a great way to share your code with others. If you are interested in learning more about creating R packages, check out the R Packages book[c] by Wickham & Bryan (2023).

[a]https://r4ds.had.co.nz/functions.html
[b]https://r4ds.had.co.nz/
[c]https://r-pkgs.org/

Before we leave the topic of functions, let's consider where to put functions after we write them. Here are a few options:

1. In the same script as the code that uses the function.
2. In a separate script, such as *functions.R*.
3. In a package, which is loaded by the script that uses the function.

The general heuristic for choosing where to put functions is to put them in the same script as the code that uses them if the function is only used in that script. If the function is used in multiple scripts or the function or number of functions clutters the readability of the code, then put it in a separate script. If the function is used in multiple projects, then put it in an R package.

In this case, we will put the function in a separate file, *functions.R*, in the same directory as the other process files as in Snippet 5.5.

Snippet 5.5. Project structure with *functions.R* file

```
project/
├── process/
│   ├── 1_acquire_data.qmd
│   ├── ...
│   └── functions.R
├── .../
```

> **⚠ Warning**
> Note that the *functions.R* file is an R script, not a Quarto document. Therefore code blocks that are used in *.qmd* files are not used, only the R code and code comments.

To include this, or other functions in the R session of the process file that uses them, use the `source()` function, with the correct relative path to the file, as seen in Example 5.17.

Example 5.17.

```
# Source functions
source("functions.R")
```

It is common to source functions at the top of the process file as part of the package setup.

Given the utility of this function to my projects and potentially others', I've included the `get_talkbank_data()` function in {qtkit}. You can view the source code by calling the function without parentheses `()`, or on the {qtkit} GitHub repository.

After running the `get_talkbank_data()` function, we can see that the data has been acquired and written to the *data/original/cabnc/* directory in Snippet 5.6.

Snippet 5.6. Project structure with CABNC data files

```
data/
├── analysis
├── derived
└── original
    └── cabnc
        ├── participants.csv
        ├── token_types.csv
        ├── tokens.csv
        ├── transcripts.csv
        └── utterances.csv
```

Add comments to your code in *1-acquire-data.qmd* and create and complete the data origin documentation file for this resource, and the acquisition is complete.

Activities

Building on the activities in the previous chapter, these activities will focus on the implementation of the data acquisition process. Key programming concepts including writing custom functions, control statements, and applying functions iteratively will be covered in addition to packages and functions which provide access to data from the web.

> **Recipe**
> **What**: Collecting and documenting data
> **How**: Read Recipe 5, complete comprehension check, and prepare for Lab 5.
> **Why**: To refine programming strategies introduced in the lesson for controlling program flow and making code more reusable in the service of programmatically acquiring and documenting data.

> **Lab**
> **What**: Harvesting research data
> **How**: Fork, clone, and complete the steps in Lab 5.
> **Why**: To investigate data sources, plan data collection strategies, and apply skills and knowledge to use R to collect and document data.

Summary

In this chapter, we have covered a lot of ground. On the surface, we have discussed a few methods for acquiring corpus data for use in text analysis. In the process, we have examined various aspects of the R programming language. Some key concepts include writing control statements and custom functions. We have also considered topics that are more general in nature and concern interacting with data found on the internet.

Each of these methods should be approached in a way that is transparent to the researcher and to would-be collaborators and the general research community. For this reason, the documentation of the steps taken to acquire data are key both in the code and in human-facing documentation.

At this point you have both a bird's eye view of the data available on the web and strategies on how to access a great majority of it. It is now time to turn to the next step in our data analysis project: data curation. In the next chapter, I will cover how to wrangle your raw data into a tidy dataset.

6

Curate

> **Outcomes**
>
> - Describe the importance of data curation in text analysis
> - Recognize the different types of data formats
> - Associate the types data formats with the appropriate R programming techniques to curate the data

In this chapter, we will now look at the next step in a text analysis project: data curation. That is, the process of converting the original data we acquire to a tidy dataset. Acquired data can come in a wide variety of formats. These formats tend to signal the richness of the metadata that is included in the file content. We will consider three general types of content formats: (1) unstructured data, (2) structured data, and (3) semi-structured data. Regardless of the file type and the structure of the data, it will be necessary to consider how to curate a dataset such that the structure reflects the basic unit of analysis that we wish to investigate. The resulting dataset will form the base from which we will work to further transform the dataset such that it aligns with the unit(s) of observation required for the analysis method that we will implement. Once the dataset is curated, we will create a data dictionary that describes the dataset and the variables that are included in the dataset for transparency and reproducibility.

> **>_ Lessons**
>
> **What**: Pattern Matching, Tidy Datasets
>
> **How**: In an R console, load {swirl}, run `swirl()`, and follow prompts to select the lesson.
>
> **Why**: To familiarize yourself with the basics of using the pattern matching syntax Regular Expressions and the {dplyr} package to manipulate data into Tidy datasets.

10.4324/9781003393764.6

6.1 Unstructured

The bulk of textual data is of the unstructured variety. Unstructured data is data that has not been organized to make the information contained within machine-readable. Remember that text in itself is not information. Only when given explicit context in the form of metadata does text become informative. Metadata can be linguistic or non-linguistic in nature. So for unstructured data there is little to no metadata directly associated with the data.

6.1.1 Reading data

Some of the common file formats which contain unstructured data include TXT, PDF, and DOCX. Although these formats are unstructured, they are not the same. Reading these files into R requires different techniques and tools.

There are many ways to read TXT files into R and many packages that can be used to do so. For example, using {readr}, we can choose to read the entire file into a single vector of character strings with `read_file()` or read the file by lines with `read_lines()` in which each line is a character string in a vector.

Less commonly used in prepared data resources, PDF and DOCX files are more complex than TXT files as they contain formatting and embedded document metadata. However, these attributes are primarily for visual presentation and not for machine-readability. Needless to say, we need an alternate strategy to extract the text content from these files and potentially some of the metadata. For example, using {readtext} (Benoit & Obeng, 2024), we can read the text content from PDF and DOCX files into a single vector of character strings with `readtext()`.

Whether in TXT, PDF, or DOCX format, the resulting data structure will require further processing to convert the data into a tidy dataset.

6.1.2 Orientation

As an example of curating an unstructured source of corpus data, let's take a look at the Europarl Parallel Corpus[1] (Koehn, 2005). This corpus contains parallel texts (source and translated documents) from the European Parliamentary proceedings between 1996 and 2011 for some 21 European languages.

Let's assume we selected this corpus because we are interested in researching Spanish to English translations. After consulting the corpus website, downloading the archive file, and inspecting the unarchived structure, we have the file structure seen in Snippet 6.1.

[1]https://www.statmt.org/europarl/

Snippet 6.1. Project directory structure for the Europarl Parallel Corpus

```
project/
├── process/
│   ├── 1-acquire-data.qmd
│   ├── 2-curate-data.qmd
│   └── ...
├── data/
│   ├── analysis/
│   ├── derived/
│   └── original/
│       |── europarl_do.csv
│       └── europarl/
│           ├── europarl-v7.es-en.en
│           └── europarl-v7.es-en.es
├── reports/
├── DESCRIPTION
├── Makefile
└── README
```

The *europarl_do.csv* file contains the data origin information documented as part of the acquisition process. The contents are seen in Table 6.1.

Table 6.1: Data origin: Europarl Corpus

attribute	description
Resource name	Europarl Parallel Corpus
Data source	https://www.statmt.org/europarl/
Data sampling frame	Spanish transcripts from the European Parliament proceedings
Data collection date(s)	1996–2011
Data format	TXT files with '.es' for source (Spanish) and '.en' for target (English) files.
Data schema	Line-by-line unannotated parallel text
License	See: https://www.europarl.europa.eu/legal-notice/en/
Attribution	Please cite the paper: Koehn, P. 2005. 'Europarl: A Parallel Corpus for Statistical Machine Translation.' *MT Summit X*, 12–16.

Now let's get familiar with the corpus directory structure and the files. In Snippet 6.1, we see that there are two corpus files, *europarl-v7.es-en.es* and *europarl-v7.es-en.en*, that contain the source and target language texts, respectively. The file names indicate that the files contain Spanish-English parallel texts. The *.es* and *.en* extensions indicate the language of the text.

Looking at the beginning of the *.es* and *.en* files, in Snippet 6.2 and Snippet 6.3, we see that the files contain a series of lines in either the source or target language.

Snippet 6.2. *europarl-v7.es-en.es* file

```
Reanudación del período de sesiones
Declaro reanudado el período de sesiones del Parlamento Europeo,
↪  interrumpido el viernes 17 de diciembre pasado, y reitero a Sus Señorías
↪  mi deseo de que hayan tenido unas buenas vacaciones.
Como todos han podido comprobar, el gran "efecto del año 2000" no se ha
↪  producido. En cambio, los ciudadanos de varios de nuestros países han
↪  sido víctimas de catástrofes naturales verdaderamente terribles.
Sus Señorías han solicitado un debate sobre el tema para los próximos días,
↪  en el curso de este período de sesiones.
A la espera de que se produzca, de acuerdo con muchos colegas que me lo han
↪  pedido, pido que hagamos un minuto de silencio en memoria de todas las
↪  víctimas de las tormentas, en los distintos países de la Unión Europea
↪  afectados.
```

We can clearly appreciate that the data is unstructured. That is, there is no explicit metadata associated with the data. The data is just a series of character strings separated by lines. The only information that we can surmise from structure of the data is that the texts are line-aligned and that the data in each file corresponds to source and target languages.

Snippet 6.3. *europarl-v7.es-en.en* file

```
Resumption of the session
I declare resumed the session of the European Parliament adjourned on Friday
↪  17 December 1999, and I would like once again to wish you a happy new
↪  year in the hope that you enjoyed a pleasant festive period.
Although, as you will have seen, the dreaded 'millennium bug' failed to
↪  materialise, still the people in a number of countries suffered a series
↪  of natural disasters that truly were dreadful.
You have requested a debate on this subject in the course of the next few
↪  days, during this part-session.
In the meantime, I should like to observe a minute' s silence, as a number
↪  of Members have requested, on behalf of all the victims concerned,
↪  particularly those of the terrible storms, in the various countries of
↪  the European Union.
```

Now, before embarking on a data curation process, it is recommendable to define the structure of the data that we want to create. I call this the "**idealized structure**" of the data. For a curated dataset, we want to reflect the contents of the original data, yet in a tidy format, to maintain the integrity of and connection with the data.

Given what we know about the data, we can define the idealized structure of the data as seen in Table 6.2.

Table 6.2: Idealized structure for the curated Europarl Corpus datasets

variable	name	type	description
type	Document type	character	Contains the type of document, either 'Source' or 'Target'
line	Line	character	Contains the text of each line in the document

Our task now is to develop code that will read the original data and render the idealized structure as a curated dataset for each corpus file. We will then write the datasets to the *data/derived/* directory. The code we develop will be added to the *2-curate-data.qmd* file. And finally, the datasets will be documented with a data dictionary file.

6.1.3 Tidy the data

To create the idealized dataset structure in Table 6.2, let's start by reading the files by lines into R. As the files are aligned by lines, we will use the `read_lines()` function to read the files into character vectors.

Example 6.1.

```r
# Load package
library(readr)

# Read Europarl files .es and .en
europarl_es_chr <-
  read_lines("../data/original/europarl-v7.es-en.es")

europarl_en_chr <-
  read_lines("../data/original/europarl-v7.es-en.en")
```

Using the `read_lines()` function, we read each line of the files into a character vector. Since the Europarl corpus is a parallel corpus, the lines in the source and target files are aligned. This means that the first line in the source file corresponds to the first line in the target file, the second line in the source file corresponds to the second line in the target file, and so on. This alignment is important for the analysis of parallel corpora, as it allows us to compare the source and target texts line by line.

Let's inspect our character vectors to ensure that they are of the length and appear to be structured as we expect. We can use the `length()` function to get the number of lines in each file and the `head()` function to preview the first few lines of each file.

Example 6.2.

```
# Inspect Spanish character vector
length(europarl_es_chr)
```

```
[1] 1965734
```

```
head(europarl_es_chr, 5)
```

```
[1] "Reanudación del período de sesiones"
[2] "Declaro reanudado el período de sesiones del Parlamento Europeo, interrumpido
el viernes 17 de diciembre pasado, y reitero a Sus Señorías mi deseo de que hayan
tenido unas buenas vacaciones."
[3] "Como todos han podido comprobar, el gran \"efecto del año 2000\" no se ha
producido. En cambio, los ciudadanos de varios de nuestros países han sido víctimas
de catástrofes naturales verdaderamente terribles."
[4] "Sus Señorías han solicitado un debate sobre el tema para los próximos días, en
el curso de este período de sesiones."
[5] "A la espera de que se produzca, de acuerdo con muchos colegas que me lo han
pedido, pido que hagamos un minuto de silencio en memoria de todas las víctimas de
las tormentas, en los distintos países de la Unión Europea afectados."
```

```
# Inspect English character vector
length(europarl_en_chr)
```

```
[1] 1965734
```

```
head(europarl_en_chr, 5)
```

```
[1] "Resumption of the session"
[2] "I declare resumed the session of the European Parliament adjourned on Friday
17 December 1999, and I would like once again to wish you a happy new year in the
hope that you enjoyed a pleasant festive period."
[3] "Although, as you will have seen, the dreaded 'millennium bug' failed to
materialise, still the people in a number of countries suffered a series of natural
disasters that truly were dreadful."
[4] "You have requested a debate on this subject in the course of the next few
days, during this part-session."
[5] "In the meantime, I should like to observe a minute' s silence, as a number of
Members have requested, on behalf of all the victims concerned, particularly those
of the terrible storms, in the various countries of the European Union."
```

The output of Example 6.2 shows that the number of lines in each file is the same. This is good. If the number of lines in each file was different, we would need to figure out why and fix it. We also see that the content of the files is aligned as expected.

Let's now create a dataset for each of the character vectors. We will use the `tibble()` function from {tibble} to create a data frame object with the character vectors as the `line` column and add a `type` column with the value 'Source' for the Spanish file and 'Target' for the English file. We will assign the output two new objects `europarl_source_df` and `europarl_target_df`, respectively, as seen in Example 6.3.

Example 6.3.

```r
# Create source data frame
europarl_source_df <-
  tibble(
    type = "Source",
    lines = europarl_es_chr
  )
# Create target data frame
europarl_target_df <-
  tibble(
    type = "Target",
    lines = europarl_en_chr
  )
```

Inspecting these data frames with `glimpse()` in Example 6.4, we can see if the data frames have the structure we expect.

Example 6.4.

```r
# Preview source
glimpse(europarl_source_df)

# Preview target
glimpse(europarl_target_df)
```

```
Rows: 1,965,734
Columns: 2
$ type  <chr> "Source", "Source", "Source", "Source", "Source", "Source", "Sou~
$ lines <chr> "Reanudación del período de sesiones", "Declaro reanudado el per~
Rows: 1,965,734
Columns: 2
$ type  <chr> "Target", "Target", "Target", "Target", "Target", "Target", "Tar~
$ lines <chr> "Resumption of the session", "I declare resumed the session of t~
```

We now have our `type` and `lines` columns and the associated observations for our idealized dataset, in Table 6.2. We can now write these datasets to the *data/derived/* directory using `write_csv()` and create corresponding data dictionary files.

6.2 Structured

Structured data already reflects the physical and semantic structure of a tidy dataset. This means that the data is already in a tabular format and the relationships between columns and rows are already well-defined. Therefore, the heavy lifting of curating the data is already done. There are two remaining questions, however, that need to be taken into account. One, logistical question, is what file format the dataset is in and how to read it into R. And the second, more research-based, is whether the data may benefit from some additional curation and documentation to make it more amenable to analysis and more understandable to others.

6.2.1 Reading datasets

Let's consider some common formats for structured data, *i.e.* datasets, and how to read them into R. First, we will consider R-native formats, such as package datasets and RDS files. Then will consider non-native formats, such as relational databases and datasets produced by other software. Finally, we will consider software agnostic formats, such as CSV.

R and some R packages provide structured datasets that are available for use directly within R. For example, {languageR} (Baayen & Shafaei-Bajestan, 2019) provides the `dative` dataset, which is a dataset containing the realization of the dative as NP or PP in the Switchboard corpus and the Treebank Wall Street Journal collection. {janeaustenr} (Silge, 2022) provides the `austen_books` dataset, which is a dataset of Jane Austen's novels. **Package datasets** are loaded into an R session using either the `data()` function, if the package is loaded, or the `::` operator, if the package is not loaded, `data(dative)` or `languageR::dative`, respectively.

> **Dive deeper**
> To explore the available datasets in a package, you can use the `data(package = "package_name")` function. For example, `data(package = "languageR")` will list the datasets available in {languageR}. You can also explore all the datasets available in the loaded packages with the `data()` function using no arguments. For example, `data()`.

R also provides a native file format for storing R objects, the RDS file. Any R object, including data frames, can be written from an R session to disk by using the `write_rds()` function from `readr`. The *.rds* files will be written to disk in a binary format that is not human-readable, which is not ideal for transparent data sharing. However, the files and the R objects can be read back into an R session using the `read_rds()` function with all the attributes intact, such as vector types, factor levels, *etc.*

R provides a suite of tools for importing data from non-native structured sources such as databases and datasets from software such as SPSS, SAS, and Stata. For instance, if you are working with data stored in a **relational database** such as MySQL, PostgreSQL, or SQLite, you can use {DBI} (R Special Interest Group on Databases (R-SIG-DB), Wickham, & Müller, 2024) to connect to the database and {dbplyr} (Wickham, Girlich, & Ruiz, 2024) to query the database using the SQL language. Files from SPSS (*.sav*), SAS (*.sas7bdat*), and Stata (*.dta*) can be read into R using {haven} (Wickham, Miller, & Smith, 2023).

Software agnostic file formats include delimited files, such as CSV, TSV, *etc.* These file formats lack the robust structural attributes of the other formats, but balance this shortcoming by storing structured data in more accessible, human-readable format. Delimited files are plain text files which use a delimiter, such as a comma (`,`), tab (`\t`), or pipe (`|`), to separate the columns and rows. For example, a CSV file is a delimited file where the columns and rows are separated by commas, as seen in Example 6.5.

Example 6.5.

```
column_1,column_2,column_3
row 1 value 1,row 1 value 2,row 1 value 3
row 2 value 1,row 2 value 2,row 2 value 3
```

Given the accessibility of delimited files, they are a common format for sharing structured data in reproducible research. It is not surprising, then, that this is the format which we have chosen for the derived datasets in this book.

6.2.2 Orientation

With an understanding of the various structured formats, we can now turn to considerations about how the original dataset is structured and how that structure is to be used for a given research project. As an example, we will work with the CABNC datasets acquired in Chapter 5. The structure of the original dataset is shown in Snippet 6.4.

Snippet 6.4. Directory structure for the CABNC datasets

```
data/
├── analysis/
├── derived/
└── original/
    ├── cabnc_do.csv
    └── cabnc/
        ├── participants.csv
        ├── token_types.csv
        ├── tokens.csv
        ├── transcripts.csv
        └── utterances.csv
```

In addition to other important information, the data origin file *cabnc_do.csv* shown in Table 6.3 informs us the datasets are related by a common variable.

Table 6.3: Data origin: CABNC datasets

attribute	description
Resource name	CABNC.
Data source	https://ca.talkbank.org/access/CABNC.html, doi:10.21415/T55Q5R
Data sampling frame	Over 400 British English speakers from across the UK stratified age, gender, social group, and region, and recording their language output over a set period of time.
Data collection date(s)	1992.
Data format	CSV Files
Data schema	The recordings are linked by `filename` and the participants are linked by `who`.
License	CC BY NC SA 3.0
Attribution	Saul Albert, Laura E. de Ruiter, and J.P. de Ruiter (2015) CABNC: the Jeffersonian transcription of the Spoken British National Corpus. https://saulalbert.github.io/CABNC/.

The CABNC datasets are structured in a relational format, which means that the data is stored in multiple tables that are related to each other. The tables are related by a common column or set of columns, which are called **keys**. A key is used to join the tables together to create a single dataset. There are two keys in the CABNC datasets, `filename` and `who`. Each variable corresponds to recording- and/ or participant-oriented datasets.

Now, let's envision a scenario in which we are preparing our data for a study that aims to investigate the relationship between speaker demographics and utterances. In their original format, the CABNC datasets separate information about utterances and speakers in separate datasets, `cabnc_utterances` and `cabnc_participants`, respectively. Ideally, we would like to curate these datasets such that the information about the utterances and the speakers are ready to be joined as part of the dataset transformation process, while still retaining the relevant original structure. This usually involves removing redundant and/ or uninformative variables and/ or adjusting variable names and writing these datasets and their documentation files to disk.

6.2.3 Tidy the dataset

With these goals in mind, let's start the process of curation by reading the relevant datasets into an R session. Since we are working with CSV files we will use the `read_csv()` function, as seen in Example 6.6.

Example 6.6.

```
# Read the relevant datasets
cabnc_utterances <-
  read_csv("data/cabnc/original/utterances.csv")
cabnc_participants <-
  read_csv("data/cabnc/original/participants.csv")
```

The next step is to inspect the structure of the datasets. We can use the `glimpse()` function for this task.

Example 6.7.

```
#Preview the structure of the datasets
glimpse(cabnc_utterances)
glimpse(cabnc_participants)
```

```
Rows: 235,901
Columns: 10
$ filename  <chr> "KB0RE000", "KB0RE000", "KB0RE000", "KB0RE000", "KB0RE000", ~
$ path      <chr> "ca/CABNC/KB0/KB0RE000", "ca/CABNC/KB0/KB0RE000", "ca/CABNC/~
$ utt_num   <dbl> 0, 1, 2, 3, 4, 5, 6, 7, 8, 9, 10, 11, 12, 13, 14, 15, 16, 17~
$ who       <chr> "PS002", "PS006", "PS002", "PS006", "PS002", "PS006", "PS002~
$ role      <chr> "Unidentified", "Unidentified", "Unidentified", "Unidentifie~
$ postcodes <lgl> NA, NA, NA, NA, NA, NA, NA, NA, NA, NA, NA, NA, NA, NA, NA, ~
$ gems      <lgl> NA, NA, NA, NA, NA, NA, NA, NA, NA, NA, NA, NA, NA, NA, NA, ~
$ utterance <chr> "You enjoyed yourself in America", "Eh", "did you", "Oh I co~
$ startTime <dbl> 0.208, 2.656, 2.896, 3.328, 5.088, 6.208, 8.320, 8.480, 10.2~
$ endTime   <dbl> 2.67, 2.90, 3.33, 5.26, 6.02, 8.50, 9.31, 11.23, 14.34, 15.9~
```

```
Rows: 6,190
Columns: 13
$ filename  <chr> "KB0RE004", "KB0RE004", "KB0RE004", "KB0RE006", "KB0RE006", ~
$ path      <chr> "ca/CABNC/0missing/KB0RE004", "ca/CABNC/0missing/KB0RE004", ~
$ who       <chr> "PS008", "PS009", "KB0PSUN", "PS007", "PS008", "PS009", "KB0~
$ name      <chr> "John", "Gethyn", "Unknown_speaker", "Alan", "John", "Gethyn~
$ role      <chr> "Unidentified", "Unidentified", "Unidentified", "Unidentifie~
$ language  <chr> "eng", "eng", "eng", "eng", "eng", "eng", "eng", "eng", "eng~
$ monthage  <dbl> 481, 481, 13, 949, 481, 481, 13, 637, 565, 13, 637, 565, 13,~
$ age       <chr> "40;01.01", "40;01.01", "1;01.01", "79;01.01", "40;01.01", "~
$ sex       <chr> "male", "male", "male", "male", "male", "male", "male", "mal~
$ numwords  <dbl> 28, 360, 156, 1610, 791, 184, 294, 93, 3, 0, 128, 24, 0, 150~
$ numutts   <dbl> 1, 9, 27, 7, 5, 7, 6, 5, 1, 0, 11, 6, 0, 110, 74, 96, 12, 1,~
$ avgutt    <dbl> 28.00, 40.00, 5.78, 230.00, 158.20, 26.29, 49.00, 18.60, 3.0~
$ medianutt <dbl> 28, 39, 5, 84, 64, 9, 3, 15, 3, 0, 9, 3, 0, 7, 6, 4, 3, 12, ~
```

From visual inspection of the output of Example 6.7 we can see that there are common variables in both datasets. In particular, we see the `filename` and `who` variables mentioned in the data origin file *cabnc_do.csv*.

The next step is to consider the variables that will be useful for future analysis. Since we are creating a curated dataset, the goal will be to retain as much information as possible from the original datasets. There are cases, however, in which there may be variables that are not informative and, thus, will not prove useful for any analysis. These removable variables tend to be of one of two types: variables which show no variation across observations and variables where the information is redundant.

As an example case, let's look at the `cabnc_participants` data frame. We can use the `skim()` function from {skimr} to get a summary of the variables in the dataset. We can add the `yank()` function to look at variable types one at a time. We will start with the character variables, as seen in Example 6.8.

Example 6.8.

```
# Summarize character variables
cabnc_participants |>
  skim() |>
  yank("character")
```

```
-- Variable type: character ----------------------------------------------------
  skim_variable n_missing complete_rate min max empty n_unique whitespace
1 filename              0             1   8   8     0     2020          0
2 path                  0             1  21  26     0     2020          0
3 who                   0             1   4   7     0      581          0
4 name                  0             1   3  25     0      269          0
5 role                  0             1  12  12     0        1          0
6 language              0             1   3   3     0        1          0
```

```
7 age                    0          1   7   8    0      83        0
8 sex                    0          1   4   6    0       2        0
```

We see from the output in Example 6.8, that the variables `role` and `language` have a single unique value. This means that these variables do not show any variation across observations. We will remove these variables from the dataset.

Continuing on, let's look for redundant variables. We see that the variables `filename` and `path` have the same number of unique values. And if we combine this with the visual summary in Example 6.7, we can see that the `path` variable is redundant. We will remove this variable from the dataset.

Another potentially redundant set of variables are `who` and `name` —both of which are speaker identifiers. The `who` variable is a unique identifier, but there may be some redundancy with the `name` variable, that is, there may be two speakers with the same name. We can check this by looking at the number of unique values in the `who` and `name` variables from the `skim()` output in Example 6.8. `who` has 568 unique values and `name` has 269 unique values. This suggests that there are multiple speakers with the same name.

Another way to explore this is to look at the number of unique values in the `who` variable for each unique value in the `name` variable. We can do this using the `group_by()` and `summarize()` functions from {dplyr}. For each value of `name`, we will count the number of unique values in `who` with `n_distinct()` and then sort the results in descending order.

Example 6.9.

```
cabnc_participants |>
  group_by(name) |>
  summarize(n = n_distinct(who)) |>
  arrange(desc(n)) |>
  slice_head(n = 5)
```

```
# A tibble: 5 x 2
  name                          n
  <chr>                     <int>
1 None                         59
2 Unknown_speaker              59
3 Group_of_unknown_speakers    21
4 Chris                         9
5 David                         9
```

It is good that we performed the check in Example 6.9 beforehand. In addition to speakers with the same name, such as 'Chris' and 'David', we also have multiple speakers with generic codes, such as 'None' and 'Unknown_speaker'. It is clear that `name` is redundant.

With this in mind, we can then safely remove the following variables from the dataset: `role`, `language`, `name`, and `path`. To drop variables from a data frame we can use the `select()` function in combination with the - operator. The - operator tells the `select()` function to drop the variable that follows it.

Example 6.10.

```
# Drop variables
cabnc_participants <-
  cabnc_participants |>
  select(-role, -language, -name, -path)

# Preview the dataset
glimpse(cabnc_participants)
```

```
Rows: 6,190
Columns: 9
$ filename  <chr> "KB0RE004", "KB0RE004", "KB0RE004", "KB0RE006", "KB0RE006", ~
$ who       <chr> "PS008", "PS009", "KB0PSUN", "PS007", "PS008", "PS009", "KB0~
$ monthage  <dbl> 481, 481, 13, 949, 481, 481, 13, 637, 565, 13, 637, 565, 13,~
$ age       <chr> "40;01.01", "40;01.01", "1;01.01", "79;01.01", "40;01.01", "~
$ sex       <chr> "male", "male", "male", "male", "male", "male", "male", "mal~
$ numwords  <dbl> 28, 360, 156, 1610, 791, 184, 294, 93, 3, 0, 128, 24, 0, 150~
$ numutts   <dbl> 1, 9, 27, 7, 5, 7, 6, 5, 1, 0, 11, 6, 0, 110, 74, 96, 12, 1,~
$ avgutt    <dbl> 28.00, 40.00, 5.78, 230.00, 158.20, 26.29, 49.00, 18.60, 3.0~
$ medianutt <dbl> 28, 39, 5, 84, 64, 9, 3, 15, 3, 0, 9, 3, 0, 7, 6, 4, 3, 12, ~
```

Now we have a frame with 9 more informative variables which describe the participants. We would then repeat this process for the `cabnc_utterances` dataset to remove redundant and uninformative variables.

Another, optional step, is to rename and/ or organize the order the variables to make the dataset more understandable. Let's organize the columns to read left to right from most general to most specific. Again, we turn to the `select()` function, this time including the variables in the order we want them to appear in the dataset. We will take this opportunity to rename some of the variable names so that they are more informative.

Example 6.11.

```
# Rename variables
cabnc_participants <-
  cabnc_participants |>
  select(
    doc_id = filename,
    part_id = who,
    part_age = monthage,
```

```
    part_sex = sex,
    num_words = numwords,
    num_utts = numutts,
    avg_utt_len = avgutt,
    median_utt_len = medianutt
  )

# Preview the dataset
glimpse(cabnc_participants)
```

```
Rows: 6,190
Columns: 8
$ doc_id         <chr> "KB0RE004", "KB0RE004", "KB0RE004", "KB0RE006", "KB0RE0~
$ part_id        <chr> "PS008", "PS009", "KB0PSUN", "PS007", "PS008", "PS009",~
$ part_age       <dbl> 481, 481, 13, 949, 481, 481, 13, 637, 565, 13, 637, 565~
$ part_sex       <chr> "male", "male", "male", "male", "male", "male", "male",~
$ num_words      <dbl> 28, 360, 156, 1610, 791, 184, 294, 93, 3, 0, 128, 24, 0~
$ num_utts       <dbl> 1, 9, 27, 7, 5, 7, 6, 5, 1, 0, 11, 6, 0, 110, 74, 96, 1~
$ avg_utt_len    <dbl> 28.00, 40.00, 5.78, 230.00, 158.20, 26.29, 49.00, 18.60~
$ median_utt_len <dbl> 28, 39, 5, 84, 64, 9, 3, 15, 3, 0, 9, 3, 0, 7, 6, 4, 3,~
```

The variable order is organized after running Example 6.11. Now let's sort the rows by `doc_id` and `part_id` so that the dataset is sensibly organized. The `arrange()` function takes a data frame and a list of variables to sort by, in the order they are listed.

Example 6.12.

```
# Sort rows
cabnc_participants <-
  cabnc_participants |>
  arrange(doc_id, part_id)

# Preview the dataset
cabnc_participants |>
  slice_head(n = 5)
```

```
# A tibble: 5 x 8
  doc_id part_id part_age part_sex num_words num_utts avg_utt_len median_utt_len
  <chr>  <chr>      <dbl> <chr>        <dbl>    <dbl>       <dbl>          <dbl>
1 KB0RE~ KB0PSUN       13 male             2        2        1                 1
2 KB0RE~ PS002        721 female         759       74       10.3               7
3 KB0RE~ PS006        601 male           399       64        6.23              5
4 KB0RE~ KB0PSUN       13 male             7        3        2.33              1
5 KB0RE~ PS005        481 female         257       32        8.03              8
```

Applying the sorting in Example 6.12, we can see that the utterances are now our desired order, a dataset that reads left to right from document to participant-oriented attributes and top to bottom by document and participant.

6.3 Semi-structured

Between unstructured and structured data falls semi-structured data. And as the name suggests, it is a hybrid data format. This means that there will be important structured metadata included with unstructured elements. The file formats and approaches to encoding the structured aspects of the data vary widely from resource to resource and therefore often require more detailed attention to the structure of the data and often include more sophisticated programming strategies to curate the data to produce a tidy dataset.

6.3.1 Reading data

The file formats associated with semi-structured data include a wide range. These include file formats conducive to more structured-leaning data, such as XML, HTML, and JSON, and file formats with more unstructured-leaning data, such as annotated TXT files. Annotated TXT files may in fact appear with the *.txt* extension, but may also appear with other, sometimes resource-specific, extensions, such as *.utt* for the Switchboard Dialog Act Corpus or *.cha* for the Child Language Data Exchange System (CHILDES) annotation files, for example.

The more structured file formats use standard conventions and therefore can be read into an R session with format-specific functions. Say, for example, we are working with data in a JSON file format. We can read the data into an R session with the `read_json()` function from {jsonlite} (Ooms, 2023). For XML and HTML files, {rvest} (Wickham, 2024) provides the `read_xml()` and `read_html()` functions.

Semi-structured data in TXT files can be read either as a file or by lines. The choice of which approach to take depends on the structure of the data. If the data structure is line-based, then `read_lines()` often makes more sense than `read_file()`. However, in some cases, the data may be structured in a way that requires the entire file to be read into an R session and then subsequently parsed.

6.3.2 Orientation

To provide an example of the curation process using semi-structured data, we will work with the Europarl corpus of native, non-native and translated texts (ENNTT) corpus (Nisioi, Rabinovich, Dinu, & Wintner, 2016). The ENNTT corpus contains native and translated English drawn from European Parliament proceedings. Let's look at the directory structure for the ENNTT corpus in Snippet 6.5.

Snippet 6.5. Data directory structure for the ENNTT corpus

```
data/
├── analysis/
├── derived/
└── original/
    ├── enntt_do.csv
    └── enntt/
        ├── natives.dat
        ├── natives.tok
        ├── nonnatives.dat
        ├── nonnatives.tok
        ├── translations.dat
        └── translations.tok
```

We now inspect the data origin file for the ENNTT corpus, *enntt_do.csv*, in Table 6.4.

Table 6.4: Data origin: ENNTT Corpus

attribute	description
Resource name	Europarl corpus of Native, Non-native and Translated Texts — ENNTT
Data source	https://github.com/senisioi/enntt-release
Data sampling frame	English, European Parliament texts, transcribed discourse, political genre
Data collection date(s)	Not specified in the repository
Data format	.tok, .dat
Data schema	.tok files contain the actual text; .dat files contain the annotations corresponding to each line in the .tok files.
License	Not specified. Contact the authors for more information.
Attribution	Nisioi, S., Rabinovich, E., Dinu, L. P., & Wintner, S. (2016). A corpus of native, non-native and translated texts. *Proceedings of the Tenth International Conference on Language Resources and Evaluation (LREC 2016).*

According to the data origin file, there are two important file types, *.dat* and *.tok*. The *.dat* files contain annotations and the *.tok* files contain the actual text. Let's inspect the first couple of lines in the *.dat* file for the native speakers, *nonnatives.dat*, in Snippet 6.6.

Snippet 6.6. Example *.dat* file for the non-native speakers

```
<LINE STATE="Poland" MEPID="96779" LANGUAGE="EN" NAME="Danuta Hübner,"
↪  SEQ_SPEAKER_ID="184" SESSION_ID="ep-05-11-17"/>
<LINE STATE="Poland" MEPID="96779" LANGUAGE="EN" NAME="Danuta Hübner,"
↪  SEQ_SPEAKER_ID="184" SESSION_ID="ep-05-11-17"/>
```

We see that the *.dat* file contains annotations for various session and speaker attributes. The format of the annotations is XML-like. XML is a form of markup language, such as YAML, JSON, *etc.* **Markup languages** are used to annotate text with additional information about the structure, meaning, and/ or presentation of text. In XML, structure is built up by nesting of nodes. The nodes are named with tags, which are enclosed in angle brackets, < and >. Nodes are opened with `<TAG>` and closed with `</TAG>`. In Snippet 6.7 we see an example of a simple XML file structure.

Snippet 6.7. Example *.xml* file structure

```
<?xml version="1.0" encoding="UTF-8"?>
<book category="fiction">
  <title lang="en">The Catcher in the Rye</title>
  <author>J.D. Salinger</author>
  <year>1951</year>
</book>
```

In Snippet 6.7 there are four nodes, three of which are nested inside of the `<book>` node. The `<book>` node in this example is the root node. XML files require a root node. Nodes can also have attributes, such as the `category` attribute in the `<book>` node, but they are not required. Furthermore, XML files also require a declaration, which is the first line in Snippet 6.7. The declaration specifies the version of XML used and the encoding.

So the *.dat* file is not strict XML, but is similar in that it contains nodes and attributes. An XML variant you are likely familiar with, HTML, has more relaxed rules than XML. HTML is a markup language used to annotate text with information about the organization and presentation of text on the web that does not require a root node or a declaration —much like our *.dat* file. So suffice it to say that the *.dat* file can safely be treated as HTML.

And the *.tok* file for native speakers, *nonnatives.tok*, in Snippet 6.8, shows the actual text for each line in the corpus.

Snippet 6.8. Example *.tok* file for the non-native speakers

```
The Commission is following with interest the planned construction of a
↪ nuclear power plant in Akkuyu , Turkey and recognises the importance of
↪ ensuring that the construction of the new plant follows the highest
↪ internationally accepted nuclear safety standards .
According to our information , the decision on the selection of a bidder has
↪ not been taken yet .
```

In a study in which we are interested in contrasting the language of natives and non-natives, we will want to combine the *.dat* and *.tok* files for these groups of speakers.

The question is what attributes we want to include in the curated dataset. Given the research focus, we will not need the `LANGUAGE` or `NAME` attributes. We may want to modify the attribute names so they are a bit more descriptive.

An idealized version of the curated dataset based on this criteria is shown in Table 6.5.

Table 6.5: Idealized structure for the curated ENNTT Corpus datasets

variable	name	type	description
session_id	Session ID	character	Unique identifier for each session.
speaker_id	Speaker ID	integer	Unique identifier for each speaker.
state	State	character	The political state of the speaker.
type	Type	character	Indicates whether the text is native or non-native
session_seq	Session Sequence	integer	The sequence of the text in the session.
text	Text	character	Contains the text of the line, and maintains the structure of the original data.

6.3.3 Tidy the data

Now that we have a better understanding of the corpus data and our target curated dataset structure, let's work to extract and organize the data from the native and non-native files.

The general approach we will take is, for native and then non-natives, to read in the *.dat* file as an HTML file and then extract the line nodes and their attributes combining them into a data frame. Then we'll read in the *.tok* file as a text file and then combine the two into a single data frame.

Starting with the natives, we use {rvest} to read in the *.dat* file as an XML file with the `read_html()` function and then extract the line nodes with the `html_elements()` function as in Example 6.13.

Example 6.13.

```
# Load packages
library(rvest)

# Read in *.dat* file as HTML
ns_dat_lines <-
  read_html("../data/original/enntt/natives.dat") |>
  html_elements("line")

# Inspect
class(ns_dat_lines)
typeof(ns_dat_lines)
length(ns_dat_lines)
```

```
[1] "xml_nodeset"
[1] "list"
[1] 116341
```

We can see that the `ns_dat_lines` object is a special type of list, `xml_nodeset` which contains 116,341 line nodes. Let's now jump out of sequence and read in the *.tok* file as a text file, in Example 6.14, again by lines using `read_lines()`, and compare the two to make sure that our approach will work.

Example 6.14.

```
# Read in *.tok* file by lines
ns_tok_lines <-
  read_lines("../data/enntt/original/natives.tok")

# Inspect
class(ns_tok_lines)
typeof(ns_tok_lines)
length(ns_tok_lines)
```

```
[1] "character"
[1] "character"
[1] 116341
```

We do, in fact, have the same number of lines in the *.dat* and *.tok* files. So we can proceed with extracting the attributes from the line nodes and combining them with the text from the *.tok* file.

Let's start by listing the attributes of the first line node in the `ns_dat_lines` object. To do this we will draw on the `pluck()` function from {purrr} (Wickham & Henry, 2023) to extract the first line node. Then, we use the `html_attrs()` function to get the attribute names and the values, as in Example 6.15.

Example 6.15.

```
# Load package
library(purrr)

# List attributes line node 1
ns_dat_lines |>
  pluck(1) |>
  html_attrs()
```

```
           state               mepid           language              name
"United Kingdom"              "2099"               "EN" "Evans, Robert J"
  seq_speaker_id          session_id
             "2"      "ep-00-01-17"
```

No surprise here, these are the same attributes we saw in the *.dat* file preview in Snippet 6.6. At this point, it's good to make a plan on how to associate the attribute names with the column names in our curated dataset.

- `session_id` = `session_id`
- `speaker_id` = `MEPID`
- `state` = `state`
- `session_seq` = `seq_speaker_id`

We can do this one attribute at a time using the `html_attr()` function and then combine them into a data frame with the `tibble()` function as in Example 6.16.

Example 6.16.

```
# Extract attributes from first line node
session_id <- ns_dat_lines |> pluck(1) |> html_attr("session_id")
speaker_id <- ns_dat_lines |> pluck(1) |> html_attr("mepid")
state <- ns_dat_lines |> pluck(1) |> html_attr("state")
session_seq <- ns_dat_lines |> pluck(1) |> html_attr("seq_speaker_id")

# Combine into data frame
tibble(session_id, speaker_id, state, session_seq)
```

```
# A tibble: 1 x 4
  session_id  speaker_id state          session_seq
  <chr>       <chr>      <chr>          <chr>
1 ep-00-01-17 2099       United Kingdom 2
```

The results from Example 6.16 show that the attributes have been extracted and mapped to our idealized column names, but this would be tedious to do for each line node. A function to extract attributes and values from a line and add them to a data frame would help simplify this process. The function in Example 6.17 does just that.

Example 6.17.

```
# Function to extract attributes from line node
extract_dat_attrs <- function(line_node) {
  session_id <- line_node |> html_attr("session_id")
  speaker_id <- line_node |> html_attr("mepid")
  state <- line_node |> html_attr("state")
  session_seq <- line_node |> html_attr("seq_speaker_id")

  tibble(session_id, speaker_id, state, session_seq)
}
```

It's a good idea to test out the function to verify that it works as expected. We can do this by passing the various indices to the `ns_dat_lines` object to the function as in Example 6.18.

Example 6.18.

```
# Test function
ns_dat_lines |> pluck(1) |> extract_dat_attrs()
ns_dat_lines |> pluck(20) |> extract_dat_attrs()
ns_dat_lines |> pluck(100) |> extract_dat_attrs()
```

```
# A tibble: 1 x 4
  session_id  speaker_id state          session_seq
  <chr>       <chr>      <chr>          <chr>
1 ep-00-01-17 2099       United Kingdom 2
# A tibble: 1 x 4
  session_id  speaker_id state          session_seq
  <chr>       <chr>      <chr>          <chr>
1 ep-00-01-17 1309       United Kingdom 40
# A tibble: 1 x 4
  session_id  speaker_id state          session_seq
  <chr>       <chr>      <chr>          <chr>
1 ep-00-01-18 4549       United Kingdom 28
```

It looks like the `extract_dat_attrs()` function is ready for prime-time. Let's now apply it to all of the line nodes in the `ns_dat_lines` object using the `map_dfr()` function from {purrr} as in Example 6.19.

Example 6.19.

```
# Extract attributes from all line nodes
ns_dat_attrs <-
  ns_dat_lines |>
  map_dfr(extract_dat_attrs)

```

```
# Inspect
glimpse(ns_dat_attrs)
```

```
Rows: 116,341
Columns: 4
$ session_id  <chr> "ep-00-01-17", "ep-00-01-17", "ep-00-01-17", "ep-00-01-17"~
$ speaker_id  <chr> "2099", "2099", "2099", "4548", "4548", "4541", "4541", "4~
$ state       <chr> "United Kingdom", "United Kingdom", "United Kingdom", "Uni~
$ session_seq <chr> "2", "2", "2", "4", "4", "12", "12", "12", "12", "12", "12~
```

> **Dive deeper**
> The `map*()` functions from {purrr} are a family of functions that apply a function to each element of a vector, list, or data frame. The `map_dfr()` function is a variant of the `map()` function that returns a data frame that is the result of row-binding the results, hence `*_dfr`.

We can see that the `ns_dat_attrs` object is a data frame with 116,341 rows and 4 columns, just has we expected. We can now combine the `ns_dat_attrs` data frame with the `ns_tok_lines` vector to create a single data frame with the attributes and the text. This is done with the `mutate()` function assigning the `ns_tok_lines` vector to a new column named `text` as in Example 6.20.

Example 6.20.

```
# Combine attributes and text
ns_dat <-
  ns_dat_attrs |>
  mutate(text = ns_tok_lines)

# Inspect
glimpse(ns_dat)
```

```
Rows: 116,341
Columns: 5
$ session_id  <chr> "ep-00-01-17", "ep-00-01-17", "ep-00-01-17", "ep-00-01-17"~
$ speaker_id  <chr> "2099", "2099", "2099", "4548", "4548", "4541", "4541", "4~
$ state       <chr> "United Kingdom", "United Kingdom", "United Kingdom", "Uni~
$ session_seq <chr> "2", "2", "2", "4", "4", "12", "12", "12", "12", "12", "12~
$ text        <chr> "You will be aware from the press and television that ther~
```

This is the data for the native speakers. We can now repeat this process for the non-native speakers, or we can create a function to do it for us.

Consider this
Using the previous code as a guide, consider what steps you would need to take to create a function to combine the *.dat* and *.tok* files for the non-native speakers (and/ or the translations). What arguments would the function take? What would the function return? What would the processing steps be? In what order would the steps be executed?

After applying the curation steps to both the native and non-native datasets, we will have two data frames, `enntt_ns_df` and `enntt_nns_df`, respectively that meet the idealized structure for the curated ENNTT Corpus datasets, as shown in Table 6.5. The `enntt_ns_df` and `enntt_nns_df` data frames are ready to be written to disk and documented.

6.4 Documentation

After applying the curation steps to our data, we will now want to write the dataset to disk and to do our best to document the process and the resulting dataset.

Since data frames are a tabular, we will have various options for the file type to write. Many of these formats are software-specific, such as `*.xlsx` for Microsoft Excel, `*.sav` for SPSS, `*.dta` for Stata, and `*.rds` for R. We will use the `*.csv` format since it is a common format that can be read by many software packages. We will use the `write_csv()` function from {readr} to write the dataset to disk.

Now the question is where to save our CSV file. Since our dataset is derived by our work, we will added it to the *derived/* directory. If you are working with multiple data sources within the same project, it is a good idea to create a sub-directory for each dataset. This will help keep the project organized and make it easier to find and access the datasets.

The final step, as always, is to provide documentation. For datasets the documentation is a data dictionary, as discussed in Section 2.3.2. As with data origin files, you can use spreadsheet software to create and edit the data dictionary.

Tip
The `create_data_dictionary()` function from {qtkit} provides a rudimentary data dictionary template by default. However, the `model` argument let's you take advantage of OpenAI's text generation models to generate a more detailed data dictionary for you to edit. See the function documentation for more information.

In {qtkit} we have a function, `create_data_dictionary()` that will generate the scaffolding for a data dictionary. The function takes two arguments, `data` and `file_path`. It reads the dataset columns and provides a template for the data dictionary.

An example of a data dictionary, a data dictionary for the `enntt_ns_df` dataset is shown in Table 6.6.

Table 6.6: Data dictionary: `enntt_ns_df` dataset

variable	name	type	description
session_id	Session ID	categorical	Unique identifier for each session
speaker_id	Speaker ID	categorical	Unique identifier for each speaker
state	State	categorical	Name of the state or country the session is linked to
session_seq	Session Sequence	ordinal	Sequence number in the session
text	Text	categorical	Text transcript of the session
type	Type	categorical	The type of the speaker, whether native or nonnative

Activities

The following activities build on your skills and knowledge to use R to read, inspect, and write data and datasets in R. In these activities you will have an opportunity to learn and apply your skills and knowledge to the task of curating datasets. This is a vital component of text analysis research that uses unstructured and semi-structured data.

> **Recipe**
> **What**: Organizing and documenting datasets
> **How**: Read Recipe 6, complete comprehension check, and prepare for Lab 6.
> **Why**: To rehearse methods for deriving tidying datasets to use as the base for further project-specific purposes. We will explore how regular expressions are helpful in developing strategies for matching, extracting, and/ or replacing patterns in character sequences and how to organize datasets in rows and columns. We will also explore how to document datasets in a data dictionary.

Lab
What: Taming data
How: Fork, clone, and complete the steps in Lab 6.
Why: To gain experience working with coding strategies to manipulate data using Tidyverse functions and regular expressions, to practice reading/ writing data from/ to disk, and to implement organizational strategies for organizing and documenting a dataset in reproducible fashion.

Summary

In this chapter we looked at the process of structuring data into a dataset. This included a discussion on three main types of data —unstructured, structured, and semi-structured. The level of structure of the original data(set) will vary from resource to resource and by the same token so will the file format used to support the level of metadata included. The results from data curation results in a dataset that is saved separate from the original data in order to maintain modularity between what the data(set) look like before we intervene and afterwards. Since there can be multiple analysis approaches applied to the original data in a research project, this curated dataset serves as the point of departure for each of the subsequent datasets derived from the transformational steps. In addition to the code we use to derive the curated dataset's structure, we also include a data dictionary which documents the variables and measures in the curated dataset.

7

Transform

> **Outcomes**
>
> - Understand the role of data transformation in a text analysis project.
> - Identify the main types of transformations used to prepare datasets for analysis.
> - Recognize the importance of planning and documenting the transformation process.

In this chapter, we will focus on transforming curated datasets to refine and possibly expand their relational characteristics to align with our research. I will approach the transformation process by breaking it down into two sub-processes: preparation and enrichment. The preparation process involves normalizing and tokenizing text. The enrichment process involves generating, recoding, and integrating variables. These processes are not sequential but may occur in any order based on the researcher's evaluation of the dataset characteristics and the desired outcome.

> **>_ Lessons**
>
> **What**: Reshape Datasets by Rows, Reshape datasets by Columns
>
> **How**: In an R console, load {swirl}, run `swirl()`, and follow prompts to select the lesson.
>
> **Why**: Explore data preprocessing skills to manipulate rows and columns using powerful packages like {dplyr} and {tidytext} to normalization, tokenize, and integrate datasets equipping you with the essential techniques to structure datasets for analysis.

7.1 Preparation

In this section, we will cover the processes of normalization and tokenization. These processes are particularly relevant for text analysis, as text conventions can introduce unwanted variability in the data and, therefore, the unit of observation may need to be adjusted to align with the research question.

10.4324/9781003393764.7

To illustrate these processes, we will use a curated version of the Europarl Parallel Corpus (Koehn, 2005). This dataset contains transcribed source language (Spanish) and translated target language (English) from the proceedings of the European Parliament. The unit of observation is the `lines` variable whose values are lines of dialog. We will use this dataset to explore the normalization and tokenization processes.

The contents of the data dictionary for this dataset appears in Table 7.1.

Table 7.1: Data dictionary for the curated Europarl Parallel Corpus.

variable name		type	description
doc_id	Document ID	numeric	Unique identification number for each document
type	Document Type	categorical	Type of document; either 'Source' (Spanish) or 'Target' (English)
line_id	Line ID	numeric	Unique identification number for each line in each document type
lines	Lines	categorical	Content of the lines in the document

Let's read in the dataset CSV file with `read_csv()` and inspect the first lines of the dataset with `slice_head()` in Example 7.1.

Example 7.1.

```
# Read in the dataset
europarl_tbl <-
  read_csv(file = "../data/derived/europarl_curated.csv")

# Preview the first 10 lines
europarl_tbl |>
  slice_head(n = 10)
```

```
# A tibble: 10 x 4
    doc_id type   line_id lines
     <dbl> <chr>    <dbl> <chr>
 1 1965735 Source       1 "Reanudación del período de sesiones"
 2       1 Target       1 "Resumption of the session"
 3 1965736 Source       2 "Declaro reanudado el período de sesiones del Parlame~
 4       2 Target       2 "I declare resumed the session of the European Parlia~
 5 1965737 Source       3 "Como todos han podido comprobar, el gran \"efecto de~
 6       3 Target       3 "Although, as you will have seen, the dreaded 'millen~
 7 1965738 Source       4 "Sus Señorías han solicitado un debate sobre el tema ~
 8       4 Target       4 "You have requested a debate on this subject in the c~
 9 1965739 Source       5 "A la espera de que se produzca, de acuerdo con mucho~
10       5 Target       5 "In the meantime, I should like to observe a minute' ~
```

This dataset includes 3,931,468 observations and four variables. The key variable for our purposes is the `lines` variable. This variable contains the text we will be working with. The other variables are metadata that may be of interest for our analyses.

7.1.1 Normalization

The process of normalizing datasets in essence is to sanitize the values of a variable or set of variables such that there are no artifacts that will contaminate subsequent processing. It may be the case that non-linguistic metadata may require normalization, but more often than not, linguistic information is the most common target for normalization as text often includes artifacts from the acquisition process which will not be desired in the analysis.

Simply looking at the first 10 lines of the dataset from Example 7.1 gives us a clearer sense of the dataset structure, but, in terms of normalization procedures we might apply, it is likely not sufficient. We want to get a sense of any potential inconsistencies in the dataset, in particular in the `lines` variable. Since this is a large dataset with 3,931,468 observations, we will need to explore the dataset in more detail using procedures for summarizing and filtering data.

After exploring variations in the `lines` variable, I identified a number of artifacts in this dataset that we will want to consider addressing. These are included in Table 7.2.

Table 7.2: Characteristics of the Europarl Parallel Corpus dataset that may require normalization

Description	Examples
Non-speech annotations	`(Abucheos)`, `(A4-0247/98)`, `(The sitting was opened at 09:00)`
Inconsistent whitespace (␣)	`5␣%␣`, `␣`, `Palacio'␣s`
Non-sentence punctuation	`-`, `:`, `...`, `;`
(Non-)Abbreviations	`Mr.`, `Sr.`, `Mme.`, `Mr`, `Sr`, `Mme`, `Mister`, `Señor`, `Madam`
Text case	`The`, `the`, `White`, `white`

These artifacts either may not be of interest or may introduce unwanted variability that could prove problematic for subsequent processing (*e.g* tokenization, calculating frequencies, *etc.*).

The majority of text normalization procedures incorporate {stringr} (Wickham, 2023b). This package provides a number of functions for manipulating text strings. The workhorse functions we will use for our tasks are the `str_remove()` and `str_replace()` functions. These functions give us the ability to remove or replace text based on literal strings, actual text, or Regular Expressions. **Regular Expressions** (regex, *pl.* regexes) are a powerful tool for pattern matching and text manipulation which employs a syntax that allows for the specification of complex search patterns.

Our first step, however, is to identify the patterns we want to remove or replace. For demonstration purposes, let's focus on removing non-speech annotations from the `lines` variable. To develop a search pattern to identify these annotations, there are various possibilities, `str_view()`, `str_detect()` inside a `filter()` call, or `str_extract()` inside a `mutate()` call. No matter which approach we choose, we need to be sure that our search pattern does not over- or under-generalize the text we want to remove or replace. If we are too general, we may end up removing or replacing text that we want to keep. If we are too specific, we may not remove or replace all the text we want to remove or replace.

In Example 7.2, I've used `str_detect()` which detects a pattern in a character vector and returns a logical vector, `TRUE` if the pattern is detected and `FALSE` if it is not. In combination with `filter()` we can identify a variable with rows that match a pattern. I've added the `slice_sample()` function at the end to return a small, random sample of the dataset to get a better sense how well our pattern works across the dataset.

Now, how about our search pattern? From the examples in Table 7.2 above, we can see that the instances of non-speech are wrapped with parentheses `(` and `)`. The text within the parentheses can vary, so we need a regex to do the heavy lifting. To start out we can match any one or multiple characters with `.+`. But it is important to recognize the `+` (and also the `*`) operators are **'greedy'**, meaning that if there are multiple matches (in this case multiple sets of parentheses) in a single line of text, the longest match will be returned. That is, the match will extend as far as possible. This is not what we want in this case. We want to match the shortest match. To do this we can append the `?` operator to make the `+` operator **'lazy'**. This will match the shortest match.

Example 7.2.

```
# Load package
library(stringr)

# Identify non-speech lines
europarl_tbl |>
  filter(str_detect(lines, "\\(.+?\\)")) |>
  slice_sample(n = 10)
```

```
# A tibble: 10 x 4
    doc_id type   line_id lines
     <dbl> <chr>    <dbl> <chr>
 1 3225772 Source 1260038 (PT) Señor Presidente, quisiera plantear dos pregunta~
 2 3715842 Source 1750108 (El Parlamento decide la devolución a la Comisión)
 3 1961715 Target 1961715 (Parliament adopted the resolution)
 4 1429470 Target 1429470 27, originally Greens/EFA amendment in FEMM); binding~
 5   51632 Target   51632 Question No 8 by (H-0376/00):
 6 2482671 Source  516937 La Comisión propone proporcionar a las Agencias nacio~
 7 1059628 Target 1059628 (The President cut off the speaker)
 8 1507254 Target 1507254 in writing. - (LT) I welcomed this document, because ~
 9 2765325 Source  799591 (Aplausos)
10 2668536 Source  702802    Las preguntas que, por falta de tiempo, no han rec~
```

The results from Example 7.2 show that we have identified the lines that contain at least one of the parliamentary session description annotations. A more targeted search to identify specific instances of the parliamentary session descriptions can be accomplished adding the `str_extract_all()` function as seen in Example 7.3.

Example 7.3.

```
# Extract non-speech fragments
europarl_tbl |>
  filter(str_detect(lines, "\\(.+?\\)")) |>
  mutate(non_speech = str_extract_all(lines, "\\(.+?\\)")) |>
  slice_sample(n = 10)
```

```
# A tibble: 10 x 5
    doc_id type   line_id lines                                        non_speech
     <dbl> <chr>    <dbl> <chr>                                        <list>
 1 3225772 Source 1260038 (PT) Señor Presidente, quisiera plantear d~ <chr [1]>
 2 3715842 Source 1750108 (El Parlamento decide la devolución a la C~ <chr [1]>
 3 1961715 Target 1961715 (Parliament adopted the resolution)          <chr [1]>
 4 1429470 Target 1429470 27, originally Greens/EFA amendment in FEM~ <chr [1]>
 5   51632 Target   51632 Question No 8 by (H-0376/00):                <chr [1]>
 6 2482671 Source  516937 La Comisión propone proporcionar a las Age~ <chr [2]>
 7 1059628 Target 1059628 (The President cut off the speaker)          <chr [1]>
 8 1507254 Target 1507254 in writing. - (LT) I welcomed this documen~ <chr [1]>
 9 2765325 Source  799591 (Aplausos)                                   <chr [1]>
10 2668536 Source  702802    Las preguntas que, por falta de tiempo,~ <chr [1]>
```

OK, that might not be what you expected. The `str_extract_all()` function returns a list of character vectors. This is because for any given line in `lines` there may be a different number of matches. To maintain the data frame as rectangular, a list is returned for each value of `non_speech`. We could expand the list into a data frame with the `unnest()` function if our goal were to work with these matches. But that is not our aim. Rather, we want to know if we have multiple matches per line. Note that the information provided for the `non_speech` column by the data frame object tells use that we have some lines with multiple matches, as we can see in line 6 of our small sample. So good thing we checked!

Let's now remove these non-speech annotations from each line in the `lines` column. We turn to `str_remove_all()`, a variant of `str_remove()`, that, as you expect, will remove multiple matches in a single line. We will use the `mutate()` function to overwrite the `lines` column with the modified text. The code is seen in Example 7.4.

Example 7.4.

```
# Remove non-speech fragments
europarl_tbl <-
  europarl_tbl |>
  mutate(lines = str_remove_all(lines, "\\(.+?\\)"))
```

I recommend spot checking the results of this normalization step by running the code in Example 7.2 again, if nothing appears we've done our job.

When you are content with the results, drop the observations that have no text in the `lines` column. These were rows where the entire line was non-speech annotation. This can be done with the `is.na()` function and the `filter()` function as seen in Example 7.5.

Example 7.5.

```
# Drop empty lines
europarl_tbl <-
  europarl_tbl |>
  filter(!is.na(lines))
```

Normalization goals will vary from dataset to dataset but the procedures often follow a similar line of attack to those outlined in this section.

7.1.2 Tokenization

Tokenization is the process of segmenting units of language into components relevant for the research question. This includes breaking text in curated datasets into smaller units, such as words, ngrams, sentences, *etc.* or combining smaller units into larger units.

The process of tokenization is fundamentally row-wise. Changing the unit of observation changes the number of rows. It is important both for the research and the text processing to operationalize our language units beforehand For example, while it may appear obvious to you what 'word' or 'sentence' means, a computer, and your reproducible research, needs a working definition. This can prove trickier than it seems. For example, in English, we can segment text into words by splitting on whitespace. This works fairly well, but there are some cases where this is not ideal. For example, in the case of contractions, such as `don't`, `won't`, `can't`, *etc.* the apostrophe is not a whitespace character. If we want to consider these contractions as separate words, then perhaps we need to entertain a different tokenization strategy.

> **Consider this**
> Consider the following paragraph:
>
> "As the sun dipped below the horizon, the sky was set ablaze with shades of orange-red, illuminating the landscape. It's a sight Mr. Johnson, a long-time observer, never tired of. On the lakeside, he'd watch with friends, enjoying the ever-changing hues—especially those around 6:30 p.m.—and reflecting on nature's grand display. Even in the half-light, the water's glimmer, coupled with the echo of distant laughter, created a timeless scene. The so-called 'magic hour' was indeed magical, yet fleeting, like a well-crafted poem; it was the essence of life itself."
>
> What text conventions would pose issues for word tokenization based on a whitespace criterion?

Furthermore, tokenization strategies can vary between languages. In German, for example, words are often compounded together, meaning many 'words' will not be captured by the whitespace convention. Whitespace may not even be relevant for word tokenization in logographic writing systems, such as Chinese characters. The take-home message is there is no one-size-fits-all tokenization strategy.

> **Dive deeper**
> For processing Chinese text, including tokenization, see {jiebaR} (Wenfeng & Yanyi, 2019) and {gibasa} (Kato, Ichinose, & Kudo, 2024).

Let's continue to work with the Europarl Parallel Corpus dataset to demonstrate tokenization. We will start by tokenizing the text into words. If we envision what this should look like, we might imagine something like Table 7.3.

Table 7.3: Example of tokenizing the `lines` variable into word tokens

doc_id	type	line_id	token
1	Target	2	I
1	Target	2	declare
1	Target	2	resumed
1	Target	2	the
1	Target	2	session

Comparing Table 7.3 to the fourth row of the output of Example 7.1, we can see that we want to segment the words in `lines` and then have each segment appear as a separate observation, retaining the relevant metadata variables.

Tokenization that maintains the tidy dataset structure is a very common task in text analysis using R. So common, in fact, that {tidytext} (Robinson & Silge, 2024) includes a function, `unnest_tokens()` that tokenizes text in just such a way. Various tokenization types can be specified including 'characters', 'words', 'ngrams', 'sentences' among others. We will use the 'word' tokenization type to recreate the structure we envisioned in Table 7.3.

In Example 7.6, we set our output variable to `token` and our input variable to `lines`.

Example 7.6.

```
# Load package
library(tidytext)

# Tokenize the lines into words
europarl_unigrams_tbl <-
  europarl_tbl |>
  unnest_tokens(
    output = token,
    input = lines,
    token = "words"
  )
```

Let's preview the very same lines we modeled in Table 7.3 to see the results of our tokenization.

Example 7.7.

```
# Preview
europarl_unigrams_tbl |>
  filter(type == "Target", line_id == 2) |>
  slice_head(n = 10)
```

```
# A tibble: 10 x 4
   doc_id type   line_id token
    <dbl> <chr>    <dbl> <chr>
 1      2 Target       2 i
 2      2 Target       2 declare
 3      2 Target       2 resumed
 4      2 Target       2 the
 5      2 Target       2 session
 6      2 Target       2 of
 7      2 Target       2 the
```

```
8        2 Target        2 european
9        2 Target        2 parliament
10       2 Target        2 adjourned
```

In Example 7.7, the `token` column now contains our word tokens. One thing to note, however, is that text is lowercased and punctuation is stripped by default. If we want to retain the original case or punctuation, keep the original variable, or change the tokenization strategy, we can update the `to_lower`, `strip_punct`, `drop`, or `token` parameters, respectively.

As we derive datasets to explore, let's also create bigram tokens. We can do this by changing the `token` parameter to `"ngrams"` and specifying the value for n with the `n` parameter. I will assign the result to `europarl_bigrams_tbl` as we will have two-word tokens, as seen in Example 7.8.

Example 7.8.

```
# Tokenize the lines into bigrams
europarl_bigrams_tbl <-
  europarl_tbl |>
  unnest_tokens(
    output = token,
    input = lines,
    token = "ngrams",
    n = 2
  )
# Preview
europarl_bigrams_tbl |>
  filter(type == "Target", line_id == 2) |>
  slice_head(n = 10)
```

```
# A tibble: 10 x 4
   doc_id type   line_id token
    <dbl> <chr>    <dbl> <chr>
 1      2 Target       2 i declare
 2      2 Target       2 declare resumed
 3      2 Target       2 resumed the
 4      2 Target       2 the session
 5      2 Target       2 session of
 6      2 Target       2 of the
 7      2 Target       2 the european
 8      2 Target       2 european parliament
 9      2 Target       2 parliament adjourned
10      2 Target       2 adjourned on
```

Dive deeper

{tidytext} is one of a number of packages that provide tokenization functions. Some other notable packages include {tokenizers} (Mullen, 2022) and {textrecipes} (Hvitfeldt, 2023). In fact, the functions from {tokenizers} are used under the hood in {tidytext}. {textrecipes} is part of the Tidymodels framework and is designed to work with a suite of packages for computational modeling. It is particularly useful for integrating tokenization with other preprocessing steps and machine learning models, as we will see in Chapter 9.

The most common tokenization strategy is to segment text into smaller units, often words. However, there are times when we may want text segments to be larger than the existing token unit, effectively collapsing over rows. Let's say that we are working with a dataset like the one we created in `europarl_unigrams_tbl` and we want to group the words into sentences. We can again turn to the `unnest_tokens()` function to accomplish this. In Example 7.9, we use the `token = "sentences"` and `collapse = c("type", "line_id")` parameters to group the words into sentences by the `type` and `line_id` variables.

Example 7.9.

```
# Tokenize the lines into sentences
europarl_sentences_tbl <-
  europarl_unigrams_tbl |>
  unnest_tokens(
    output = token,
    input = token,
    token = "sentences",
    collapse = c("type", "line_id")
  )

# Preview
europarl_sentences_tbl |>
  slice_head(n = 5)
```

```
# A tibble: 5 x 3
  type   line_id token
  <chr>    <dbl> <chr>
1 Source       1 reanudación del período de sesiones
2 Target       1 resumption of the session
3 Source       2 declaro reanudado el período de sesiones del parlamento europe~
4 Target       2 i declare resumed the session of the european parliament adjou~
5 Source       3 como todos han podido comprobar el gran efecto del año 2000 no~
```

In this example, we have collapsed the word tokens into sentences. But note, the `token` column contained no punctuation so all the tokens grouped by `type` and `line_id` were concatenated together. This works for our test dataset as lines are sentences. However, in other scenarios, we would need punctuation to ensure that the sentences are properly segmented —if, in fact, punctuation is the cue for sentence boundaries.

7.2 Enrichment

Where preparation steps are focused on sanitizing and segmenting the text, enrichment steps are aimed towards augmenting the dataset either through recoding, generating, or integrating variables. These processes can prove invaluable for aligning the dataset with the research question and facilitating the analysis.

As a practical example of these types of transformations, we'll posit that we are conducting translation research. Specifically, we will set up an investigation into the effect of translation on the syntactic simplification of text. The basic notion is that when translators translate text from one language to another, they subconsciously simplify the text, relative to native texts (Liu & Afzaal, 2021).

To address this research question, we will use the ENNTT corpus, introduced in Section 6.3.2. This data contains European Parliament proceedings and the type of text (native, non-native, or translation) from which the text was extracted. There is one curated dataset for each of the text types.

The data dictionary for the curated native dataset appears in Table 7.4.

Table 7.4: Data dictionary for the curated native ENNTT dataset.

variable	name	type	description
session_id	Session ID	categorical	Unique identifier for each session
speaker_id	Speaker ID	categorical	Unique identifier for each speaker
state	State	categorical	The country or region the speaker is from
session_seq	Session Sequence	ordinal	The order in which the session occurred
text	Text	categorical	The spoken text during the session
type	Type	categorical	The type of speaker. Natives in this dataset.

All three curated datasets have the same variables. The unit of observation for each dataset is the `text` variable.

Before we get started, let's consider what the transformed dataset might look like and what its variables mean. First, we will need to operationalize what we mean by syntactic simplification There are many measures of syntactic complexity (Szmrecsanyi, 2004). For our purposes, we will focus on two measures of syntactic complexity: number of T-units and sentence length (in words). A T-unit is a main clause and all of its subordinate clauses. To calculate the number of T-units, we will need to identify the main clauses and their subordinate clauses. The sentence length is straightforward to calculate after word tokenization.

An idealized transformed dataset dictionary for this investigation should look something like Table 7.5.

Table 7.5: Idealized transformed dataset for the syntactic simplification investigation

variable	name	type	description
doc_id	Document ID	integer	Unique identifier for each document.
type	Type	character	Type of text (native or translated).
t_units	T-units	integer	Number of T-units in the text.
word_len	Word Length	integer	Number of words in the text.

We will be using the native and translated datasets for our purposes, so let's go ahead and read in these datasets.

```
# Read in curated natives
enntt_natives_tbl <-
  read_csv("data/enntt_natives_curated.csv")

# Read in curated translations
enntt_translations_tbl <-
  read_csv("data/enntt_translations_curated.csv")
```

7.2.1 Generation

The process of generation involves the addition of information to a dataset. This differs from other transformation procedures in that instead of manipulating, classifying, and/ or deriving information based on characteristics explicit in a dataset, generation involves deriving new information based on characteristics implicit in a dataset.

The most common type of operation involved in the generation process is the addition of **linguistic annotation**. This process can be accomplished manually by a researcher or research team or automatically through the use of pre-trained linguistic resources and/ or software. Ideally, the annotation of linguistic information can be conducted automatically.

To identify the main clauses and their subordinate clauses in our datasets, we will need to derive syntactic annotation information from the ENNTT `text` variable.

As fun as it would be to hand-annotate the ENNTT corpus, we will instead turn to automatic linguistic annotation. {udpipe} (Wijffels, 2023) provides an interface for annotating text using pre-trained models from the Universal Dependencies[1] (UD) project (Nivre et al., 2020). The UD project is an effort to develop cross-linguistically consistent syntactic annotation for a variety of languages.

Our first step, then, is to peruse the available pre-trained models for the languages we are interested in and selected the most register-aligned models. The models, model names, and licensing information are documented in the {udpipe} documentation for the `udpipe_download_model()` function. For illustrative purposes, we will use the `english` treebank model from the *https://github.com/bnosac/udpipe.models.ud* repository which is released under a CC-BY-SA license[2]. This model is trained on various sources including news, Wikipedia, and web data of various genres.

Let's set the stage by providing an overview of the annotation process.

1. Load {udpipe}.
2. Select the pre-trained model to use and the directory where the model will be stored in your local environment.
3. Prepare the dataset to be annotated (if necessary). This includes ensuring that the dataset has a column of text to be annotated and a grouping column. By default, the names of these columns are expected to be `text` and `doc_id`, respectively. The `text` column needs to be a character vector and the `doc_id` column needs to be a unique index for each text to be annotated.
4. Annotate the dataset. The result returns a data frame.

[1] https://universaldependencies.org/
[2] https://creativecommons.org/licenses/by-sa/4.0/

Since we are working with two datasets, steps 3 and 4 will be repeated. For brevity, I will only show the code for the dataset for the natives. Additionally, I will subset the dataset to 10,000 randomly selected lines for both datasets. Syntactic annotation is a computationally expensive operation and the natives and translations datasets contain 116,341 and 738,597 observations, respectively. This subset will suffice for illustrative purposes.

> **Dive deeper**
> In your own research computationally expensive operations cannot be avoided, but they can be managed. One strategy is to work with a subset of the data until your code is working as expected. Once you are confident that your code is working as expected, then you can scale up to the full dataset. If you are using Quarto, you can use the `cache: true` metadata field in your code blocks to cache the results of computationally expensive code blocks. This will allow you to run your code once and then use the cached results for subsequent runs. Parallel processing is another strategy for managing computationally expensive code. Some packages, such as {udpipe}, have built-in support for parallel processing. Other packages, such as {tidytext}, do not. In these cases, you can use {future} (Bengtsson, 2024) to parallelize your code.

With the subsetted `enntt_natives_tbl` object, let's execute steps 1 through 4, as seen in Example 7.10.

Example 7.10.

```
# Load package
library(udpipe)

# Model and directory
model <- "english"
model_dir <- "../data/"

# Prepare the dataset to be annotated
enntt_natives_prepped_tbl <-
  enntt_natives_tbl |>
  mutate(doc_id = row_number()) |>
  select(doc_id, text)

# Annotate the dataset
enntt_natives_ann_tbl <-
  udpipe(
    x = enntt_natives_prepped_tbl,
    object = model,
    model_dir = model_dir
  ) |>
  tibble()
```

```
# Preview
glimpse(enntt_natives_ann_tbl)
```

```
Rows: 264,124
Columns: 17
$ doc_id        <chr> "1", "1", "1", "1", "1", "1", "1", "1", "1", "1", "1", "~
$ paragraph_id  <int> 1, 1, 1, 1, 1, 1, 1, 1, 1, 1, 1, 1, 1, 1, 1, 1, 1, 1, 1,~
$ sentence_id   <int> 1, 1, 1, 1, 1, 1, 1, 1, 1, 1, 1, 1, 1, 1, 1, 1, 1, 1, 1,~
$ sentence      <chr> "It is extremely important that action is taken to ensur~
$ start         <int> 1, 4, 7, 17, 27, 32, 39, 42, 48, 51, 58, 63, 66, 73, 77,~
$ end           <int> 2, 5, 15, 25, 30, 37, 40, 46, 49, 56, 61, 64, 71, 75, 82~
$ term_id       <int> 1, 2, 3, 4, 5, 6, 7, 8, 9, 10, 11, 12, 13, 14, 15, 16, 1~
$ token_id      <chr> "1", "2", "3", "4", "5", "6", "7", "8", "9", "10", "11",~
$ token         <chr> "It", "is", "extremely", "important", "that", "action", ~
$ lemma         <chr> "it", "be", "extremely", "important", "that", "action", ~
$ upos          <chr> "PRON", "AUX", "ADV", "ADJ", "SCONJ", "NOUN", "AUX", "VE~
$ xpos          <chr> "PRP", "VBZ", "RB", "JJ", "IN", "NN", "VBZ", "VBN", "TO"~
$ feats         <chr> "Case=Nom|Gender=Neut|Number=Sing|Person=3|PronType=Prs"~
$ head_token_id <chr> "4", "4", "4", "0", "8", "8", "8", "4", "10", "8", "13",~
$ dep_rel       <chr> "expl", "cop", "advmod", "root", "mark", "nsubj:pass", "~
$ deps          <chr> NA, NA, NA, NA, NA, NA, NA, NA, NA, NA, NA, NA, NA, NA, ~
$ misc          <chr> NA, NA, NA, NA, NA, NA, NA, NA, NA, NA, NA, NA, NA, NA, ~
```

There is quite a bit of information which is returned from `udpipe()`. Note that the input lines have been tokenized by word. Each token includes the `token`, `lemma`, part of speech (`upos` and `xpos`)[3], morphological features (`feats`), and syntactic relationships (`head_token_id` and `dep_rel`). The `token_id` keeps track of the token's position in the sentence and the `sentence_id` keeps track of the sentence's position in the original text. Finally, the `doc_id` column and its values correspond to the `doc_id` in the `enntt_natives_tbl` dataset.

The number of variables in the `udpipe()` annotation output is quite overwhelming. However, these attributes come in handy for manipulating, extracting, and plotting information based on lexical and syntactic patterns. See the dependency tree in Figure 7.1 for an example of the syntactic information that can be extracted from the `udpipe()` annotation output.

> **Dive deeper**
> The plot in Figure 7.1 was created using {rsyntax} (Welbers & van Atteveldt, 2022). In addition to creating dependency tree plots, {rsyntax} can be used to extract syntactic patterns from the `udpipe()` annotation output.

[3]The Universal POS tags are defined by the Universal Dependencies project. The `upos` tag is a coarse-grained POS tag and the `xpos` (Penn) tag is a fine-grained POS tag. For more information, see the UD Project https://universaldependencies.org/u/pos/.

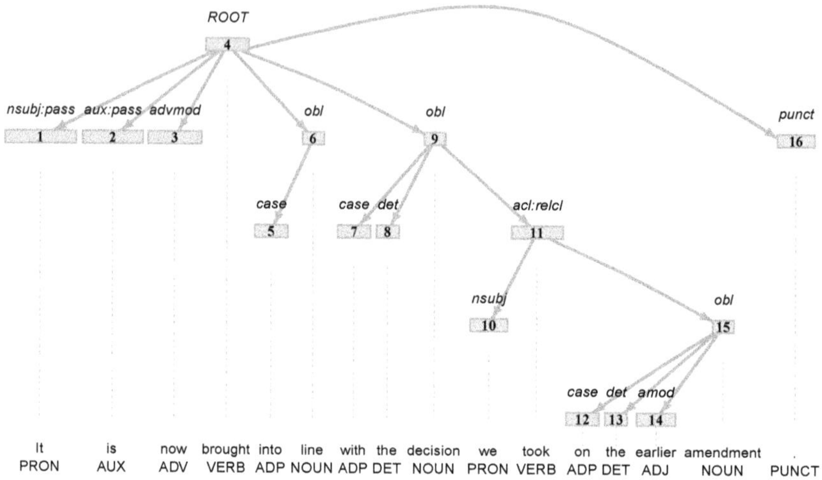

Figure 7.1: Plot of the syntactic tree for a sentence in the ENNTT natives dataset

In Figure 7.1 we see the syntactic tree for a sentence in the ENNTT natives dataset. Each node is labeled with the `token_id` which provides the linear ordering of the sentence. Above the nodes the `dep_relation`, or dependency relationship label is provided. These labels are based on the UD project's dependency relations. We can see that the 'ROOT' relation is at the top of the tree and corresponds to the verb 'brought'. 'ROOT' relations mark predicates in the sentence. Not seen in the example tree, 'cop' relation is a copular, or non-verbal predicate and should be included. These are the key syntactic pattern we will use to identify main clauses for T-units.

7.2.2 Recoding

Recoding processes can be characterized by the creation of structural changes which are derived from values in variables effectively recasting values as new variables to enable more direct access in our analyses.

Specifically, we will need to identify and count the main clauses and their subordinate clauses to create a variable `t_units` from our natives and translations annotations objects. In the UD project's listings, the relations 'ccomp' (clausal complement), 'xcomp' (open clausal complement), and 'acl:relcl' (relative clause) are subordinate clauses. Furthermore, we will also need to count the number of words in each sentence to create a variable `word_len`.

To calculate T-units and words per sentence we turn to {dplyr}. We will use the `group_by()` function to group the dataset by `doc_id` and `sentence_id` and then use the `summarize()` function to calculate the number of T-units and words per sentence, where a T-unit is the combination of the sum of main clauses and sum of subordinate clauses. The code is seen in Example 7.11.

Example 7.11.

```
# Calculate the number of T-units and words per sentence
enntt_natives_syn_comp_tbl <-
  enntt_natives_ann_tbl |>
  group_by(doc_id, sentence_id) |>
  summarize(
    main_clauses = sum(dep_rel %in% c("ROOT", "cop")),
    subord_clauses = sum(dep_rel %in% c("ccomp", "xcomp", "acl:relcl")),
    t_units = main_clauses + subord_clauses,
    word_len = n()
  ) |>
  ungroup()

# Preview
glimpse(enntt_natives_syn_comp_tbl)
```

```
Rows: 10,199
Columns: 6
$ doc_id         <chr> "1", "10", "100", "1000", "10000", "1001", "1002", "100~
$ sentence_id    <int> 1, 1, 1, 1, 1, 1, 1, 1, 1, 1, 1, 1, 1, 1, 1, 1, 1, 1, 1~
$ main_clauses   <int> 1, 0, 0, 0, 2, 0, 0, 1, 1, 0, 1, 1, 1, 0, 2, 0, 1, 1, 1~
$ subord_clauses <int> 3, 2, 1, 0, 1, 2, 1, 1, 0, 2, 1, 0, 3, 2, 0, 4, 2, 1, 1~
$ t_units        <int> 4, 2, 1, 0, 3, 2, 1, 2, 1, 2, 2, 1, 4, 2, 2, 4, 3, 2, 2~
$ word_len       <int> 21, 25, 27, 15, 40, 43, 29, 23, 13, 30, 33, 9, 68, 35, ~
```

A quick spot check of some sentences calculations `enntt_natives_syn_comp_tbl` dataset against the `enntt_natives_ann_tbl` is good to ensure that the calculation is working as expected. In Figure 7.2 we see a sentence that has a word length of 13 and a T-unit value of 5.

Now we can drop the intermediate columns we created to calculate our key syntactic complexity measures using `select()` to indicate those that we do want to keep, as seen in Example 7.12.

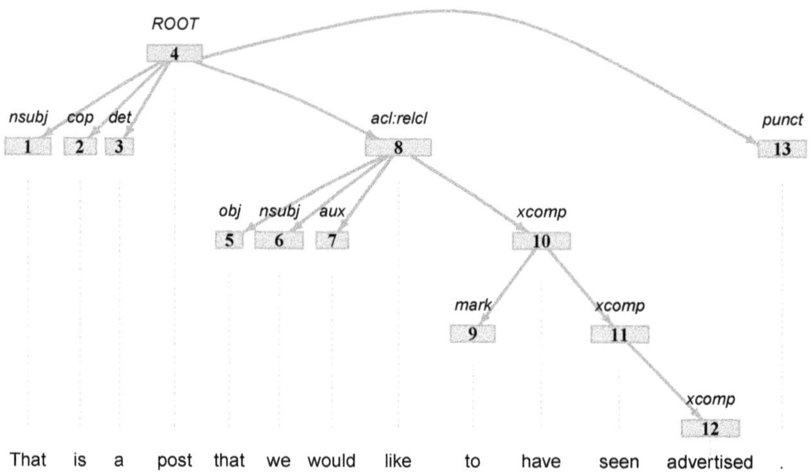

Figure 7.2: Sentence with a word length of 13 and a T-unit value of 5

Example 7.12.

```
# Select columns
enntt_natives_syn_comp_tbl <-
  enntt_natives_syn_comp_tbl |>
  select(doc_id, sentence_id, t_units, word_len)
```

Now we can repeat the process for the ENNTT translated dataset. I will assign the result to `enntt_translations_syn_comp_tbl`. The next step is to join the `sentences` from the annotated data frames into our datasets so that we have the information we set out to generate for both datasets. Then, we will combine the native and translations datasets into a single dataset. These steps are part of the transformation process and will be covered in the next section.

7.2.3 Integration

One final class of transformations that can be applied to curated datasets to enhance their informativeness for a research project is the process of integrating two or more datasets. There are two integration types: joins and concatenation. **Joins** can be row- or column-wise operations that combine datasets based on a common attribute or set of attributes. **Concatenation** is exclusively a row-wise operation that combines datasets that share the same attributes.

Of the two types, joins are the most powerful and sometimes more difficult to understand. When two datasets are joined at least one common variable must be shared between the two datasets. The common variable(s) are referred to as **keys**. The keys are used to match observations in one dataset with observations in another dataset by serving as an index.

There are a number of join types. The most common are left, full, semi, and anti. The type of join determines which observations are retained in the resulting dataset. Let's see this in practice. First, let's create two datasets to join with a common variable `key`, as seen in Example 7.13.

Example 7.13.

```
a_tbl <-
  tibble(
    key = c(1, 2, 3, 5, 8),
    a = letters[1:5]
  )

a_tbl
b_tbl <-
  tibble(
    key = c(1, 2, 4, 6, 8),
    b = letters[6:10]
  )

b_tbl
```

```
# A tibble: 5 x 2
    key a
  <dbl> <chr>
1     1 a
2     2 b
3     3 c
4     5 d
5     8 e
```

```
# A tibble: 5 x 2
    key b
  <dbl> <chr>
1     1 f
2     2 g
3     4 h
4     6 i
5     8 j
```

The a_tbl and the b_tbl datasets share the key variable, but the values in the key variable are not identical. The two datasets share values 1, 2, and 8. The a_tbl dataset has values 3 and 5 in the key variable and the b_tbl dataset has values 4 and 6 in the key variable.

If we apply a **left join** to the a_tbl and b_tbl datasets, the result will be a dataset that retains all of the observations in the a_tbl dataset and only those observations in the b_tbl dataset that have a match in the a_tbl dataset. The result is seen in Example 7.14.

Example 7.14.

```
left_join(x = a_tbl, y = b_tbl, by = "key")
```

```
# A tibble: 5 x 3
    key a     b
  <dbl> <chr> <chr>
1     1 a     f
2     2 b     g
3     3 c     <NA>
4     5 d     <NA>
5     8 e     j
```

Now, if the key variable has the same name, R will recognize and assume that this is the variable to join on and we don't need the by = argument, but if there are multiple potential key variables, we use by = to specify which one to use.

A **full join** retains all observations in both datasets, as seen in Example 7.15.

Example 7.15.

```
full_join(x = a_tbl, y = b_tbl)
```

```
# A tibble: 7 x 3
    key a     b
  <dbl> <chr> <chr>
1     1 a     f
2     2 b     g
3     3 c     <NA>
4     5 d     <NA>
5     8 e     j
6     4 <NA>  h
7     6 <NA>  i
```

Left and full joins maintain or increase the number of observations. On the other hand, semi and anti joins aim to decrease the number of observations. A **semi join** retains only those observations in the left dataset that have a match in the right dataset, as seen in Example 7.16.

Example 7.16.

```
semi_join(x = a_tbl, y = b_tbl)
```

```
# A tibble: 3 x 2
    key a
  <dbl> <chr>
1     1 a
2     2 b
3     8 e
```

And an **anti join** retains only those observations in the left dataset that do not have a match in the right dataset, as seen in Example 7.17.

Example 7.17.

```
anti_join(x = a_tbl, y = b_tbl)
```

```
# A tibble: 2 x 2
    key a
  <dbl> <chr>
1     3 c
2     5 d
```

Of these join types, the left join and the anti join are some of the most common to encounter in research projects.

> **Consider this**
> In addition to datasets that are part of an acquired resource or derived from a corpus resource, there are also a number of datasets that are included in R packages that are particularly relevant for text analysis. For example, {tidytext} includes `sentiments` and `stop_words` datasets. {lexicon} (Rinker, 2019) includes large number of datasets that include sentiment lexicons, stopword lists, contractions, and more.

With this in mind, let's return to our syntactic simplification investigation. Recall that we started with two curated ENNTT datasets: the natives and translations. We manipulated these datasets subsetting them to 10,000 randomly selected lines, prepped them for annotation by adding a `doc_id` column and dropping all columns except `text`, and then annotated them using {udpipe}. We then calculated the number of T-units and words per sentence and created the variables `t_units` and `word_len` for each.

These steps produced two datasets for both the natives and for the translations. The first dataset for each is the annotated data frame. The second is the data frame with the syntactic complexity measures we calculated. The `enntt_natives_ann_tbl` and `enntt_translations_ann_tbl` contain the annotations and `enntt_natives_syn_comp_tbl` and `enntt_translations_syn_comp_tbl` the syntactic complexity measures. In the end, we want a dataset that take the form in Table 7.6.

Table 7.6: Idealized integrated dataset for the syntactic simplification

doc_id	type	t_units	word_len	text
1	natives	1	5	I am happy right now.
2	translation	3	11	I think that John believes that Mary is a good person.

To create this unified dataset, we will need to apply joins and concatenation. First, we will join the prepped datasets with the annotated datasets. Then, we will concatenate the two resulting datasets.

Let's start first by joining the annotated datasets with the datasets with the syntactic complexity calculations. In these joins, we can see that the prepped and calculated datasets share a couple variables, `doc_id` and `sentence_id`, in Example 7.18.

Example 7.18.

```
# Preview datasets to join
glimpse(enntt_natives_ann_tbl)
glimpse(enntt_natives_syn_comp_tbl)
```

```
Rows: 264,124
Columns: 17
$ doc_id        <chr> "1", "1", "1", "1", "1", "1", "1", "1", "1", "1", "1", "~
$ paragraph_id  <int> 1, 1, 1, 1, 1, 1, 1, 1, 1, 1, 1, 1, 1, 1, 1, 1, 1, 1, 1,~
$ sentence_id   <int> 1, 1, 1, 1, 1, 1, 1, 1, 1, 1, 1, 1, 1, 1, 1, 1, 1, 1, 1,~
$ sentence      <chr> "It is extremely important that action is taken to ensur~
$ start         <int> 1, 4, 7, 17, 27, 32, 39, 42, 48, 51, 58, 63, 66, 73, 77,~
$ end           <int> 2, 5, 15, 25, 30, 37, 40, 46, 49, 56, 61, 64, 71, 75, 82~
$ term_id       <int> 1, 2, 3, 4, 5, 6, 7, 8, 9, 10, 11, 12, 13, 14, 15, 16, 1~
$ token_id      <chr> "1", "2", "3", "4", "5", "6", "7", "8", "9", "10", "11",~
$ token         <chr> "It", "is", "extremely", "important", "that", "action", ~
$ lemma         <chr> "it", "be", "extremely", "important", "that", "action", ~
$ upos          <chr> "PRON", "AUX", "ADV", "ADJ", "SCONJ", "NOUN", "AUX", "VE~
$ xpos          <chr> "PRP", "VBZ", "RB", "JJ", "IN", "NN", "VBZ", "VBN", "TO"~
$ feats         <chr> "Case=Nom|Gender=Neut|Number=Sing|Person=3|PronType=Prs"~
$ head_token_id <chr> "4", "4", "4", "0", "8", "8", "8", "4", "10", "8", "13",~
```

```
$ dep_rel       <chr> "expl", "cop", "advmod", "root", "mark", "nsubj:pass", "~
$ deps          <chr> NA, NA, NA, NA, NA, NA, NA, NA, NA, NA, NA, NA, NA, NA, ~
$ misc          <chr> NA, NA, NA, NA, NA, NA, NA, NA, NA, NA, NA, NA, NA, NA, ~
Rows: 10,199
Columns: 4
$ doc_id      <chr> "1", "10", "100", "1000", "10000", "1001", "1002", "1003",~
$ sentence_id <int> 1, 1, 1, 1, 1, 1, 1, 1, 1, 1, 1, 1, 1, 1, 1, 1, 1, 1, 1, 1~
$ t_units     <int> 4, 2, 1, 0, 3, 2, 1, 2, 1, 2, 2, 1, 4, 2, 2, 4, 3, 2, 2, 1~
$ word_len    <int> 21, 25, 27, 15, 40, 43, 29, 23, 13, 30, 33, 9, 68, 35, 16,~
```

The `doc_id` and `sentence_id` variables are both keys that we will use to join the datasets. The reason being that if we only use one of the two we will not align the two datasets at the sentence level. Only the combination of `doc_id` and `sentence_id` isolates the sentences for which we have syntactic complexity measures.

Beyond having a common variable (or variables in our case), we must also ensure that join key variables are of the same vector type in both data frames and that we are aware of any differences in the values. From the output in Example 7.18, we can see that the `doc_id` and `sentence_id` variables aligned in terms of vector type; `doc_id` is character and `sentence_id` is integer in both data frames. If they happened not to be, their types would need to be adjusted.

Now, we need to check for differences in the values. We can do this by using the `setequal()` function. This function returns `TRUE` if the two vectors are equal and `FALSE` if they are not. If the two vectors are not equal, the function will return the values that are in one vector but not the other. So if one has `10001` and the other doesn't we will get `FALSE`. Let's see this in practice, as seen in Example 7.19.

Example 7.19.

```
# Check for differences in the values
setequal(
  enntt_natives_ann_tbl$doc_id,
  enntt_natives_syn_comp_tbl$doc_id
)

setequal(
  enntt_natives_ann_tbl$sentence_id,
  enntt_natives_syn_comp_tbl$sentence_id
)
```

```
[1] TRUE
[1] TRUE
```

So the values are the same. The final check is to see if the vectors are of the same length. We know the values are the same, but we don't know if the values are repeated. We do this by simply comparing the length of the vectors, as seen in Example 7.20.

Example 7.20.

```
# Check for differences in the length
length(enntt_natives_ann_tbl$doc_id) ==
  length(enntt_natives_syn_comp_tbl$doc_id)

length(enntt_natives_ann_tbl$sentence_id) ==
  length(enntt_natives_syn_comp_tbl$sentence_id)
```

```
[1] FALSE
[1] FALSE
```

So they are not the same length. Using the `nrow()` function, I can see that the annotated dataset has 264,124 observations and the calculated dataset has 10,199 observations. The annotation data frames will have many more observations due to the fact that the unit of observations is word tokens. The recoded syntactic complexity data frames' unit of observation is the sentence.

To appreciate the difference in the number of observations, let's look at the first 10 observations of the natives annotated frame for just the columns of interest, as seen in Example 7.21.

Example 7.21.

```
# Preview the annotated dataset
enntt_natives_ann_tbl |>
  select(doc_id, sentence_id, sentence, token) |>
  slice_head(n = 10)
```

```
# A tibble: 10 x 4
   doc_id sentence_id sentence                                             token
   <chr>        <int> <chr>                                                <chr>
 1 1                1 It is extremely important that action is taken to e~ It
 2 1                1 It is extremely important that action is taken to e~ is
 3 1                1 It is extremely important that action is taken to e~ extr~
 4 1                1 It is extremely important that action is taken to e~ impo~
 5 1                1 It is extremely important that action is taken to e~ that
 6 1                1 It is extremely important that action is taken to e~ acti~
 7 1                1 It is extremely important that action is taken to e~ is
 8 1                1 It is extremely important that action is taken to e~ taken
 9 1                1 It is extremely important that action is taken to e~ to
10 1                1 It is extremely important that action is taken to e~ ensu~
```

The annotated data frames have a lot of redundancy in for the join variables and the `sentence` variable that we want to add to the calculated data frames. We can reduce the redundancy by using the `distinct()` function from {dplyr}. In this case we want all observations where `doc_id`, `sentence_id` and `sentence` are distinct. We then select these variables with `distinct()`, as seen in Example 7.22.

Example 7.22.

```
# Reduce annotated data frames to unique sentences
enntt_natives_ann_distinct <-
  enntt_natives_ann_tbl |>
  distinct(doc_id, sentence_id, sentence)

enntt_translations_ann_distinct <-
  enntt_translations_ann_tbl |>
  distinct(doc_id, sentence_id, sentence)
```

We now have two datasets that are ready to be joined with the recoded datasets. The next step is to join the two. We will employ a left join where the syntactic complexity data frames are on the left and the join variables will be both the `doc_id` and `sentence_id` variables. The code is seen in Examples 7.23 and 7.24.

Example 7.23.

```
# Join the native datasets
enntt_natives_transformed_tbl <-
  left_join(
    x = enntt_natives_syn_comp_tbl,
    y = enntt_natives_ann_distinct,
    by = c("doc_id", "sentence_id")
  )

# Preview
glimpse(enntt_natives_transformed_tbl)
```

```
Rows: 10,199
Columns: 5
$ doc_id      <chr> "1", "10", "100", "1000", "10000", "1001", "1002", "1003",~
$ sentence_id <int> 1, 1, 1, 1, 1, 1, 1, 1, 1, 1, 1, 1, 1, 1, 1, 1, 1, 1, 1, 1~
$ t_units     <int> 4, 2, 1, 0, 3, 2, 1, 2, 1, 2, 2, 1, 4, 2, 2, 4, 3, 2, 2, 1~
$ word_len    <int> 21, 25, 27, 15, 40, 43, 29, 23, 13, 30, 33, 9, 68, 35, 16,~
$ sentence    <chr> "It is extremely important that action is taken to ensure ~
```

Example 7.24.

```
# Join the translations datasets
enntt_translations_transformed_tbl <-
  left_join(
    x = enntt_translations_syn_comp_tbl,
    y = enntt_translations_ann_distinct,
    by = c("doc_id", "sentence_id")
  )

# Preview
glimpse(enntt_translations_transformed_tbl)
```

```
Rows: 10,392
Columns: 5
$ doc_id      <chr> "1", "10", "100", "1000", "10000", "1001", "1002", "1003",~
$ sentence_id <int> 1, 1, 1, 1, 1, 1, 1, 1, 1, 1, 1, 1, 1, 1, 1, 1, 1, 1, 1, 1~
$ t_units     <int> 0, 2, 0, 1, 3, 0, 3, 2, 3, 3, 2, 0, 1, 0, 3, 1, 0, 1, 2, 2~
$ word_len    <int> 24, 31, 5, 39, 44, 26, 67, 23, 46, 28, 24, 68, 19, 18, 36,~
$ sentence    <chr> "To my great surprise , on leaving the sitting , I found t~
```

The two data frames now have the same columns and we are closer to our final dataset. The next step is to move toward concatenating the two datasets. Before we do that, we need to do some preparation. First, and most important, we need to add a `type` column to each dataset. This column will indicate whether the sentence is a native or a translation. The second is that our `doc_id` does not serve as a unique identifier for the sentences. Only in combination with `sentence_id` can we uniquely identify a sentence.

So our plan will be to add a `type` column to each dataset specifying the values for all the observations in the respective dataset. Then we will concatenate the two datasets. Note, if we combine them before, distinguishing the type will be more difficult. After we concatenate the two datasets, we will add a `doc_id` column that will serve as a unique identifier for the sentences and drop the `sentence_id` column. OK, that's the plan. Let's execute it in Example 7.25.

Example 7.25.

```
# Add a type column
enntt_natives_transformed_tbl <-
  enntt_natives_transformed_tbl |>
  mutate(type = "natives")

enntt_translations_transformed_tbl <-
  enntt_translations_transformed_tbl |>
  mutate(type = "translations")

```

```
# Concatenate the datasets
enntt_transformed_tbl <-
  bind_rows(
    enntt_natives_transformed_tbl,
    enntt_translations_transformed_tbl
  )

# Overwrite the doc_id column with a unique identifier
enntt_transformed_tbl <-
  enntt_transformed_tbl |>
  mutate(doc_id = row_number()) |>
  select(doc_id, type, t_units, word_len, text = sentence)

# Preview
glimpse(enntt_transformed_tbl)
```

```
Rows: 20,591
Columns: 5
$ doc_id   <int> 1, 2, 3, 4, 5, 6, 7, 8, 9, 10, 11, 12, 13, 14, 15, 16, 17, 18~
$ type     <chr> "natives", "natives", "natives", "natives", "natives", "nativ~
$ t_units  <int> 4, 2, 1, 0, 3, 2, 1, 2, 1, 2, 2, 1, 4, 2, 2, 4, 3, 2, 2, 1, 1~
$ word_len <int> 21, 25, 27, 15, 40, 43, 29, 23, 13, 30, 33, 9, 68, 35, 16, 53~
$ text     <chr> "It is extremely important that action is taken to ensure tha~
```

The output of Example 7.25 now looks structurally like the idealized form in Table 7.6. We have a dataset that has the syntactic complexity measures for both the natives and the translations. We can now write this dataset to disk and document it in the data dictionary.

Activities

In the following activities, you will review the concept of transforming data to prepare it for analysis and working to implement these steps with R. This includes preparation and enrichment of curated datasets using normalization, tokenization, recoding, generation, and/ or integration strategies.

> **Recipe**
> **What**: Transforming and documenting datasets
> **How**: Read Recipe 7, complete comprehension check, and prepare for Lab 7.
> **Why**: To work with two primary types of transformations, tokenization and joins. Tokenization is the process of recasting textual units into units of other sizes. The process of joining datasets aims to incorporate other datasets to augment or filter the dataset of interest.

Lab
What: Dataset alchemy
How: Fork, clone, and complete the steps in Lab 7.
Why: To gain experience working with coding strategies for transforming datasets using tidyverse functions and regexes, practice reading from and writing to disk, and implement organizational strategies for organizing and documenting a dataset in reproducible fashion.

Summary

In this chapter we covered the process of transforming datasets. The goal is to manipulate the curated dataset to make it align better for analysis.

We covered various types of transformation procedures from text normalization to data frame integrations. In any given research project some or all of these steps will be employed —but not necessarily in the order presented in this chapter. It is not uncommon to mix procedures as well. The etiology of the transformation is as unique as the data that you are working with.

Since you are applying techniques that have a significant factor on the shape and contents of your dataset(s) it is important to perform data checks to ensure that the transformations are working as expected. You may not catch everything, and some things may not be caught until later in the analysis process, but it is important to do as much as you can as early as you can.

In line with the reproducible research principles, it is important to write the transformed dataset to disk and to document it in the data dictionary. This is especially important if you are working with multiple datasets. Good naming conventions also come into play. Choosing descriptive names is so easily overlooked by your present self but so welcomed by your future self.

Part IV

Analysis

This part turns to the analysis of datasets, the evaluation of results, and the interpretation of the findings. We will outline the three main types of analyses: exploratory data analysis (EDA), predictive data analysis (PDA), and inferential data analysis (IDA). Each of these analysis types have distinct, non-overlapping aims and therefore should be determined from the outset of the research project and included as part of the research blueprint. The aim of this section is to establish a clearer picture of the goals, methods, and value of each of these approaches.

8

Explore

Outcomes

- Determine the suitability of exploratory data analysis for a research project.
- Understand descriptive analysis and unsupervised learning methods, their strengths in pattern recognition and data summarization.
- Interpret insights from data summarization and pattern recognition, considering their potential to guide further research.

In this chapter, we examine a wide range of strategies for exploratory data analysis. The chapter outlines two main branches of exploratory data analysis: descriptive analysis which statistically and/or visually summarizes a dataset and unsupervised learning which is a machine learning approach that does not assume any particular relationship between variables in a dataset. Either through descriptive or unsupervised learning methods, exploratory data analysis employs quantitative methods to summarize, reduce, and sort complex datasets and statistically and visually interrogate a dataset in order to provide the researcher novel perspective to be qualitatively assessed.

>_ Lessons
What: Advanced objects
How: In an R console, load {swirl}, run `swirl()`, and follow prompts to select the lesson.
Why: To learn about advanced objects in R, including lists and matrices, and create, inspect, access, and manipulate these objects.

10.4324/9781003393764.8

8.1 Orientation

The goal of exploratory data analysis is to discover, describe, and posit new hypotheses. This analysis approach is best-suited for research questions where the literature is scarce, where the gap in knowledge is wide, or where new territories are being explored. The researcher may not know what to expect, but they are willing to let the data speak for itself. The researcher is open to new insights and new questions that may emerge from the analysis process.

While exploratory data analysis allows flexibility, it is essential to have a guiding research question that provides a focus for the analysis. This question will help to determine the variables of interest and the methods to be used. The research question will also help to determine the relevance of the results and the potential for the results to be used in further research.

The general workflow for exploratory data analysis is shown in Table 8.1.

Table 8.1: Workflow for exploratory data analysis

Step	Name	Description
1	Identify	Consider the research question and identify variables of potential interest to provide insight into our question.
2	Inspect	Check for missing data, outliers, *etc.* and check data distributions and transform if necessary.
3	Interrogate	Submit the selected variables to descriptive (frequency, keyword, co-occurrence analysis, *etc.*) or unsupervised learning (clustering, dimensionality reduction, vector spacing modeling, *etc.*) methods to provide quantitative measures to evaluate.
4	Interpret	Evaluate the results and determine if they are valid and meaningful to respond to the research question.
5	Iterate (Optional)	Repeat steps 1-4 as new questions emerge from your interpretation.

8.2 Analysis

To frame our demonstration and discussion of exploratory data analysis, let's tackle a task. The task will be to identify relevant materials for an English-language learner (ELL) textbook. This will involve multiple research questions and allow us to illustrate some very fundamental concepts that emerge across text analysis research in both descriptive and unsupervised learning approaches.

Since our task is geared towards English language use, we will want a representative data sample. For this, we will use the Manually Annotated Sub-Corpus of American English (MASC) of the American National Corpus (Ide et al., 2008).

The data dictionary for the dataset we will use as our point of departure is shown in Table 8.2.

Table 8.2: Data dictionary for the MASC dataset

variable	name	type	description
doc_id	Document ID	numeric	Unique identifier for each document
modality	Modality	categorical	The form in which the document is presented (written or spoken)
genre	Genre	categorical	The category or type of the document
term_num	Term Number	numeric	Index number term per document
term	Term	categorical	Individual word forms in the document
lemma	Lemma	categorical	Base or dictionary form of the term
pos	Part of Speech	categorical	Grammatical category of the term (modified PENN Treebank tagset)

First, I'll read in and preview the dataset in Example 8.1.

Example 8.1.

```
# Read the dataset
masc_tbl <-
  read_csv("../data/masc/masc_transformed.csv")

# Preview the MASC dataset
glimpse(masc_tbl)
```

```
Rows: 591,036
Columns: 7
$ doc_id   <dbl> 1, 1, 1, 1, 1, 1, 1, 1, 1, 1, 1, 1, 1, 1, 1, 1, 1, 1, 1, 1, 1~
$ modality <chr> "Written", "Written", "Written", "Written", "Written", "Writt~
$ genre    <chr> "Letters", "Letters", "Letters", "Letters", "Letters", "Lette~
$ term_num <dbl> 0, 1, 2, 3, 4, 5, 6, 7, 8, 9, 10, 11, 12, 13, 14, 15, 16, 17,~
$ term     <chr> "December", "1998", "Your", "contribution", "to", "Goodwill",~
$ lemma    <chr> "december", "1998", "your", "contribution", "to", "goodwill",~
$ pos      <chr> "NNP", "CD", "PRP$", "NN", "TO", "NNP", "MD", "VB", "JJR", "I~
```

From the output in Example 8.1, we get some sense of the structure of the dataset. However, we also need to perform diagnostic and descriptive procedures. This will include checking for missing data and anomalies and assessing central tendency, dispersion, and/or distributions of the variables. This may include using {skimr}, {dplyr}, {stringr}, {ggplot2}, *etc.* to identify the most relevant variables for our task and to identify any potential issues with the dataset.

After a descriptive and diagnostic assessment of the dataset, not included here, I identified and addressed missing data and anomalies (including many non-words). I also recoded the `doc_id` variable to a character variable. The dataset now has 486,368 observations, a reduction from the original 591,036 observations. There are 392 documents, 2 modalities, 18 genres, almost 38k unique terms (which are words), almost 26k lemmas, and 34 distinct POS tags.

8.2.1 Descriptive analysis

Descriptive analysis includes common techniques such as frequency analysis to determine the most frequent words or phrases, dispersion analysis to see how terms are distributed throughout a document or corpus, keyword analysis to identify distinctive terms, and/or co-occurrence analysis to see what terms tend to appear together.

Using the MASC dataset, we will entertain questions such as:

- What are the most common terms a beginning ELL should learn?
- Are there term differences between spoken and written discourses that should be emphasized?
- What are some of the most common verb particle constructions?

Along the way, we will discuss frequency, dispersion, and co-occurrence measures. In addition, we will apply various descriptive analysis techniques and visualizations to explore the dataset and identify new questions and new variables of interest.

Frequency analysis

At its core, frequency analysis is a descriptive method that counts the number of times a linguistic unit occurs in a dataset. The results of frequency analysis can be used to describe the dataset and to identify terms that are linguistically distinctive or distinctive to a particular group or sub-group in the dataset.

Raw frequency

Let's consider what the most common words in the MASC dataset are as a starting point to making inroads on our task by identifying relevant vocabulary for an ELL textbook.

In the `masc_tbl` data frame we have the linguistic unit `term` which corresponds to the word-level annotation of the MASC. The `lemma` corresponds to the base form of each term, for words with inflectional morphology, the lemma is the word sans the inflection (*e.g.* is/be, are/be). For other words, the `term` and the `lemma` will be the same (*e.g.* the/the, in/in). These two variables pose a choice point for us: do we consider words to be the actual forms or the base forms? There is an argument to be made for both. In this case, I will operationalize our linguistic unit as the `lemma` variable, as this will allow us to group words with distinct inflectional morphology together.

To perform a basic word frequency analysis, we can apply `summarize()` in combination with `n()` or the convenient `count()` function from {dplyr}. Our sorted lemma counts appear in Example 8.2.

Example 8.2.

```
# Lemma count, sorted in descending order
masc_tbl |>
  count(lemma, sort = TRUE)
```

```
# A tibble: 25,923 x 2
   lemma     n
   <chr> <int>
 1 the   26137
 2 be    19466
 3 to    13548
 4 and   12528
 5 of    12005
 6 a     10461
 7 in     8374
 8 i      7783
 9 that   7082
10 you    5276
# i 25,913 more rows
```

The output of this raw frequency tabulation in Example 8.2 is a data frame with two columns: `lemma` and `n`.

As we discussed in Section 3.1.3, the frequency of linguistic units in a corpus tends to be highly right-skewed distribution, approximating the Zipf distribution. If we calculate the **cumulative frequency**, a rolling sum of the frequency term by term, of the lemmas in the `masc_tbl` data frame, we can see that the top 10 types account for around 25% of the lemmas used in the entire corpus —by 100 types that increases to near 50% and 1,000 around 75%, as seen in Figure 8.1.

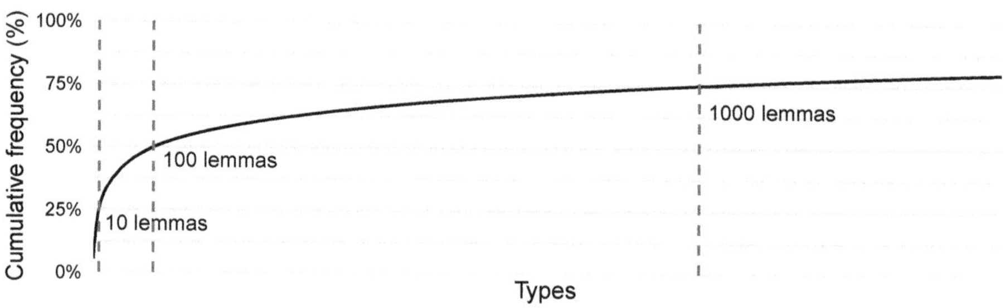

Figure 8.1: Cumulative frequency of lemmas

If we look at the types that appear within the first 50 most frequent, you can likely also appreciate another thing about language use. Let's list the top 50 types in Table 8.3.

Table 8.3: Top 50 lemma types

the	have	at	your	all
be	it	from	an	there
to	for	he	say	me
and	on	but	what	would
of	do	by	so	about
a	with	will	his	know
in	we	my	if	get
i	as	or	's	make
that	this	n't	can	out
you	not	they	go	up

For the most part, the most frequent words are function words. **Function words** are a closed class of relatively few words that are used to express grammatical relationships between content words (*e.g.* determiners, prepositions, pronouns, and auxiliary verbs). Given the importance of these words, it then is no surprise that they comprise many of the most frequent words in a corpus.

Another key observation is that for those the content words (*e.g.* nouns, verbs, adjectives, adverbs) that do figure in the most frequent words, we find that they are quite generic semantically speaking. That is, they are words that are used in a wide range of contexts and take a wide range of meanings. Take for example the adjective 'good'. It can be used to describe a wide range of nouns, such as 'good food', 'good people', 'good times', *etc.* A sometimes near-synonym of 'good', for example 'good student', is the word 'studious'. Yet, 'studious' is not as frequent as 'good' as it is used to describe a narrower range of nouns, such as 'studious student', 'studious scholar', 'studious researcher', *etc.* In this way, 'studious' is more semantically specific than 'good'.

> **Consider this**
> Based on what you now know about the expected distribution of words in a corpus, what if your were asked to predict what the most frequent English word used is in each U.S. State? What would you predict? How confident would you be in your prediction? What if you were asked to predict what the most frequent word used is in the language of a given country? What would you want to know before making your prediction?

So common across corpus samples, in some analyses these function words (and sometimes generic content words) are considered irrelevant and are filtered out. In our ELL materials task, however, we might exclude them for the simple fact that it will be a given that we will teach these words given their overall frequency. Let's aim to focus solely on the content words in the dataset.

One approach to filtering out these words is to use a list of words to exclude, known as a **stopwords** lexicon. {tidytext} includes a data frame `stop_words` which includes stopword lexicons for English. We can select a lexicon from `stop_words` and use `anti_join()` to filter out the words that appear in the `word` variable from the `lemma` variable in the `masc_tbl` data frame.

Eliminating words in this fashion, however, may not always be the best approach. Available lists of stopwords vary in their contents and are determined by other researchers for other potential uses. We may instead opt to create our own stopword list that is tailored to the task, or we may opt to use a statistical approach based on their distribution in the dataset using frequency and/or dispersion measures.

For our case, however, we have another available strategy. Since our task is to identify relevant vocabulary, beyond the fundamental function words in English, we can use the POS tags to reduce our dataset to just the content words, that is nouns, verbs, adjectives, and adverbs. Using the Penn tagset as reference, we can create a vector with the POS tags we want to retain and then use the `filter()` function on the datasets. I will assign this new data frame to `masc_content_tbl` to keep it separate from our main data frame `masc_tbl`, seen in Example 8.3.

Example 8.3.

```
# Penn Tagset for content words
# Nouns: NN, NNS,
# Verbs: VB, VBD, VBG, VBN, VBP, VBZ
# Adjectives: JJ, JJR, JJS
# Adverbs: RB, RBR, RBS

content_pos <- c("NN", "NNS", "VB", "VBD", "VBG", "VBN", "VBP", "VBZ", "JJ",
↪ "JJR", "JJS", "RB", "RBR", "RBS")

# Select content words
masc_content_tbl <-
  masc_tbl |>
  filter(pos %in% content_pos)
```

Let's now preview the top 50 lemmas in the `masc_content_tbl` data frame to see how the most frequent words have changed in Table 8.4.

Table 8.4: Frequency of tokens after filtering out lemmas with POS tags that are not content words

be	think	work	also	t
have	more	year	need	first
do	just	come	way	help
not	time	use	back	day
n't	so	well	here	many
say	other	look	new	man
go	see	then	find	ask
know	people	right	give	very
get	take	only	thing	much
make	now	want	tell	even

The resulting list in Table 8.4 paints a different picture of the most frequent words in the dataset. The most frequent words are now content words, and included in most frequent words are more semantically specific words. We now have reduced the number of observations by 50% focusing on the content words. We are getting closer to identifying the vocabulary that we want to include in our ELL materials, but we will need some more tools to help us identify the most relevant vocabulary.

Dispersion

Dispersion is a measure of how evenly distributed a linguistic unit is across a dataset. This is a key concept in text analysis, as important as frequency. It is important to recognize that frequency and dispersion are measures of different characteristics. We can have two words that occur with the same frequency, but one word may be more evenly distributed across a dataset than the other. Depending on the researcher's aims, this may be an important distinction to make. For our task, it is likely the case that we want to capture words that are well-dispersed across the dataset, as words that have a high frequency and a low dispersion tend to be connected to a particular context, whether that be a particular genre, a particular speaker, a particular topic, *etc.* In other research, the aim may be the reverse; to identify words that are highly frequent and highly concentrated in a particular context to identify words that are distinctive to that context.

There are a variety of measures that can be used to estimate the distribution of types across a corpus. Let's focus on three measures: document frequency (df), inverse document frequency (idf), and Gries' Deviation of Proportions (dp).

The most basic measure is **document frequency** (df). This is the number of documents in which a type appears at least once. For example, if a type appears in 10 documents, then the document frequency is 10. This is a very basic measure, but it is a decent starting point.

A nuanced version of document frequency is **inverse document frequency** (idf). This measure takes the total number of documents and divides it by the document frequency. This results in a measure that is inversely proportional to the document frequency. That is, the higher the document frequency, the lower the inverse document frequency. This measure is often log-transformed to spread out the values.

One thing to consider about df and idf is that neither takes into account the length of the documents in which the type appears nor the spread of each type within each document. To take these factors into account, we can use Gries' **deviation of proportions** (dp) measure (Gries, 2023, pp. 87–88). The dp measure considers the proportion of a type's frequency in each document relative to its total frequency. This produces a measure that is more sensitive to the distribution of types within and across documents in a corpus.

Let's consider how these measures differ with three scenarios:

1. Scenario A: A type with a token frequency of 100 appears in each of the 10 documents in a corpus. Each document is 100 words long, and the type appears 10 times in each document.
2. Scenario B: The same type with a token frequency of 100 appears in each of the 10 documents, each 100 words long. However, in this scenario, the type appears once in 9 documents and 91 times in 1 document.
3. Scenario C: Nine of the documents constitute 99% of the corpus. The type appears once in each of these 9 documents and 91 times in the 10th document.

In these scenarios, Scenario A is the most dispersed, Scenario B is less dispersed, and Scenario C is the least dispersed. Despite these differences, the type's document frequency (df) and inverse document frequency (idf) scores remain the same across all three scenarios. However, the dispersion (dp) score will accurately reflect the increasing concentration of the type's dispersion from Scenario A to Scenario B to Scenario C.

> **Dive deeper**
> You may wonder why we would want to use df or idf at all. The answer is some combination of the fact that they are computationally less expensive to calculate, they are widely used (especially idf), and/or in many practical situations they often highly correlated with dp.

So for our task we will use dp as our measure of dispersion. {qtkit} includes the `calc_type_metrics()` function which calculates, among other metrics, the dispersion metrics df, idf, and/or dp. Let's select `dp` and assign the result to `masc_lemma_disp`, as seen in Example 8.4.

Example 8.4.

```
# Load package
library(qtkit)

# Calculate deviance of proportions (DP)
masc_lemma_disp <-
  masc_content_tbl |>
  calc_type_metrics(
    type = lemma,
    documents = doc_id,
    dispersion = "dp"
  ) |>
  arrange(dp)
```

```
# Preview
masc_lemma_disp |>
  slice_head(n = 10)
```

```
# A tibble: 10 x 3
   type       n    dp
   <chr> <dbl> <dbl>
 1 be    19231 0.123
 2 have   5136 0.189
 3 not    2279 0.240
 4 make   1149 0.266
 5 other   882 0.269
 6 more   1005 0.276
 7 take    769 0.286
 8 only    627 0.286
 9 time    931 0.314
10 see     865 0.327
```

We would like to identify lemmas that are frequent and well-dispersed. But an important question arises, what is the threshold for frequency and dispersion that we should use to identify the lemmas that we want to include in our ELL materials?

There are statistical approaches to identifying natural breakpoints but a visual inspection is often good enough for practical purposes. Let's create a density plot to see if there is a natural break in the distribution of our dispersion measure, as seen in Figure 8.2.

Example 8.5.

```
# Density plot of dp
masc_lemma_disp |>
  ggplot(aes(x = dp)) +
  geom_density() +
  scale_x_continuous(breaks = seq(0, 1, .1)) +
  labs(x = "Deviation of Proportions", y = "Density")
```

What we are looking for is a distinctive bend in the distribution of dispersion measures. In Figure 8.2, we can see one roughly between 0.87 and 0.97. The inflection point appears to be near 0.95. This bend is called an elbow, and using this bend to make informed decisions about thresholds is called the **elbow method**.

In Example 8.6, I filter out lemmas that have a dispersion measure less than 0.95.

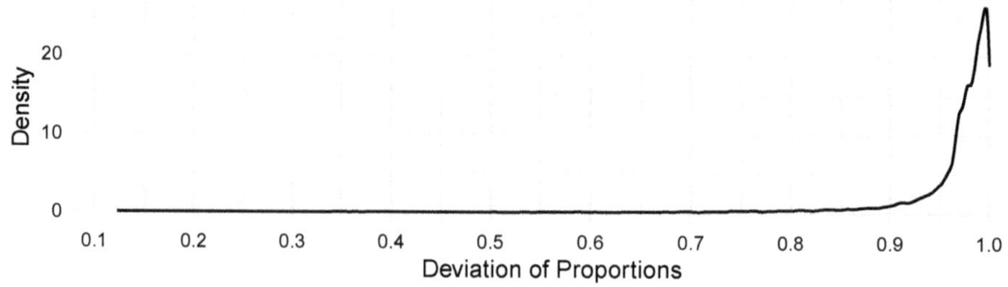

Figure 8.2: Density plot of lemma dispersion

Example 8.6.

```
# Filter for lemmas with dp <= 0.95
masc_lemma_disp_thr <-
  masc_lemma_disp |>
  filter(dp <= 0.95) |>
  arrange(desc(n))
```

Then in Tables 8.5 and 8.6, I preview the top and bottom 25 lemmas in the dataset.

Table 8.5: Top 25 lemmas after our dispersion threshold

be	say	think	other	work
have	go	more	see	year
do	know	just	people	come
not	get	time	take	use
n't	make	so	now	well

Table 8.6: Bottom 25 lemmas after our dispersion threshold

ramification	contradiction	deckhand	injustice	imaginative
trickled	flatly	graveyard	intimately	pastime
conceivably	mindset	rooftop	preoccupation	rickety
charade	mischaracterized	wharf	specifics	scroll
traipse	shameful	commend	checkered	uphill

We now have a solid candidate list of common vocabulary that is spread well across the corpus.

Relative frequency

Gauging frequency and dispersion across the entire corpus sets the foundation for any frequency analysis, but it is often the case that we want to compare the frequency and/or dispersion of linguistic units across corpora or sub-corpora.

In the case of the MASC dataset, for example, we may want to compare metrics across the two modalities or the various genres. Simply comparing raw frequency counts across these sub-corpora is not a good approach, and can be misleading, as the sub-corpora will likely vary in size. For example, if one sub-corpus is twice as large as another sub-corpus, then, all else being equal, the frequency counts will be twice as large in the larger sub-corpus. This is why we use relative frequency measures, which are normalized by the size of the sub-corpus.

> **Consider this**
> A variable in the MASC dataset that has yet to be used is the `pos` variable. How could we use this POS variable to refine our frequency and dispersion analysis of lemma types?
> Hint: consider lemma forms that may be tagged with different parts of speech.

To normalize the frequency of linguistic units across sub-corpora, we can use the **relative frequency** (rf) measure. This is the frequency of a linguistic unit divided by the total number of linguistic units in the sub-corpus. This bakes in the size of the sub-corpus into the measure. The notion of relative frequency is key to all research working with text, as it is the basis for the statistical approach to text analysis where comparisons are made.

There are some field-specific terms that are used to refer to relative frequency measures. For example, in NLP literature, the relative frequency measure is often referred to as the **term frequency** (tf). In corpus linguistics, the relative frequency measure is often modified slightly to include a constant (*e.g.* $rf * 100$) which is known as the **observed relative frequency** (orf). Although the observed relative frequency per number of tokens is not strictly necessary, it is often used to make the values more interpretable as we can now talk about an observed relative frequency of 1.5 as a linguistic unit that occurs 1.5 times per 100 linguistic units.

Let's consider how we might compare the frequency and dispersion of lemmas across the two modalities in the MASC dataset, spoken and written. To make this a bit more interesting and more relevant, let's add the `pos` variable to our analysis. The intent, then, will be to identify lemmas tagged with particular parts of speech that are particularly indicative of each modality.

We can do this by collapsing the `lemma` and `pos` variables into a single variable, `lemma_pos`, with the `str_c()` function, as seen in Example 8.7.

Example 8.7.

```
# Collapse lemma and pos into type
masc_content_tbl <-
  masc_content_tbl |>
  mutate(lemma_pos = str_c(lemma, pos, sep = "_"))

# Preview
masc_content_tbl |>
  slice_head(n = 5)
```

```
# A tibble: 5 x 8
  doc_id modality genre   term_num term         lemma        pos   lemma_pos
  <chr>  <chr>    <chr>      <dbl> <chr>        <chr>        <chr> <chr>
1 1      Written  Letters        3 contribution contribution NN    contribution~
2 1      Written  Letters        7 mean         mean         VB    mean_VB
3 1      Written  Letters        8 more         more         JJR   more_JJR
4 1      Written  Letters       12 know         know         VB    know_VB
5 1      Written  Letters       15 help         help         VB    help_VB
```

Now this will increase the number of lemma types in the dataset as we are now considering lemmas where the same lemma form is tagged with different parts of speech.

Getting back to calculating the frequency and dispersion of lemmas in each modality, we can use the `calc_type_metrics()` function with `lemma_pos` as our type argument. We will, however, need to apply this function to each sub-corpus independently and then concatenate the two data frames. This function returns a (raw) frequency (n) measure by default, but we can specify the `frequency` argument to `rf` to calculate the relative frequency of the linguistic units as in Example 8.8.

Example 8.8.

```
# Calculate relative frequency
# Spoken
masc_spoken_metrics <-
  masc_content_tbl |>
  filter(modality == "Spoken") |>
  calc_type_metrics(
    type = lemma_pos,
    documents = doc_id,
    frequency = "rf",
    dispersion = "dp"
  ) |>
  mutate(modality = "Spoken") |>
  arrange(desc(n))
```

```
# Written
masc_written_metrics <-
  masc_content_tbl |>
  filter(modality == "Written") |>
  calc_type_metrics(
    type = lemma_pos,
    documents = doc_id,
    frequency = "rf",
    dispersion = "dp"
  ) |>
  mutate(modality = "Written") |>
  arrange(desc(n))

# Concatenate metrics
masc_metrics <-
  bind_rows(masc_spoken_metrics, masc_written_metrics)

# Preview
masc_metrics |>
  slice_head(n = 5)
```

```
# A tibble: 5 x 5
  type          n     rf     dp modality
  <chr>     <dbl>  <dbl>  <dbl> <chr>
1 be_VBZ     2612 0.0489 0.0843 Spoken
2 be_VBP     1282 0.0240 0.111  Spoken
3 be_VBD     1020 0.0191 0.300  Spoken
4 n't_RB      829 0.0155 0.139  Spoken
5 have_VBP    766 0.0143 0.152  Spoken
```

With the `rf` measure, we are now in a position to compare 'apples to apples', as you might say. We can now compare the relative frequency of lemmas across the two modalities. Let's preview the top 5 lemmas in each modality, as seen in Example 8.9.

Example 8.9.

```
# Preview top 10 lemmas in each modality
masc_metrics |>
  group_by(modality) |>
  slice_max(n = 10, order_by = rf)
```

```
# A tibble: 20 x 5
# Groups:   modality [2]
   type          n      rf     dp modality
   <chr>     <dbl>   <dbl>  <dbl> <chr>
 1 be_VBZ     2612 0.0489  0.0843 Spoken
 2 be_VBP     1282 0.0240  0.111  Spoken
 3 be_VBD     1020 0.0191  0.300  Spoken
 4 n't_RB      829 0.0155  0.139  Spoken
 5 have_VBP    766 0.0143  0.152  Spoken
 6 do_VBP      728 0.0136  0.180  Spoken
 7 be_VB       655 0.0123  0.147  Spoken
 8 not_RB      638 0.0119  0.137  Spoken
 9 just_RB     404 0.00757 0.267  Spoken
10 so_RB       387 0.00725 0.357  Spoken
11 be_VBZ     4745 0.0249  0.230  Written
12 be_VBD     3317 0.0174  0.366  Written
13 be_VBP     2617 0.0137  0.237  Written
14 be_VB      1863 0.00976 0.218  Written
15 not_RB     1640 0.00859 0.259  Written
16 have_VBP   1227 0.00643 0.291  Written
17 n't_RB      905 0.00474 0.540  Written
18 have_VBD    859 0.00450 0.446  Written
19 have_VBZ    777 0.00407 0.335  Written
20 say_VBD     710 0.00372 0.609  Written
```

We can appreciate, now, that there are similarities and a few differences between the most frequent lemmas for each modality. First, there are similar lemmas in written and spoken modalities, such as 'be', 'have', and 'not'. Second, the top 10 include verbs and adverbs. Now we are looking at the most frequent types, so it is not surprising that we see more in common than not. However, looking close we can see that contracted forms are more frequent in the spoken modality, such as 'isn't', 'don't', and 'can't' and that ordering of the verb tenses differs to some degree. Whether these are important distinctions for our task is something we will need to consider.

We can further cull our results by filtering out lemmas that are not well-dispersed across the sub-corpora. Although it may be tempting to use the threshold we used earlier, we should consider that the sizes of the sub-corpora are different and the distribution of the dispersion measure may be different. With this in mind, we need to visualize the distribution of the dispersion measure for each modality and apply the elbow method to identify a threshold for each modality.

After assessing the density plots for the dispersion of each modality via the elbow method, we update our thresholds. We maintain the 0.95 threshold for the written sub-corpus and use a 0.79 threshold for the spoken sub-corpus. I apply these filters as seen in Example 8.10.

Example 8.10.

```
# Filter for lemmas with
# dp <= 0.95 for written and
# dp <= .79 for spoken
masc_metrics_thr <-
  masc_metrics |>
  filter(
    (modality == "Written" & dp <= 0.95) |
    (modality == "Spoken" & dp <= .79)
  ) |>
  arrange(desc(rf))
```

Filtering the less-dispersed types reduces the dataset from 33,428 to 7,459 observations. This will provide us with a more succinct list of common and well-dispersed lemmas that are used in each modality.

As much as the frequency and dispersion measures can provide us with a starting point, it does not provide an understanding of what types are more indicative of a particular sub-corpus, modality sub-corpora in our case. We can do this by calculating the log odds ratio of each lemma in each modality.

The **log odds ratio** is a measure that quantifies the difference between the frequencies of a type in two corpora or sub-corpora. In spirit and in name, it compares the odds of a type occurring in one corpus versus the other. The values range from negative to positive infinity, with negative values indicating that the type is more frequent in the first corpus and positive values indicating that the lemma is more frequent in the second corpus. The magnitude of the value indicates the strength of the association.

{tidylo} provides a convenient function `bind_log_odds()` to calculate the log odds ratio, and a weighed variant, for each type in each sub-corpus. The weighted log odds ratio measure provides a more robust and interpretable measure for comparing term frequencies across corpora, especially when term frequencies are low or when corpora are of different sizes. The weighting (or standardization) also makes it easier to identify terms that are particularly distinctive or characteristic of one corpus over another.

Let's calculate the weighted log odds ratio for each lemma in each modality and preview the top 10 lemmas in each modality, as seen in Example 8.11.

Example 8.11.

```r
# Load package
library(tidylo)

# Calculate log odds ratio
masc_metrics_thr <-
  masc_metrics_thr |>
  bind_log_odds(
    set = modality,
    feature = type,
    n = n
  )

# Preview top 10 lemmas in each modality
masc_metrics_thr |>
  group_by(modality) |>
  slice_max(n = 10, order_by = log_odds_weighted)
```

```
# A tibble: 20 x 6
# Groups:   modality [2]
   type             n       rf     dp modality log_odds_weighted
   <chr>        <dbl>    <dbl>  <dbl> <chr>                <dbl>
 1 be_VBZ        2612 0.0489   0.0843 Spoken               20.7
 2 n't_RB         829 0.0155   0.139  Spoken               13.6
 3 be_VBP        1282 0.0240   0.111  Spoken               13.4
 4 do_VBP         728 0.0136   0.180  Spoken               13.2
 5 have_VBP       766 0.0143   0.152  Spoken               11.4
 6 think_VBP      350 0.00655  0.259  Spoken               10.2
 7 be_VBD        1020 0.0191   0.300  Spoken                9.18
 8 well_RB        334 0.00626  0.283  Spoken                8.90
 9 know_VBP       282 0.00528  0.260  Spoken                8.78
10 just_RB        404 0.00757  0.267  Spoken                8.53
11 t_NN           475 0.00249  0.778  Written               9.62
12 figure_NN      140 0.000733 0.868  Written               5.21
13 financial_JJ   138 0.000723 0.880  Written               5.18
14 city_NN        137 0.000718 0.766  Written               5.16
15 email_NN       133 0.000697 0.866  Written               5.08
16 eye_NNS        129 0.000676 0.731  Written               5.00
17 style_NN       108 0.000566 0.829  Written               4.58
18 mail_NN        106 0.000555 0.876  Written               4.54
19 channel_NN     103 0.000540 0.919  Written               4.47
20 text_NN        103 0.000540 0.845  Written               4.47
```

Let's imagine we would like to extract the most indicative verbs for each modality using the weighted log odds as our measure. We can do this with a little regex magic. Let's use the `str_subset()` function to filter for lemmas that contain `_V` and then use `slice_max()` to extract the top 10 most indicative verb lemmas, as seen in Example 8.12.

Example 8.12.

```
# Preview (ordered by log_odds_weighted)
masc_metrics_thr |>
  group_by(modality) |>
  filter(str_detect(type, "_V")) |>
  slice_max(n = 10, order_by = log_odds_weighted) |>
  select(-n)
```

```
# A tibble: 20 x 5
# Groups:   modality [2]
   type                rf     dp modality log_odds_weighted
   <chr>            <dbl>  <dbl> <chr>                <dbl>
 1 be_VBZ        0.0489   0.0843 Spoken                20.7
 2 be_VBP        0.0240   0.111  Spoken                13.4
 3 do_VBP        0.0136   0.180  Spoken                13.2
 4 have_VBP      0.0143   0.152  Spoken                11.4
 5 think_VBP     0.00655  0.259  Spoken                10.2
 6 be_VBD        0.0191   0.300  Spoken                 9.18
 7 know_VBP      0.00528  0.260  Spoken                 8.78
 8 go_VBG        0.00534  0.207  Spoken                 8.29
 9 do_VBD        0.00603  0.321  Spoken                 8.03
10 be_VB         0.0123   0.147  Spoken                 7.92
11 post_VBN      0.000372 0.928  Written                3.71
12 don_VB        0.000361 0.839  Written                3.66
13 doe_VBZ       0.000351 0.870  Written                3.61
14 walk_VBD      0.000320 0.790  Written                3.44
15 associate_VBN 0.000304 0.777  Written                3.35
16 reply_VBD     0.000293 0.837  Written                3.30
17 develop_VBG   0.000288 0.812  Written                3.27
18 require_VBN   0.000272 0.793  Written                3.18
19 fall_VBD      0.000267 0.757  Written                3.15
20 meet_VB       0.000241 0.729  Written                2.99
```

Note that the log odds are larger for the spoken modality than the written modality. This indicates that theses types are more strongly indicative of the spoken modality than the types in the written modality are indicative of the written modality. This is not surprising, as the written modality is typically more diverse in terms of lexical usage than the spoken modality, where the terms tend to be repeated more often, including verbs.

Co-occurrence analysis

Moving forward on our task, we have a general idea of the vocabulary that we want to include in our ELL materials and can identify lemma types that are particularly indicative of each modality. Another useful approach to complement our analysis is to identify words that co-occur with our target lemmas (verbs). In English, it is common for verbs to appear with a preposition or adverb, such as 'give up', 'look after'. These 'phrasal verbs' form a semantic unit that is distinct from the verb alone.

In a case such as this, we are aiming to do a co-occurrence analysis. Co-occurrence analysis is a set of methods that are used to identify words that appear in close proximity to a target type.

An exploratory, primarily qualitative, approach is to display the co-occurrence of words in a Keyword in Context (KWIC) search. **KWIC** produces a table that displays the target word in the center of the table and the words that appear before and after the target word within some defined window context. This is a useful approach for spot identifying co-occurring patterns which include the target word or phrase. However, it can be a time-consuming process to manually inspect these results and is likely not a feasible approach for large datasets.

> **Tip**
> KWIC tables are a common tool in corpus linguistics and can be used either before or after a quantitative analysis. If you are interested, {quanteda} includes a function `kwic()` that can be used to create a KWIC table.

A straightforward quantitative way to explore co-occurrence is to set the unit of observation to an ngram of word terms. Then, the frequency and dispersion metrics can be calculated for each ngram. Yet, there is an issue with this approach for our purposes. The frequency and dispersion of ngrams does not necessarily relate to whether the two words form a semantic unit. For example, in any given corpus there will be highly frequent pairings of function words, such as 'of the', 'in the', 'to the', *etc*. These combinations our bound to occur frequently in large part because the high frequency of each individual word. However, these combinations do not have the same semantic cohesion as other, likely lower-frequency, ngrams such as 'look after', 'give up', *etc*.

To better address our question, we can use a statistical measure to estimate collocational strength between two words. A **collocation** is a sequence of words that co-occur more often than would be expected by chance. A common measure of collocation is the **pointwise mutual information** (PMI) measure. PMI scores reflect the likelihood of two words occurring together given their individual frequencies and compares this to the actual co-occurrence frequency. A high PMI indicates a strong semantic association between the words.

One consideration that we need to take into account for our goal to identify verb particle constructions, is how we ultimately want to group our `lemma_pos` values. This is particularly important given the fact that our `pos` tags for verbs include information about the verb's tense and person attributes. This means that a verb in a verb particle bigram, such as 'look after', will be represented by multiple `lemma_pos` values, such as `look_VB`, `look_VBP`, `look_VBD`, and `look_VBG`. We want to group the verb particle bigrams by a single verb value, so we need to reclassify the `pos` values for verbs. We can do this with the `case_when()` function from {dplyr}.

In Example 8.13, I recode the `pos` values for verbs to `V` and then join the `lemma` and `pos` columns into a single string.

Example 8.13.

```
masc_lemma_pos_tbl <-
  masc_tbl |>
  mutate(pos = case_when(
    str_detect(pos, "^V") ~ "V",
    TRUE ~ pos
  )) |>
  group_by(doc_id) |>
  mutate(lemma_pos = str_c(lemma, pos, sep = "_")) |>
  ungroup()
```

Let's calculate the PMI for all the bigrams in the MASC dataset. We can use the `calc_assoc_metrics()` function from {qtkit}. We need to specify the `association` argument to `pmi` and the `type` argument to `bigrams`, as seen in Example 8.14.

Example 8.14.

```
masc_lemma_pos_assoc <-
  masc_lemma_pos_tbl |>
  calc_assoc_metrics(
    doc_index = doc_id,
    token_index = term_num,
    type = lemma_pos,
    association = "pmi"
  )

# Preview
masc_lemma_pos_assoc |>
  arrange(desc(pmi)) |>
  slice_head(n = 10)
```

```
# A tibble: 10 x 4
   x                 y                   n   pmi
   <chr>             <chr>           <dbl> <dbl>
 1 #Christian_NN     bigot_NN            1  12.4
 2 #FAIL_NN          phenomenally_RB     1  12.4
 3 #NASCAR_NN        #indycar_NN         1  12.4
 4 #PALM_NN          merchan_NN          1  12.4
 5 #Twitter_NN       #growth_NN          1  12.4
 6 #college_NN       #jobs_NN            1  12.4
 7 #education_NN     #teaching_NN        1  12.4
 8 #faculty_NN       #cites_NN           1  12.4
 9 #fb_NN            siebel_NNP          1  12.4
10 #glitchmyass_NN reps_NNP              1  12.4
```

One caveat to using the PMI measure is that it is sensitive to the frequency of the words. If the words in a bigram pair are infrequent, and especially if they only occur once, then the PMI measure will be unduly inflated. To mitigate this issue, we can apply a frequency threshold to the bigrams before calculating the PMI measure. Let's filter out bigrams that occur less than 10 times and have a positive PMI, and while we are at it, let's also filter `x` and `y` for the appropriate forms we are targeting, either `_V` and `_IN`, as seen Example 8.15.

Example 8.15.

```
# Filter for target bigrams
masc_verb_part_assoc <-
  masc_lemma_pos_assoc |>
  filter(n >= 10 & pmi > 0) |>
  filter(str_detect(x, "_V")) |>
  filter(str_detect(y, "_IN"))

# Preview
masc_verb_part_assoc |>
  slice_max(order_by = pmi, n = 10)
```

```
# A tibble: 10 x 4
   x           y            n   pmi
   <chr>       <chr>    <dbl> <dbl>
 1 figure_V    out_IN      17  4.93
 2 worry_V     about_IN    27  4.78
 3 walk_V      up_IN       10  4.62
 4 talk_V      about_IN   114  4.57
 5 sound_V     like_IN     15  4.42
 6 post_V      by_IN       57  4.29
 7 derive_V    from_IN     17  4.27
 8 stem_V      from_IN     10  4.13
 9 deal_V      with_IN     53  4.12
10 associate_V with_IN     48  4.05
```

We have a working method for identify verb particle constructions. We can clean up the results a bit by removing the POS tags from the x and y variables, up our minimum PMI value, and create a network plot to visualize the results. A **network plot** is a type of graph that shows relationships between entities. In this case, the entities are verbs and particles, and the relationships are the PMI values between them. The connections between are represented by edges, and the thickness of the edges is proportional to the PMI value.

Figure 8.3: Network plot of verb particle constructions

> **Dive deeper**
> {ggplot2} cannot create network plots directly, so we use {ggraph} (Pedersen, 2024) and {igraph} (Csárdi et al., 2024) to create the network plot. For more information on creating network plots, see the {ggraph} documentation.

From Figure 8.3, and from the underlying data, we can explore verb particle constructions. We could go further and apply our co-occurrence methods to each modality separately, if we wanted to identify verb particle constructions that are distinctive to each modality. We could also apply our co-occurrence methods to other parts of speech, such as adjectives and nouns, to identify collocations of these parts of speech. There is much more to explore with co-occurrence analysis, but this should give you a good idea of the types of questions that can be addressed.

8.2.2 Unsupervised learning

Aligned in purpose with descriptive approaches, unsupervised learning approaches to exploratory data analysis are used to identify patterns in the data from an algorithmic perspective. Common methods in text analysis include principal component analysis, clustering, and vector space modeling.

We will continue to use the MASC dataset as we develop materials for our ELL textbook to illustrate unsupervised learning methods. In the process, we will explore the following questions:

- Can we identify and group documents based on linguistic features or co-occurrence patterns of the data itself?
- Do the groups of documents relate to categories in the dataset?
- Can we estimate the semantics of words based on their co-occurrence patterns?

Through these questions we will build on our knowledge of frequency, dispersion, and co-occurrence analysis and introduce concepts and methods associated with machine learning.

Clustering

Clustering is an unsupervised learning technique that can be used to group similar items in the text data, helping to organize the data into distinct categories and discover relationships between different elements in the text. The main steps in the procedure includes identifying the relevant linguistic features to use for clustering, representing the features in a way that can be used for clustering, applying a clustering algorithm to the data, and then interpreting the results.

In our ELL textbook task, we may very well want to explore the similarities and/or differences between the documents based on the distribution of linguistic features. This provides us a view to evaluate to what extent the variables in the dataset, say genre for this demonstration, map to the distribution of linguistic features. Based on this evaluation, we may want to consider re-categorizing the documents, collapsing categories, or even adding new categories.

Instead of relying entirely on the variables' values in the MASC dataset, we can let the data itself say something about how documents may or may not be related. Yet, a pivotal question is what linguistic features we will use, otherwise known as **feature selection**. We could use terms or lemmas, but we may want to consider other features, such as parts of speech or some co-occurrence pattern. We are not locked into using one criterion, and we can perform clustering multiple times with different features, but we should consider the implications of our feature selection for our interpretation of the results.

Imagine that among the various features that we are interested in associating documents, we consider lemma use and POS use. However, we need to operationalize what we mean by 'use'. In machine learning, this process is known as **feature engineering**. We likely want to use some measure of frequency. Since we are comparing documents, a relative frequency measure will be most useful. Another consideration it means to use lemmas or POS tags as our features. Each represents a different linguistic of the documents. Lemmas represent the lexical diversity of the documents while POS tags approximate the grammatical diversity of the documents (Petrenz & Webber, 2011).

Let's assume that our interest is to gauge the grammatical diversity of the documents, so we will go with POS tags. With this approach, we aim to distinguish between documents in a way that may allow us to consider whether genre-document categories are meaningful, along grammatical lines.

The next question to address in any analysis is how to represent the features. In machine learning, the most common way to represent document-feature relationships is in a matrix. In our case, we want to create a matrix with the documents in the rows and the features in the columns. The values in the matrix will be the operationalization of grammatical diversity in each document. This configuration is known as a **document-term matrix** (DTM).

To recast a data frame into a DTM, we can use the `cast_dtm()` function from {tidytext}. This function takes a data frame with a document identifier, a feature identifier, and a value for each observation and casts it into a matrix. Operations such as normalization are easily and efficiently performed in R on matrices, so initially we can cast a frequency table of POS tags into a matrix and then normalize the matrix by documents.

Let's see how this works with the MASC dataset in Example 8.16.

Example 8.16.

```
# Load package
library(tidytext)

# Create a document-term matrix of POS tags
masc_pos_dtm <-
  masc_tbl |>
  count(doc_id, pos) |>
  cast_dtm(doc_id, pos, n) |>
  as.matrix()

# Inspect
dim(masc_pos_dtm)

```

```
# Preview
masc_pos_dtm[1:5, 1:5]
```

```
[1] 392  32
     Terms
Docs  CC DT EX IN JJ
  1   14 35  1 44 27
  10  11 38  0 39 18
  100  0  2  0  2  3
  101  3 16  0 23  7
  102 20 29  0 34 20
```

The matrix `masc_pos_dtm` has 392 documents and 32 POS tags. The values in the matrix are the frequency of each POS tag in each document. Note to preview a subset of the contents of a matrix, such as in Example 8.16, we use bracket syntax `[]` instead of the `head()` function.

We can now normalize the matrix by documents. We can do this by dividing each feature count by the total count in each document. This is a row-wise transformation, so we can use the `rowSums()` function from base R to calculate the total count in each document. Then each count divided by its row's total count, as seen in Example 8.17.

Example 8.17.

```
# Normalize pos matrix by documents
masc_pos_dtm <-
  masc_pos_dtm / rowSums(masc_pos_dtm)
```

There are two concerns to address before we can proceed with clustering. First, clustering algorithm performance tends to degrade with the number of features. Second, clustering algorithms perform better with more informative features. That is to say, features that are more distinct across the documents provide better information for deriving useful clusters.

We can address both of these concerns by reducing the number of features and increasing the informativeness of the features. To accomplish this is to use dimensionality reduction. **Dimensionality reduction** is a set of methods that are used to reduce the number of features in a dataset while retaining as much information as possible. The most common method for dimensionality reduction is **principal component analysis** (PCA). PCA is a method that transforms a set of correlated variables into a set of uncorrelated variables, known as principal components. The principal components are ordered by the amount of variance that they explain in the data. The first principal component explains the most variance, the second principal component explains the second most variance, and so on.

We can apply PCA to the matrix and assess how well it accounts for the variation in the data and how the variation is distributed across components. The `prcomp()` function from base R can be used to perform PCA.

Let's apply PCA to the matrix, as seen in Example 8.18.

Example 8.18.

```
set.seed(123) # for reproducibility

# Apply PCA to matrix
masc_pos_pca <-
  masc_pos_dtm |>
  prcomp()
```

We can visualize the amount of variance explained by each principal component with a scree plot. A **scree plot** is a bar plot ordered by the amount of variance explained by each principal component. The `fviz_eig()` function from {factoextra} implements a scree plot on a PCA object. We can set the number of components to visualize with `ncp =`, as seen in Example 8.19.

Example 8.19.

```
# Load package
library(factoextra)

# Scree plot: POS relative frequency
fviz_eig(masc_pos_pca, ncp = 10)
```

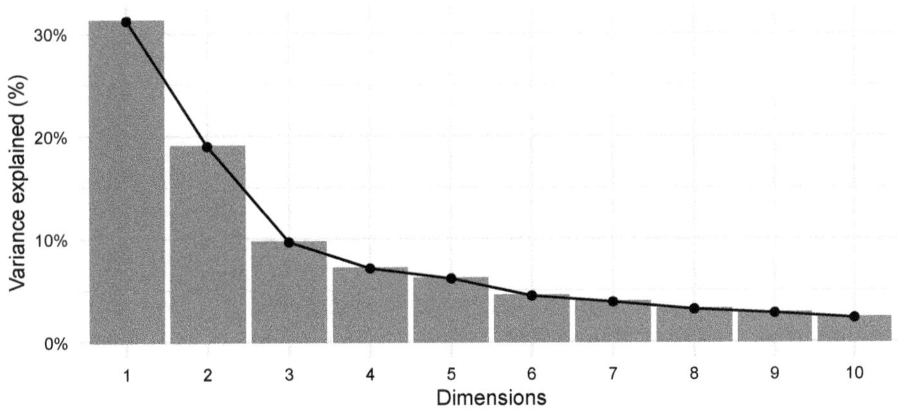

Figure 8.4: Scree plot of the principal components of the POS relative frequency

Dive deeper

As with many modeling techniques we will encounter, it is possible to extract the importance of features that contribute to the model. In the case of PCA, we can extract the feature values from the principal components using the `get_pca_var()` function from {factoextra}. Feature importance provides more detailed insight into the inner workings of the algorithms we employ in our research and therefore can serve to inform our interpretation of the results.

From the scree plot for the matrix in Figure 8.4, we can see that the first component shows the most variance explained, around just over 30%, and then drops for subsequent drops as the number of dimensions increase. Visually we will apply the elbow method to identify the number of dimensions to use for clustering. It appears the variance explained decreases after 4 dimensions. This is a good indication that we should use 4 dimensions for our clustering algorithm.

Let's go ahead and create a matrix of the first four principal components for the POS data, as seen in Example 8.20.

Example 8.20.

```
# Create a matrix of the first four principal components
masc_pos_pca_pc <-
  masc_pos_pca$x[, 1:4]
```

Now that we have identified the features that we want to use for clustering and we have represented the features in a way that can be used for clustering, we can apply a clustering algorithm to the data.

Some algorithms are better suited for certain types of data and certain types of tasks. For example, **hierarchical clustering** is best when we are not sure how many clusters we want to identify, as it does not require us to specify the number of clusters from the outset. However, it is not ideal when we have a large dataset, as it can be computationally expensive compared to some other algorithms. **k-means clustering**, on the other hand, is a good choice when we want to identify a pre-defined number of clusters, and the aim is to gauge how well the data fit the clusters. These two clustering techniques, therefore, complement each other, with hierarchical clustering being favored for initial exploration and k-means clustering being better suited for targeted evaluation.

Since we are exploring the usefulness of the 18 genre labels used in the MASC dataset we have an idea of how many clusters we want to start with. This is a good case to employ the k-means clustering algorithm.

In k-means clustering, we specify the number of clusters that we want to identify. For each cluster number, a random center is generated. Then each observation is assigned to the cluster with the nearest center. The center of each cluster is then recalculated based on the distribution of the observations in the cluster. This process iterates either a pre-defined number of times, or until the centers converge (*i.e.* observations stop switching clusters).

The `kmeans()` function from base R takes the matrix of features as its first argument and the number of clusters as its second argument. We can specify the number of clusters with the `centers` argument. Other arguments `nstart` and `iter.max` can be used to specify the number of random starts and the maximum number of iterations, respectively. Since the starting point for centers is random, it is recommendable to run the algorithm multiple times with different starting points. Furthermore, we will limit the iterations to avoid the algorithm running indefinitely.

Our goal, then, will be to assess how well this number of clusters fits the data. After finding the optimal number of clusters, we can then compare the results with the genre variable to see how well the clusters map to the values of this variable.

One way to assess the fit of the clustering algorithm is to visualize the results, interpret, and adjust the number of clusters, if necessary, any number of times. Another, more efficient, approach is to algorithmically assess the variability of the clusters based on differing number of clusters and then select the number of clusters that best fits the data.

We will take the later approach and plot the **within-cluster sum of squares** (WSS) for a range of values for k. The WSS is the sum of the squared distance between each observation and its cluster center. With a plot of the WSS for a range of values for k, we can identify the value for k where the WSS begins to level off, using the elbow method. It is not always clear where the elbow is, yet it is a good starting point for identifying the optimal number of clusters.

The `fviz_nbclust()` function can be used to plot the WSS for a range of values for k. The `fviz_nbclust()` function takes the `kmeans()` function as its first argument and the matrix of features as its second argument. The `fviz_nbclust()` function also takes arguments `method = "wss"` to specify the WSS method and `k.max = 20` to specify the maximum number of clusters to plot. Let's plot the WSS for a range of values for k, as seen in Figure 8.5, using the code in Example 8.21.

Example 8.21.

```
masc_pos_pca_pc |>
  fviz_nbclust(
    FUNcluster = kmeans,
    method = "wss", # method
    k.max = 20,
    nstart = 25,
    iter.max = 20
  )
```

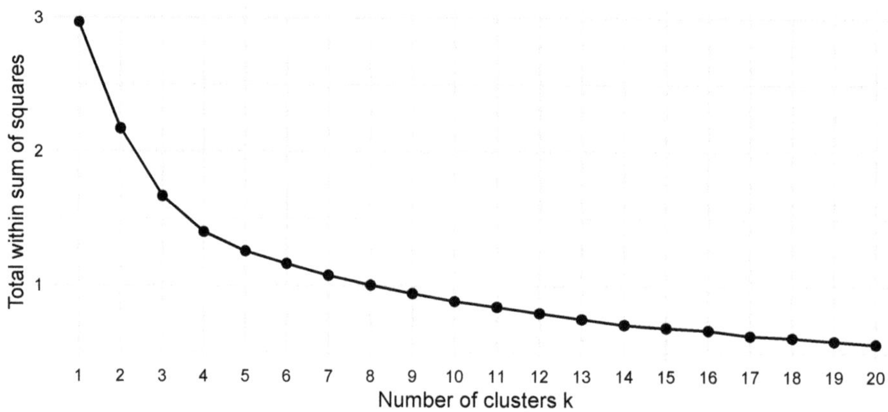

Figure 8.5: Elbow method for k-means clustering

It is clear that there are significant gains in cluster fit from 1 to 4 clusters, but the gains begin to level off after 5 clusters.

Now we have an informed selection for k. Let's use 4 clusters in the `kmeans()` function and collect the results, as seen in Example 8.22.

Example 8.22.

```
set.seed(123) # for reproducibility

# k-means: for 4 clusters
masc_pos_kmeans_fit <-
  masc_pos_pca_pc |>
  kmeans(
    centers = 4,
    nstart = 25,
    iter.max = 20
  )

```

```
# Preview
masc_pos_kmeans_fit$cluster[1:10]
```

```
 1  10 100 101 102 103 104 105 106 107
 1   1   2   3   3   2   2   2   4   3
```

The preview from Example 8.22 shows the cluster assignments for the first 10 documents (`doc_id`) in the dataset.

From this point we can join document-cluster pairings produced by the k-means algorithm with the original dataset. We can then explore the clusters in terms of the original features. We can also explore the clusters in terms of the original labels.

Let's join the cluster assignments to the original dataset, as seen in Example 8.23.

Example 8.23.

```
# Organize k-means clusters into a tibble
masc_pos_cluster_tbl <-
  tibble(
    doc_id = names(masc_pos_kmeans_fit$cluster),
    cluster = masc_pos_kmeans_fit$cluster
  )

# Join cluster assignments to original dataset
masc_cluster_tbl <-
  masc_tbl|>
  left_join(
    masc_pos_cluster_tbl,
    by = "doc_id"
  )

# Preview
masc_cluster_tbl |>
  slice_head(n = 5)
```

```
# A tibble: 5 x 8
  doc_id modality genre   term_num term         lemma        pos   cluster
  <chr>  <chr>    <chr>      <dbl> <chr>        <chr>        <chr>   <int>
1 1      Written  Letters        2 Your         your         PRP$        1
2 1      Written  Letters        3 contribution contribution NN          1
3 1      Written  Letters        4 to           to           TO          1
4 1      Written  Letters        6 will         will         MD          1
5 1      Written  Letters        7 mean         mean         VB          1
```

We now see that the cluster assignments from the k-means algorithm have been joined to the original dataset. We can now explore the clusters in terms of the original features. For example, let's look at the distribution of the clusters across genre, as seen in Example 8.24. To do this, we first need to reduce our dataset to the distinct combinations of genre and cluster. Then, we can use {janitor}'s `tabyl()` function to provided formatted percentages.

Example 8.24.

```
# Load package
library(janitor)

# Reduce to distinct combinations of genre and cluster
masc_meta_tbl <-
  masc_cluster_tbl |>
  distinct(genre, cluster)

# Tabulate: cluster by genre
masc_meta_tbl |>
  tabyl(genre, cluster) |>
  adorn_percentages("col") |>
  adorn_pct_formatting(digits = 1) |>
  as_tibble() |>
  tt(width = 1)
```

Table 8.7: Distribution of clusters by genre

genre	1	2	3	4
Blog	7.7%	20.0%	8.3%	0.0%
Email	7.7%	20.0%	8.3%	20.0%
Essay	7.7%	0.0%	8.3%	20.0%
Face-to-face	7.7%	0.0%	0.0%	0.0%
Fiction	7.7%	0.0%	8.3%	0.0%
Fictlets	7.7%	0.0%	0.0%	0.0%
Government	0.0%	0.0%	8.3%	0.0%
Jokes	7.7%	0.0%	0.0%	0.0%
Journal	7.7%	0.0%	8.3%	0.0%
Letters	7.7%	20.0%	8.3%	0.0%
Movie Script	7.7%	0.0%	8.3%	0.0%
Newspaper	7.7%	20.0%	8.3%	20.0%
Non-fiction	0.0%	0.0%	8.3%	20.0%
Technical	0.0%	0.0%	8.3%	20.0%
Telephone	7.7%	0.0%	0.0%	0.0%
Transcript	7.7%	0.0%	0.0%	0.0%
Travel Guide	0.0%	0.0%	8.3%	0.0%
Twitter	0.0%	20.0%	0.0%	0.0%

From Example 8.24, we can see that the clusters are not evenly distributed across the genres. In particular, cluster 2 tends to be more associated with 'blog', 'email', 'letters', 'twitter', and 'newspaper'. Another interesting cluster is cluster 4, which is more associated with 'non-fiction', and interestingly, 'email' and 'newspaper'. This suggest that the clusters are capturing some of the variation in the across the genres and potential within some of the genres.

We could continue to explore genre, but we could also entertain the possibility that the clusters may capture differences between modality —even some interaction between modality and genre! This highlights how exploratory data analysis through clustering can be used to identify new questions and new variables of interest.

> **Consider this**
> Given the cluster assignments derived using the distribution of POS tags, what other relationships between the clusters and the original features could one explore? What are the limitations of this approach? What are the implications of this approach for the interpretation of the results?

Vector space models

In our discussion of clustering, we targeted associations between documents based on the distribution of linguistic features. We now turn to targeting associations between linguistic features based on their distribution across documents. The technique we will introduce is known as **vector space modeling**. Vector space modeling aims to represent linguistic features as numerical vectors which reflect the various linguistic contexts in which the features appear. Together these vectors form a feature-context space in which features with similar contextual distributions are closer together.

An interesting property of vector space models is that they are able to capture semantic and/or syntactic relationships between features based on their distribution. In this way, vector space modeling can be seen as an implementation of the **distributional hypothesis** —that is, terms that appear in similar linguistic contexts tend to have similar meanings (Harris, 1954). As Firth (1957) states, "you shall know a word by the company it keeps".

Let's assume in our textbook project we are interested in gathering information about English's expression of the semantic concepts of manner and motion. For learners of English, this can be an area of difficulty as languages differ in how these semantic properties are expressed. English is an example of a "satellite-framed" language, that is that manner and motion are often encoded in the same verb with a particle encoding the motion path ("rush out", "climb up"). Other languages such as Spanish, Turkish, and Japanese are "verb-framed" languages, that is that motion but not manner is encoded in the verb ("salir corriendo", "koşarak çıkmak", "走り出す").

Case study

Garg, Schiebinger, Jurafsky, & Zou (2018) quantify and compare gender and ethnic stereotypes over time using word embeddings. The authors explore the temporal dynamics of stereotypes using word embeddings as a quantitative measure of bias. The data used includes word embeddings from the Google News dataset for contemporary analysis, as well as embeddings from the COHA and Google Books datasets for historical analysis. Additional validation is done using embeddings from the New York Times Annotated Corpus. Several word lists representing gender, ethnicity, and neutral words are collated for analysis. The main finding is that language reflects and perpetuates cultural stereotypes, and the analysis shows consistency in the relationships between embedding bias and external metrics across datasets over time. The results also highlight the impact of historical events, such as the women's movement of the 1960s, on the encoding of stereotypes.

We can use vector space modeling to attempt to represent the distribution of verbs in the MASC dataset and then target the concepts of manner and motion to then explore how English encodes these concepts. The question will be what our features will be. They could be terms, lemmas, POS tags, *etc.* Or they could be some combination. Considering the task at hand, which we will ultimately want to know something about verbs, it makes sense to include the POS information in combination with either the term or the lemma.

If we include term and POS then we have a feature for every morphological variant of the term (*e.g.* house_VB, housed_VBD, housing_VBG). This can make the model larger than it needs to be. If we include lemma and POS then we have a feature for every lemma with a distinct grammatical category (*e.g.* house_NN, house_VB). Note that as the POS tags are from the Penn tagset, many morphological variants appear in the tag itself (*e.g.* house_VB, houses_VBZ, housing_VBG). This demonstrates how the choice of features can impact the size of the model. In our case, it is not clear that we need to include the morphological variants of the verbs, so I will use lemmas and recode the POS variables as a simplified tagset.

After simplifying the features, we can then apply the vector space model (VSM) to the MASC dataset. When VSM is applied to words, it is known as **word embedding**. To calculate word embeddings there are various algorithms that can be used (BERT, word2vec, GloVe, *etc.*) We will use the **word2vec** (Mikolov, Sutskever, Chen, Corrado, & Dean, 2013) algorithm. Word2vec is a neural network-based algorithm that learns word embeddings from a large corpus of text. In the word2vec algorithm, the researcher can choose to learn embeddings from a **Continuous Bag of Words** (CBOW) or a **Skip-gram model**. The CBOW model predicts a target word based on the context words. The Skip-gram model predicts the context words based on the target word. The CBOW model is faster to train and is better for frequent words. The Skip-gram model is slower to train and is better for infrequent words.

> **Dive deeper**
> Choosing window size and dimensions for word2vec models is another important consideration. The window size is the number of words that the model will consider as context for the target word. Smaller window sizes tend to capture more syntactic information, while larger window sizes tend to capture more semantic information.
> The number of dimensions is the number of features that the model will learn. More dimensions can capture more information, but can also lead to **overfitting** —picking up on nuances that are particular to the dataset and that do not generalize well. Fewer dimensions can capture less information, but can also lead to **underfitting** —*not* picking up on nuances that are particular to the dataset and that do generalize well. The number of dimensions is a hyperparameter that can be tuned to optimize the model for the task at hand.

Another consideration to take into account is the size of the corpus used to train the model. VSM provide more reliable results when trained on larger corpora. The MASC dataset is relatively small. We've simplified our features in order to have a smaller vocabulary in hopes to offset this limitation to a degree. But the choice of either CBOW or Skip-gram can also help to offset this limitation. CBOW can be better for smaller corpora as it aggregates context information. Skip-gram can be better for larger corpora as it can capture more nuanced relationships between words.

To implement the word2vec algorithm on our lemma + POS features, we will use {word2vec}. The `word2vec()` function takes a text file and uses it to train the vector representations. To prepare the MASC dataset for training, we will need to write the lemma + POS features to a text file as a single character string. We can do this by first collapsing the `lemma_pos` variable into a single string for the entire corpus using the `str_c()` function. Then we can use the `write_lines()` function to write the string to a text file, as in Example 8.25.

Example 8.25.

```
# Write lemma + POS to text file
masc_tbl |>
  summarize(text = str_c(lemma_pos, collapse = " ")) |>
  pull(text) |>
  write_lines(
    file = "../data/analysis/masc_lemma_pos.txt"
  )
```

With the single line text file on disk, we will read it in, apply the word2vec algorithm using {word2vec} (Wijffels & Watanabe, 2023), and write the model to disk. By default, the `word2vec()` function applies the CBOW model, with 50 dimensions, a window size of 5, and a minimum word count of 5. We can change these parameters as needed, but let's apply the default algorithm to the text file splitting features by sentence punctuation, as seen in Example 8.26.

Example 8.26.

```
# Load package
library(word2vec)

# Traing word2vec model
masc_model <-
  word2vec(
    x = "../data/analysis/masc_lemma_pos.txt",
    type = "cbow", # or "skip-gram"
    dim = 100,
    split = c(" "),
    threads = 8L
  )

# Write model to disk
write.word2vec(
  masc_model,
  file = "../data/analysis/masc_lemma_pos.bin"
)
```

Writing the model to disk is important as it allows us to read the model in without having to retrain it. In cases where the corpus is large, this can save a lot of computational time.

Now that we have a trained model, we can read it in with the `read.vectors()` function from {wordVectors} as in Example 8.27.

Example 8.27.

```
# Load package
library(wordVectors)

# Read word2vec model
masc_model <-
  read.vectors(
    filename = "../data/analysis/masc_lemma_pos.bin"
  )
```

The `read.vectors()` function returns a matrix where each row is a term in the model and each column is a dimension in the vector space, as seen in Example 8.28.

Example 8.28.

```
# Inspect
dim(masc_model)

# Preview
masc_model[1:5, 1:5]
```

```
[1] 5808  100
A VectorSpaceModel object of  5  words and  5  vectors
                    [,1]   [,2]    [,3]   [,4]    [,5]
abbreviated_ADJ    1.068  1.103 -0.3439  0.386 -1.0062
absent_ADJ        -1.839 -1.753  0.0658  0.119  0.9376
absorb_VERB       -1.772 -1.528 -0.0554  0.664 -1.2453
accidentally_ADV -1.264 -0.742 -0.6870  0.613 -1.0750
aesthetic_ADJ      0.567  0.524  1.0638 -0.332 -0.0424
attr(,".cache")
<environment: 0x16fca1ac0>
```

The row-wise vector in the model is the vector representation of each feature. The notion is that these values can now be compared with other features to explore distributional relatedness. We can extract specific features from the matrix using the `[]` operator.

As an example, let's compare the vectors for noun-verb pairs for the lemmas 'run' and 'walk'. To do this we extract these features from the model. To appreciate the relatedness of these features it is best to visualize them. We can do this by first reducing the dimensionality of the vectors using principal components analysis. We can then plot the first two principal components with the code in Example 8.29 which produces Figure 8.6.

Example 8.29.

```
# Extract vectors
word_vectors <-
  masc_model[c("run_VERB", "walk_VERB", "run_NOUN", "walk_NOUN"), ] |>
  as.matrix()

set.seed(123) # for reproducibility

pca <-
  word_vectors |>
  scale() |>
```

```
  prcomp()

pca_tbl <-
  as_tibble(pca$x[, 1:2]) |>
  mutate(word = rownames(word_vectors))

pca_tbl |>
  ggplot(aes(x = PC1, y = PC2, label = word)) +
  geom_point(size = 1) +
  ggrepel::geom_text_repel(size = 2)
```

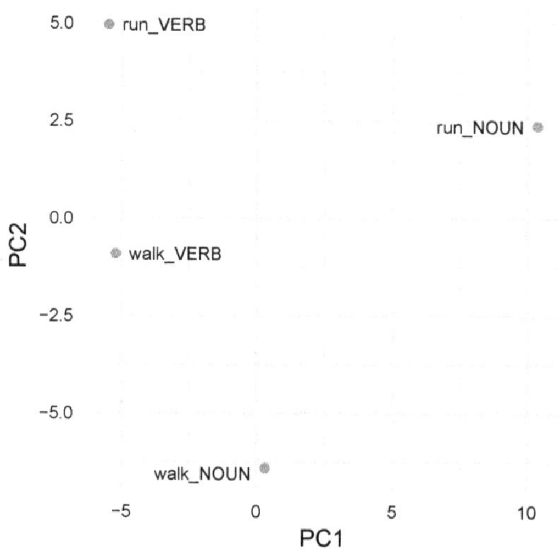

Figure 8.6: Similarity between 'run' and 'walk'

From Figure 8.6, we can see that each of these features occupies a distinct position in the reduced vector space. But on closer inspection, we can see that there is a relationship between the lemma pairs. Remember that PCA reduces the dimensionality of the data by identifying the dimensions that capture the greatest amount of variance in the data. This means that of the 50 dimensions in the model, the PC1 and PC2 correspond to orthogonal dimensions that capture the greatest amount of variance in the data. If we look along PC1, we can see that there is a distinction between POS. Looking along PC2, we see some parity between lemma meanings. Given these features, we can see that meaning and grammatical category can be approximated in the vector space.

An interesting property of vector space models is that we can build up a dimension of meaning by adding vectors that we expect to approximate that meaning. For example, we can add the vectors for typical motion verbs to create a vector for motion-similarity and one for manner-similarity. We can then compare the feature vectors for all verbs and assess their motion-similarity and manner-similarity.

To do this let's first subset the model to only include verbs, as in Example 8.30. We will also remove the POS tags from the row names of the matrix as they are no longer needed.

Example 8.30.

```
# Filter to verbs
verbs <- str_subset(rownames(masc_model), ".*_VERB")
verb_vectors <- masc_model[verbs, ]

# Remove POS tags
rownames(verb_vectors) <-
  verb_vectors |>
  rownames() |>
  str_replace_all("_VERB", "")

# Inspect
dim(verb_vectors)

# Preview
verb_vectors[1:5, 1:5]
```

```
[1] 1115  100
A VectorSpaceModel object of  5  words and  5  vectors
          [,1]   [,2]    [,3]    [,4]   [,5]
absorb  -1.772 -1.528 -0.0554  0.6642 -1.245
auction -2.083 -0.977 -0.2505 -0.0204 -0.874
bid      0.217 -0.490 -0.4588  0.1373  0.247
brief    1.215 -0.674 -0.7121  0.5072 -0.445
cap     -0.135  0.884  0.2278 -0.2563 -0.207
attr(,".cache")
<environment: 0x119d71dc0>
```

We now have `verb_vectors` which includes the vector representations for all verbs 1,115 in the MASC dataset. Next, let's seed the vectors for motion-similarity and manner-similarity and calculate the vector 'closeness' to the motion and manner seed vectors with the `closest_to()` function from {wordVectors} package, in Example 8.32.

Example 8.31.

```
# Add vectors for motion-similarity and manner-similarity
motion <-
  c("go", "come", "leave", "arrive", "enter", "exit", "depart", "return")

motion_similarity <-
  verb_vectors |> closest_to(motion, n = Inf)

# Preview
glimpse(motion_similarity)

manner <-
  c("run", "walk", "jump", "crawl", "swim", "fly", "drive", "ride")

manner_similarity <-
  verb_vectors |> closest_to(manner, n = Inf)

# Preview
glimpse(manner_similarity)
```

```
Rows: 1,115
Columns: 2
$ word                    <chr> "walk", "step", "return", "enter", "leave", "le~
$ `similarity to motion` <dbl> 0.742, 0.741, 0.732, 0.727, 0.682, 0.669, 0.664~
Rows: 1,115
Columns: 2
$ word                    <chr> "walk", "drop", "step", "hang", "rub", "shut", ~
$ `similarity to manner` <dbl> 0.865, 0.841, 0.831, 0.826, 0.826, 0.824, 0.820~
```

The `motion_similarity` and `manner_similarity` data frames each contain all the verbs with a corresponding closeness measure. We can join these two data frames by feature to create a single data frame with the motion-similarity and manner-similarity measures, as seen in Example 8.32.

Example 8.32.

```
# Join motion-similarity and manner-similarity
manner_motion_similarity <-
  manner_similarity |>
  inner_join(motion_similarity)

# Preview
glimpse(manner_motion_similarity)
```

```
Rows: 1,115
Columns: 3
$ word                    <chr> "walk", "drop", "step", "hang", "rub", "shut", ~
```

```
$ `similarity to manner` <dbl> 0.865, 0.841, 0.831, 0.826, 0.826, 0.824, 0.820~
$ `similarity to motion` <dbl> 0.742, 0.642, 0.741, 0.635, 0.624, 0.589, 0.561~
```

The result of Example 8.32 is a data frame with the motion-similarity and manner-similarity measures for all verbs in the MASC dataset. We can now visualize the distribution of motion-similarity and manner-similarity measures, as seen in Figure 8.7.

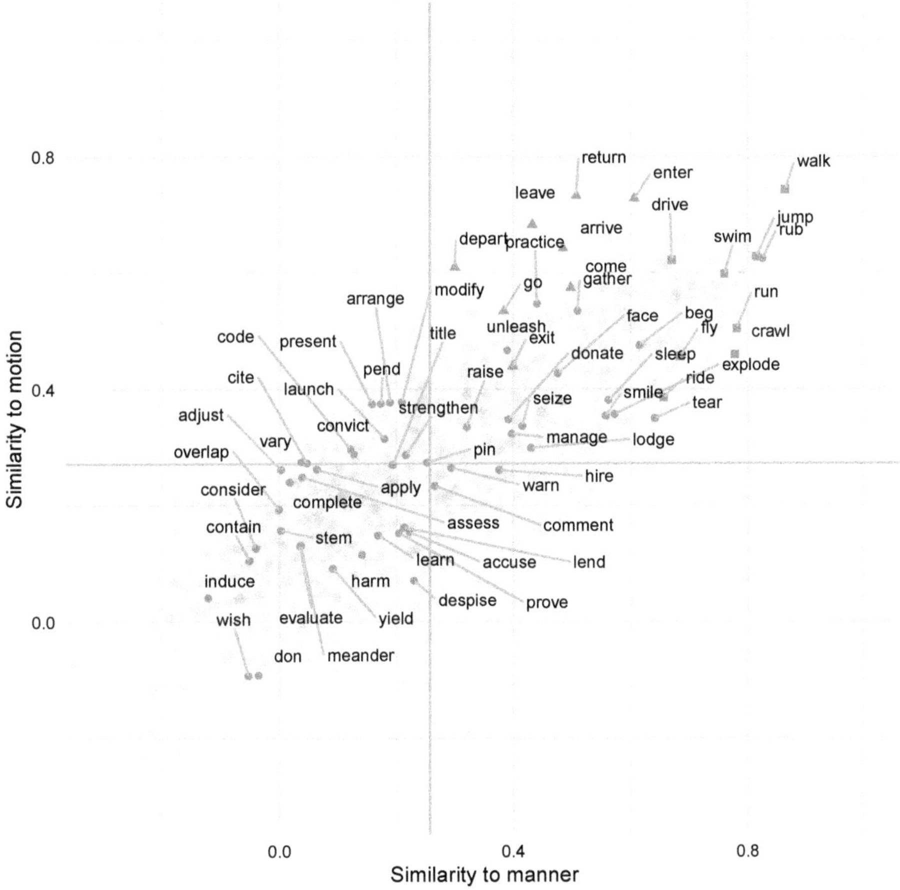

Figure 8.7: Motion-similarity and manner-similarity of verbs

From Figure 8.7, we see that manner-similarity is plotted on the x-axis and motion-similarity on the y-axis. I've added lines to divide the scatterplot into quadrants: the top-right shows high manner- and motion-similarity, while the bottom-left shows low manner- and motion-similarity. Verbs in the top-left quadrant have high motion-similarity but low manner-similarity, and verbs in the bottom-right quadrant have high manner-similarity but low motion-similarity.

I've randomly sampled 50 verbs from the dataset and plotted them with text labels, along with the motion and manner seed vectors as triangle and box points, respectively. Motion- and manner-similarity seed verbs appear together in the top-right quadrant, indicating their semantic relationship. Verbs in other quadrants exhibit lower similarity in either manner or motion, or both. Qualitatively, many verbs align with intuition, though some do not, which is expected given the model's training on a relatively small corpus. This example demonstrates how vector space modeling can explore semantic relationships between linguistic features.

Activities

Exploratory analysis is a wide-ranging term that encompasses many different methods. In these activities, we will focus on the methods that are most commonly used in the analysis of textual data. These include frequency and distributional analysis, clustering, and word embedding models. We will model how to explore iteratively using the output of one method to inform the next and ultimately to address a research question.

Recipe
What: Exploratory analysis methods
How: Read Recipe 8, complete comprehension check, and prepare for Lab 8.
Why: To illustrate how to prepare a dataset for descriptive and unsupervised machine learning methods and evaluate the results for exploratory data analysis.

Lab
What: Pattern discovery
How: Clone, fork, and complete the steps in Lab 8.
Why: To gain experience working with coding strategies to prepare, feature engineer, explore, and evaluate results from exploratory data analyses, practice transforming datasets into new object formats and visualizing relationships, and implement organizational strategies for organizing and reporting results in a reproducible fashion.

Summary

In this chapter, we surveyed a range of methods for uncovering insights from data, particularly when we do not have a predetermined hypothesis. We broke the chapter discussion along the two central branches of exploratory data analysis: descriptive analysis and unsupervised learning. Descriptive analysis offers statistical or visual summaries of datasets through frequency, dispersion, and co-occurrence measures, while unsupervised learning utilizes machine learning techniques to uncover patterns without pre-defining variable relationships. Here we covered a few unsupervised learning methods including clustering, dimensionality reduction, and vector space modeling. Through either descriptive or unsupervised learning methodologies, we probe questions in a data-driven fashion and apply methods to summarize, reduce, and sort complex datasets. This in turn facilitates novel, quantitative perspectives that can subsequently be evaluated qualitatively, offering us a robust approach to exploring and generating research questions.

9

Predict

Outcomes

- Identify the research goals of predictive data analysis
- Describe the workflow for predictive data analysis
- Recognize quantitative and qualitative methods for evaluating predictive models

In this chapter, I introduce supervised learning as an approach to text analysis. Supervised learning aims to establish a relationship between a target (or outcome) variable and a set of feature variables derived from text data. By leveraging this relationship, statistical generalizations (models) can be created to accurately predict values of the target variable based on the values of the feature variables. Throughout the chapter, we explore practical tasks and theoretical applications of statistical learning in text analysis.

>_ Lessons
What: Advanced Visualization
How: In an R console, load {swirl}, run `swirl()`, and follow prompts to select the lesson.
Why: To dive deeper into {ggplot2} to enhance visual summaries and provide an introduction to {factoextra} and {ggfortify} that extend {ggplot2} capabilities to model objects.

9.1 Orientation

Predictive data analysis (PDA) is a powerful analysis method for making predictions about new or future data based on patterns in existing data. PDA is a type of supervised learning, which means that it involves training a model on a labeled dataset where the input data and desired output are both provided. The model is able to make predictions or classifications based on the

10.4324/9781003393764.9

input data by learning the relationships between the input and output data. Supervised machine learning is an important tool for linguists studying language and communication, as it allows us to analyze language data to identify patterns or trends in language use, assess hypotheses, and prescribe actions.

The approach to conducting predictive analysis shares some commonalities with exploratory data analysis (Section 8.1) (as well as inferential analysis Chapter 10), but there are also some key differences. Consider the workflow in Table 9.1.

Table 9.1: Workflow for predictive data analysis

Step	Name	Description
1	Identify	Consider the research question and aim and identify relevant variables
2		Split the data into representative training and testing sets
3		Apply variable selection and engineering procedures
4	Inspect	Inspect the data to ensure that it is in the correct format and that the training and testing sets are representative of the data
5	Interrogate	Train and evaluate the model on the training set, adjusting models or hyperparameters as needed, to produce a final model
6	(Optional) Iterate	Repeat steps 3-5 to select new variables, models, hyperparameters
7	Interpret	Interpret the results of the final model in light of the research question or hypothesis

Focusing on the overlap with other analysis methods, we can see some fundamental steps such as identifying relevant variables, inspecting the data, interrogating the data, and interpreting the results. And if our research aim is exploratory in nature, iteration may also be a part of the workflow.

There are two main differences, however, between the PDA and the EDA workflow we discussed in Chapter 8. The first is that PDA requires partitioning the data into training and testing sets. The training set is used to develop the model, and the testing set is used to evaluate the model's performance. This strategy is used to ensure that the model is robust and generalizes well to new data. It is well known, and makes intuitive sense, that using the same data to develop and evaluate a model likely will not produce a model that generalizes well to new data. This is because the model will have potentially conflated the nuances of the data ('the noise') with any real trends ('the signal') and therefore will not be able to generalize well to new data. This is called **overfitting** and by holding out a portion of the data for testing, we can evaluate the model's performance on data that it has not seen before and therefore get a more accurate estimate of the generalizable trends in the data.

Dive deeper
Prediction modeling is a hot topic. Given the potential to make actionable predictions about future outcomes, it attracts a lot of attention from organizations which aim to leverage data to make informed decisions. It's use in research is also growing beyond the development of better models and using predictive models to address research questions and hypotheses.
We will apply predictive modeling in the context of language data as a semi-inductive method. However, it is also increasingly used in hypothesis testing scenarios, see Gries & Deshors (2014), Deshors & Gries (2016), and Baayen (2011) for examples.

Another procedure to avoid the perils of overfitting, is to use resampling methods as part of the model evaluation on the training set. Resampling is the process of repeatedly drawing samples from the training set and evaluating the model on each sample. The two most common resampling methods are **bootstrapping** (resampling with replacement) and **cross-validation** (resampling without replacement). The performance of these multiple models is summarized and the error between them is assessed. The goal is to minimize the performance differences between the models while maximizing the overall performance. These measures go a long way to avoiding overfitting and therefore maximizing the chance that the training phase will produce a model which is robust at the testing phase.

The second difference, not reflected in the workflow but inherent in predictive analysis, is that PDA requires a fixed outcome variable. This means that the outcome variable must be defined from the outset and cannot be changed during the analysis. Furthermore, the informational nature of the outcome variable will dictate what type of algorithm we choose to interrogate the data and how we will evaluate the model's performance.

If the outcome is categorical in nature, we will use a **classification algorithm** (*e.g.* logistic regression, naive Bayes, *etc.*). Classification evaluation metrics include accuracy, precision, recall, and F1 scores (a metric which balances precision and recall) which can be derived from and visualized in a cross-tabulation of the predicted and actual outcome values.

If the outcome is numeric in nature, we will use a **regression algorithm** (*e.g.* linear regression, support vector regression, *etc.*). Since the difference between prediction and actual values is numeric, metrics that quantify numerical differences, such as root mean square error (RMSE) or R^2, are used to evaluate the model's performance.

The evaluation of the model is quantitative on the one hand, but it is also qualitative in that we need to consider the implications of the model's performance in light of the research question or hypothesis. Furthermore, depending on our research question we may be interested in exploring the features that are most important to the model's performance. This is called **feature importance** and can be derived from the model's coefficients or weights. Notably, however, some of the most powerful models in use today, such as deep neural networks, are not easily interpretable and therefore feature importance is not easily derived. This is something to keep in mind when considering the research question and the type of model that will be used to address it.

9.2 Analysis

In this section, we now turn to the practical application of predictive data analysis. The discussion will be separated into classification and regression tasks, as model selection and evaluation procedures differ between the two. For each task, we will frame a research goal and work through the process of building a predictive model to address that goal. Along the way we will cover concepts and methods that are common to both classification and regression tasks and specific to each.

To frame our analyses, we will posit research aimed at identifying language usage patterns in second language use, one for a classification task and one for a regression task. Our first research question will be to assess whether Spanish language use can be used to predict natives and L1 English learners (categorical). Our second research question will be to gauge the extent to which the L1 English learners' Spanish language placement test scores (numeric) can be predicted based on their language use.

Table 9.2: Data dictionary for the CEDEL2 corpus

variable	name	type	description
doc_id	Document ID	numeric	Unique identifier for each document
subcorpus	Subcorpus	categorical	The sub-corpus to which the document belongs ('Learner' or 'Native')
place_score	Placement Score	numeric	The score obtained by the document author in a placement test. Null values indicate missing data (i.e. the document author did not take the placement test)
proficiency	Proficiency	ordinal	The level of language proficiency of the document author ('Upper intermediate', 'Lower advanced', 'Upper beginner', or 'Native')
text	Text	character	The written text provided by the document author

We will use data from the CEDEL2 corpus (Lozano, 2022). We will include a subset of the variables from this data that are relevant to our research questions. The data dictionary for this dataset is seen in Table 9.2.

Let's go ahead and read the transformed dataset and preview it in Example 9.1.

Example 9.1.

```
# Read in the dataset
cedel_tbl<-
  read_csv("../data/cedel2/cedel2_transformed.csv")

# Preview
glimpse(cedel_tbl)
```

```
Rows: 2,957
Columns: 5
$ doc_id      <dbl> 1, 2, 3, 4, 5, 6, 7, 8, 9, 10, 11, 12, 13, 14, 15, 16, 17,~
$ subcorpus   <chr> "Learner", "Learner", "Learner", "Learner", "Learner", "Le~
$ place_score <dbl> 14.0, 16.3, 16.3, 18.6, 18.6, 18.6, 20.9, 20.9, 20.9, 20.9~
$ proficiency <chr> "Lower beginner", "Lower beginner", "Lower beginner", "Low~
$ text        <chr> "Yo vivo es Alanta, Georgia. Atlanta es muy grande ciudad.~
```

The output of Example 9.1 provides some structural information about the dataset, number of rows and columns as well as variable types.

After I performed some diagnostics and made some adjustments based on a descriptive assessment, the dataset is in good order to proceed with the analysis. I updated the variables `subcorpus` and `proficiency` as factor variables and ordered them in a way that makes sense for the analysis. The `place_score` variable is distributed well across the proficiency levels. The `subcorpus` variable is less balanced, with around 65% of the texts being from learners. This is not a problem, but it is something to keep in mind when building and interpreting the predictive models.

We will be using the Tidymodels framework in R to perform these analyses. {tidymodels} is a meta-package, much like {tidyverse}, that provides a consistent interface for machine learning modeling. Some key packages unique to {tidymodels} are {recipes}, {parsnip}, {workflows}, and {tune}. {recipes} includes functions for pre-processing and engineering features. {parsnip} provides a consistent interface for specifying modeling algorithms. {worflows} allows us to combine recipes and models into a single pipeline. Finally, {tune} give us the ability to evaluate and adjust, or 'tune', the parameters of models.

Since we are using text data, we will also be using {textrecipes} which makes various functions available for pre-processing text including extracting and engineering features.

Let's go ahead and do the setup, loading the necessary packages, seen in Example 9.2.

Example 9.2.

```
# Load packages
library(tidymodels)  # modeling metapackage
library(textrecipes) # text pre-processing

# Prefer tidymodels functions
tidymodels_prefer()
```

9.2.1 Text classification

The goal of text classification analysis is to develop a model that can accurately label text samples as either native or learner. This is a binary classification problem. We will approach this problem from an exploratory perspective, and therefore our aim is to identify features from the text that best distinguish between the two classes and explore the features that are most important to the model's performance.

Let's modify the data frame to include only the variables we need for this analysis, assigning it to `cls_tbl`. In the process, we will rename the `subcorpus` variable to `outcome` to reflect that it is the outcome variable. This is seen in Example 9.3.

Example 9.3.

```
# Rename subcorpus to outcome
cls_tbl <-
  cedel_tbl |>
  select(outcome = subcorpus, proficiency, text)
```

Let's begin the workflow from Table 9.1 by identifying the features that we will use to classify the texts. There may be many features that we could use. These could be features derived from raw text (*e.g.* characters, words, ngrams, *etc.*), feature vectors (*e.g.* word embeddings), or meta-linguistic features (*e.g.* part-of-speech tags, syntactic parses, or semantic features) that have been derived from these through manual or automatic annotation.

If as part of our research question the types of features are included, then we should proceed toward deriving those features. If not, a simple approach is to use words as the predictor features. This will serve as a baseline for more complex models, if necessary.

This provides us the linguistic unit we will use, but we still need to decide how to operationalize what we mean by 'use' in our research statement. Do we use raw token counts? Do we use normalized frequencies? Do we use some type of weighting scheme? These are questions that we need to consider as we embark on this analysis. Since we are exploring, we can use trial-and-error or consider the implications of each approach and choose the one that best fits our research question —or both.

Let's approach this with a bit more nuance as we already have some domain knowledge about word use. First, we know that the frequency distribution of words is highly skewed, meaning that a few words occur very frequently and most words occur very infrequently. Second, we know that the most frequent words in a language are often function words (*e.g.* 'the', 'and', 'of', *etc.*) and that these words are not very informative for distinguishing between classes of texts. Third, we know that comparing raw counts across texts conflates the influence text class lengths.

With these considerations in mind, we will tokenize by words and apply a metric known as the **term-frequency inverse-document frequency** (tf-idf). The tf-idf measure, as the name suggests, is the product of tf and idf for each term. In effect, it produces a weighting scheme, which will downweight words that are common across all documents and upweight words that are unique to a document. It also mitigates the varying lengths of the documents. This is a common approach in text classification and is a good starting point for our analysis.

With our features and engineering approach identified, we can move on to step 2 of our workflow and split the data into training and testing sets. We make the splits to our data at this point to draw a line in the sand between the data we will use to train the model and the data we will use to test the model. A typical approach in supervised machine learning is to allocate around 75-80% of the data to the training set and the remaining 20-25% to the testing set, depending on the number of observations. We have 2957 observations in our dataset, so we can allocate 80% of the data to the training set and 20% of the data to the testing set.

In Example 9.4, we will use the `initial_split()` function from {rsample} to split the data into training and testing sets. The `initial_split()` function takes a data frame and a proportion and returns a `split` object which contains the training and testing sets. We will use the `strata` argument to stratify the data by the `outcome` variable. This will ensure that the training and testing sets have the same proportion of native and learner texts.

Example 9.4.

```
set.seed(123) # for reproducibility

# Split the data into training and testing sets
cls_split <-
  initial_split(
    data = cls_tbl,
    prop = 0.8,
    strata = outcome
  )

# Create training set
cls_train <- training(cls_split)  # 80% of data

# Create testing set
cls_test <- testing(cls_split)    # 20% of data
```

A confirmation of the distribution of the data across the training and testing sets as well as a breakdown of the outcome variable, created by {janitor}'s `tabyl()` function, can be seen in Example 9.5.

Example 9.5.

```
# View the distribution
# Training set
cls_train |>
  tabyl(outcome) |>
  adorn_totals("row") |>
  adorn_pct_formatting(digits = 1)

# Testing set
cls_test |>
  tabyl(outcome) |>
  adorn_totals("row") |>
  adorn_pct_formatting(digits = 1)
```

```
 outcome    n percent
 Learner 1524   64.5%
  Native  840   35.5%
   Total 2364  100.0%
 outcome   n percent
 Learner 382   64.4%
  Native 211   35.6%
   Total 593  100.0%
```

We can see that the split was successful. The training and testing sets have very similar proportions of native and learner texts.

We are now ready to create a 'recipe', step 3 in our analysis. A recipe is Tidymodels terminology for a set of instructions or blueprint which specifies the outcome variable and the predictor variable and determines how to pre-process and engineer the feature variables.

We will use the `recipe()` function from {recipes} to create the recipe. The `recipe()` function minimally takes a formula and a data frame and returns a `recipe` object. **R formulas** provide a way to specify relationships between variables and are used extensively in R data modeling. Formulas specify the outcome variable (y) and the predictor variable(s) ($x_1..x_n$). For example, `y ~ x` can be read as "y as a function of x". In our particular case, we will use the formula `outcome ~ text` to specify that the outcome variable is the `outcome` variable and the predictor variable is the `text` variable. The code is seen in Example 9.6.

Example 9.6.

```
# Create a recipe
base_rec <-
  recipe(
    formula = outcome ~ text, # formula
    data = cls_train
    )

# Preview
base_rec
```

```
── Recipe ──────────────────────────────────

── Inputs
Number of variables by role
outcome:   1
predictor: 1
```

The recipe object at this moment contains just one instruction, what the variables are and what their relationship is.

> **Tip**
> R formulas are a powerful way to specify relationships between variables and are used extensively in data modeling including exploratory, predictive, and inferential analysis. The basic formula syntax is `y ~ x` where `y` is the outcome variable and `x` is the feature variable. The formula syntax can be extended to include multiple feature variables, interactions, and transformations. For more information on R formulas, see R for Data Science (Wickham & Grolemund, 2017)

{recipes} provides a wide range of `step_*()` functions which can be applied to the recipe to specify how to engineer the variables in our recipe call. These include functions to scale (*e.g* `step_center()`, `step_scale()`, *etc.*) and transform (*e.g.* `step_log()`, `step_pca()`, *etc.*) numeric variables, and functions to encode (*e.g.* `step_dummy()`, `step_labelencode()`, *etc.*) categorical variables.

These step functions are great when we have selected the variables we want to use in our model and we want to engineer them in a particular way. In our case, however, we need to derive features from the text in the `text` column of datasets before we engineer them.

To ease this process, {textrecipes} provides a number of step functions for pre-processing text data. These include functions to tokenize (*e.g.* `step_tokenize()`), remove stop words (*e.g.* `step_stopwords()`), and to derive meta-features (*e.g.* `step_lemma()`, `step_stem()`, *etc.*)[1]. Furthermore, there are functions to engineer features in ways that are particularly relevant to text data, such as feature frequencies and weights (*e.g.* `step_tf()`, `step_tfidf()`, *etc.*) and token filtering (*e.g.* `step_tokenfilter()`).

> **Dive deeper** For other tokenization strategies and feature engineering methods, see {textrecipes} documentation (Hvitfeldt, 2023). There are, however, packages which provide integration with `textrecipes` for other languages, for example, {washoku} for Japanese text processing (Uryu, 2024).

So let's build on our basic recipe `cls_rec` by adding steps relevant to our task. To extract our features, we will use the `step_tokenize()` function to tokenize the text into words. The default behavior of the `step_tokenize()` function is to tokenize the text into words, but other token units can be derived and various options can be added to the function call (as {tokenizers} is used under the hood). Adding the `step_tokenize()` function to our recipe is seen in Example 9.7.

Example 9.7.

```
# Add step to tokenize the text
cls_rec <-
  base_rec |>
  step_tokenize(text) # tokenize

# Preview
cls_rec
```

[1] Note that functions for meta-features require more sophisticated text analysis software to be installed on the computing environment (e.g. {spacyr} for `step_lemma()`, `step_pos()`, *etc.*). See {textrecipes} documentation for more information.

```
── Recipe ──────────────────────────────────────────

── Inputs
Number of variables by role
outcome:   1
predictor: 1

── Operations
• Tokenization for: text
```

The recipe object `cls_rec` now contains two instructions, one for the outcome variable and one for the feature variable. The feature variable instruction specifies that the text should be tokenized into words.

We now need to consider how to engineer the word features. If we add `step_tf()` we will get a matrix of token counts by default, with the option to specify other weights. The step function `step_tfidf()` creates a matrix of term frequencies weighted by inverse document frequency.

We decided in step 1 that we will start with *tf-idf*, so we will add `step_tfidf()` to our recipe. This is seen in Example 9.8.

Example 9.8.

```
# Add step to tokenize the text
cls_rec <-
  cls_rec |>
  step_tfidf(text, smooth_idf = FALSE)

# Preview
cls_rec
```

```
── Recipe ──────────────────────────────────────────
Number of variables by role
outcome:   1
predictor: 1

── Operations
• Tokenization for: text
• Term frequency-inverse document frequency with: text
```

Tip
The `step_tfidf()` function by default adds a *smoothing term* to the inverse document frequency (idf) calculation. This setting has the effect of reducing the influence of the idf calculation. Thus, terms that appear in many (or all) documents will not be downweighted as much as they would be if the smoothing term was not added. For our purposes, we want to downweight or eliminate the influence of the most frequent terms, so we will set `smooth_idf = FALSE`.

To make sure things are in order and that the recipe performs as expected, we can use the functions `prep()` and `bake()` to inspect the recipe. The `prep()` function takes a recipe object and a data frame and returns a `prep` object. The `prep` object contains the recipe and the data frame with the feature variables engineered according to the recipe. The `bake()` function takes a `prep` object and an optional new dataset to apply the recipe to. If we only want to see the application to the training set, we can use the `new_data = NULL` argument.

In Example 9.9, we use the `prep()` and `bake()` functions to create a data frame with the feature variables. We can then inspect the data frame to see if the recipe performs as expected.

Example 9.9.

```
# Prep and bake
cls_bake <-
  cls_rec |>
  prep() |> # create a prep object
  bake(new_data = NULL) # apply to training set

# Preview
dim(cls_bake)
```

```
[1]  2364 38115
```

The resulting engineered features data frame has 2,364 observations and 38,115 variables. That is a lot of features! Given the fact that for each writing sample, only a small subset of them will actually appear, most of our cells will be filled with zeros. This is what is known as a **sparse matrix**.

Tip
When applying tokenization and feature engineering steps to text data the result is often contained in a matrix object. Using {recipes} a data frame with a matrix-like structure is returned. Remember, a matrix is a data frame where all the vector types are the same.
Furthermore, the features are prefixed with the variable name and transformation step labels. In Example 9.9 we applied tf-idf to the `text` variable. Therefore the features are prefixed with `tfidf_text_`.

But we should pause. This is an unwieldy number of features, on for every single word, for a model and it is likely that many of these features are not useful for our classification task. Furthermore, the more features we have, the more chance these features will capture the nuances of these particular writing samples increasing the likelihood we overfit the model. All in all, we need to reduce the number of features.

We can filter out features by stopword list or by frequency of occurrence. Let's start by frequency of occurrence. We can set the maximum number of the top features with an arbitrary threshold to start. The `step_tokenfilter()` function can filters out features on a number of criteria. Let's use the `max_tokens` argument to set the maximum number of features to 100.

This particular step needs to be applied before the `step_tfidf()` step, so we will add it to our recipe before the `step_tfidf()` step. This is seen in Example 9.10.

Example 9.10.

```
# Rebuild recipe with tokenfilter step
cls_rec <-
  base_rec |>
  step_tokenize(text) |>
  step_tokenfilter(text, max_tokens = 100) |>
  step_tfidf(text, smooth_idf = FALSE)

# Prep and bake
cls_bake <-
  cls_rec |>
  prep() |>
  bake(new_data = NULL)

# Preview
dim(cls_bake)

cls_bake[1:5, 1:5]
```

```
[1] 2364  101
# A tibble: 5 x 5
  outcome tfidf_text_a tfidf_text_ahora tfidf_text_al tfidf_text_amigos
  <fct>          <dbl>            <dbl>         <dbl>             <dbl>
1 Learner      0                    0             0                 0
2 Learner      0.00399              0             0                 0
3 Learner      0.00615              0             0                 0
4 Learner      0                    0             0                 0
5 Learner      0.0111               0             0                 0
```

We now have a manageable set of features, and fewer of which will have a as many zeros. Only during the interrogation step will we know if they are useful.

> **Tip**
> The `prep()` and `bake()` functions are useful for inspecting the recipe and the engineered features, but they are not required to build a recipe. When a recipe is added to a workflow, the `prep()` and `bake()` functions are called automatically as part of the process.

We are now ready to turn our attention to step 5 of our workflow, interrogating the data. In this step, we will first select a classification algorithm, then add this algorithm and our recipe to a workflow object. We will then use the workflow object to train and assess the resulting models, adjusting them until we believe we have a robust final model to apply on the testing set for our final evaluation.

There are many classification algorithms to choose from with their own strengths and shortcomings. In Table 9.3, we list some of the most common classification algorithms and their characteristics.

Table 9.3: Common classification algorithms

Algorithm	Strengths	Shortcomings	Tuning Recommendation
Logistic regression	Interpretable, fast, high-dimensional data	Linear relationship, not for complex tasks	Cross-validate regularization strength
Naive Bayes	Interpretable, fast, high-dimensional data, multi-class	Assumes feature (naive) independence, poor with small data	None
Decision trees	Nonlinear, interpretable, numerical/ categorical data	Overfitting, high variance	Cross-validate maximum tree depth
Random forest	Nonlinear, numerical/ categorical data, less overfitting	Less interpretable, poor with high-dimensional data	Cross-validate number of trees
Support vector machines	Nonlinear, high-dimensional data, numerical/ categorical	Requires parameter tuning, memory intensive	Cross-validate regularization parameter
Neural networks	Nonlinear, large data, auto feature learning	Overfitting, difficult to interpret, expensive	Cross-validate learning rate

In the process of selecting an algorithm, simple, computationally efficient, and interpretable models are preferred over complex, computationally expensive, and uninterpretable models, all things being equal. Only if the performance of the simple model is not good enough should we move on to a more complex model.

> **Tip**
> {parsnip} provides a consistent interface to many different models, 105 at the time of writing. You can peruse the list of models by running `parsnip::model_db`. You can also retrieve the list of potential engines for a given model specification with the `show_engines()` function. For example, `show_engines("logistic_reg")` will return a data frame with the engines available for the logistic regression model specification. Note, the engines represent R packages that need to be installed to use the engine.

With this end mind, we will start with a simple logistic regression model to see how well we can classify the texts in the training set with the features we have engineered. We will use the `logistic_reg()` function from {parsnip} to specify the logistic regression model. We then select the implementation engine (`glmnet` General Linear Model) and the mode of the model (`classification`). The implementation engine is the software that will be used to fit the model. The code to set up the model specification is seen in Example 9.11.

Example 9.11.

```
# Create a model specification
cls_spec <-
  logistic_reg() |>
  set_engine("glmnet")

# Preview
cls_spec
```

```
Logistic Regression Model Specification (classification)

Computational engine: glmnet
```

Now, different algorithms will have different parameters that can be adjusted which can affect the performance of the model (see Table 9.3). As not to confuse these parameters with the features, which are also parameters of the model, these are given the name **hyperparameters**. The adjustment process is called **hyperparameter tuning** and involves fitting the model to the training set with different hyperparameters and evaluating the model's performance to determine the best hyperparameter values to use for the model.

Tip
You can find the hyperparameters for a model-engine by consulting the `parsnip::model_db` object and unnesting the `parameters` column. For example, `parsnip::model_db |> filter(model == "logistic_reg") |> unnest(parameters)` will return a data frame with the hyperparameters for the logistic regression model.
To learn more about the hyperparameters for a specific model, you can consult the documentation for `parsnip` model (*e.g.* `?logistic_reg`).

For example, the logistic regression model using `glmnet` can be tuned to prevent overfitting. The regularization typically applied is the LASSO (L1) penalty[2]. The `logistic_reg()` function takes the arguments `penalty` and `mixture`. We set `mixture = 1`, but we now need to decide what value to use for the strength of the `penalty` argument. Values can range from 0 to 1, where 0 indicates no penalty and 1 indicates a maximum penalty.

Instead of guessing, we will use {tune} to tune the hyperparameters of the model. The `tune()` function serves as a placeholder for the hyperparameters we want to tune. We can add the `tune()` function to our model specification to specify the hyperparameters we want to tune. The code is seen in Example 9.12.

Example 9.12.

```
# Create a model specification (with tune)
cls_spec <-
  logistic_reg(penalty = tune(), mixture = 1) |>
  set_engine("glmnet")

# Preview
cls_spec
```

```
Logistic Regression Model Specification (classification)

Main Arguments:
  penalty = tune()
  mixture = 1

Computational engine: glmnet
```

We can see now that the `cls_spec` model specification now includes the `tune()` function as the value for the `penalty` argument.

[2]The LASSO (least absolute shrinkage and selection operator) is a type of regularization that penalizes the absolute value of the coefficients. In essence, it smooths the coefficients by shrinking them towards zero to avoid coefficients picking up on particularities of the training data that will not generalize to new data.

To tune our model, we will need to combine our recipe and model specification into a workflow object which sequences our feature selection, engineering, and model selection. We will use the `workflow()` function from {workflows} to do this. The code is seen in Example 9.13.

Example 9.13.

```
# Create a workflow
cls_wf <-
  workflow() |>
  add_recipe(cls_rec) |>
  add_model(cls_spec)

# Preview
cls_wf
```

```
══ Workflow ════════════════════════════════════════
Preprocessor: Recipe
Model: logistic_reg()

── Preprocessor ────────────────────────────────────
3 Recipe Steps

• step_tokenize()
• step_tokenfilter()
• step_tfidf()

── Model ───────────────────────────────────────────
Logistic Regression Model Specification (classification)

Main Arguments:
  penalty = tune()
  mixture = 1

Computational engine: glmnet
```

We now have a workflow `cls_wf` that includes our recipe and model specification, including the `tune()` function as a placeholder for a range of values for the penalty hyperparameter. To tune the penalty hyperparameter, we use the `grid_regular()` function from {dials} to specify a grid of values to try. Let's choose a random set of 10 values, as seen in Example 9.14.

Example 9.14.

```
# Create a grid of values for the penalty hyperparameter
cls_grid <-
  grid_regular(penalty(), levels = 10)
```

```

# Preview
cls_grid
```

```
# A tibble: 10 x 1
        penalty
          <dbl>
 1 0.0000000001
 2 0.00000000129
 3 0.0000000167
 4 0.000000215
 5 0.00000278
 6 0.0000359
 7 0.000464
 8 0.00599
 9 0.0774
10 1
```

The 10 values chosen to be in the grid range from nearly 0 to 1, where 0 indicates no penalty and 1 indicates a strong penalty.

Now to perform the tuning and arrive at an optimal value for `penalty` we need to create a tuning workflow. We do this by calling the `tune_grid()` function using our tuning model specification workflow, a resampling object, and our hyperparameter grid and return a `tune_grid` object.

Resampling is a strategy that allows us to generate multiple training and testing sets from a single dataset —in this case the training data we split at the outset. Each generated training-testing pair is called a fold. Which is why this type of resampling is called **k-fold cross-validation**. The `vfold_cv()` function from {rsample} takes a data frame and a number of folds and returns a `vfold_cv` object. We will apply the `cls_wf` workflow to the 10 folds of the training set with `tune_grid()`. For each fold, each of the 10 values of the penalty hyperparameter will be tried and the model's performance will be evaluated. The code is seen in Example 9.15.

Example 9.15.

```
set.seed(123) # for reproducibility

# Create a resampling object
cls_vfold <- vfold_cv(cls_train, v = 10)

# Tune the model
cls_tune <-
  tune_grid(
    cls_wf,
```

```
    resamples = cls_vfold,
    grid = cls_grid
    )

# Preview
cls_tune
```

```
# Tuning results
# 10-fold cross-validation
# A tibble: 10 x 4
   splits             id     .metrics          .notes
   <list>             <chr>  <list>            <list>
 1 <split [2127/237]> Fold01 <tibble [30 x 5]> <tibble [0 x 3]>
 2 <split [2127/237]> Fold02 <tibble [30 x 5]> <tibble [0 x 3]>
 3 <split [2127/237]> Fold03 <tibble [30 x 5]> <tibble [0 x 3]>
 4 <split [2127/237]> Fold04 <tibble [30 x 5]> <tibble [0 x 3]>
 5 <split [2128/236]> Fold05 <tibble [30 x 5]> <tibble [0 x 3]>
 6 <split [2128/236]> Fold06 <tibble [30 x 5]> <tibble [0 x 3]>
 7 <split [2128/236]> Fold07 <tibble [30 x 5]> <tibble [0 x 3]>
 8 <split [2128/236]> Fold08 <tibble [30 x 5]> <tibble [0 x 3]>
 9 <split [2128/236]> Fold09 <tibble [30 x 5]> <tibble [0 x 3]>
10 <split [2128/236]> Fold10 <tibble [30 x 5]> <tibble [0 x 3]>
```

The `cls_tune` object contains the results of the tuning for each fold. We can see the results of the tuning for each fold by calling the `collect_metrics()` function on the `cls_tune` object, as seen in Example 9.16. Passing the `cls_tune` object to `autoplot()` produces the visualization in Figure 9.1.

Example 9.16.

```
# Collect the results of the tuning
cls_tune_metrics <-
  collect_metrics(cls_tune)

# Visualize metrics
autoplot(cls_tune)
```

The most common metrics for model performance in classification are accuracy and the area under the **receiver operating characteristic area under the curve** (ROC-AUC). Accuracy is simply the proportion of correct predictions. The ROC-AUC provides a single score which summarizes how well the model can distinguish between classes. The closer to 1 the more discriminative power the model has.

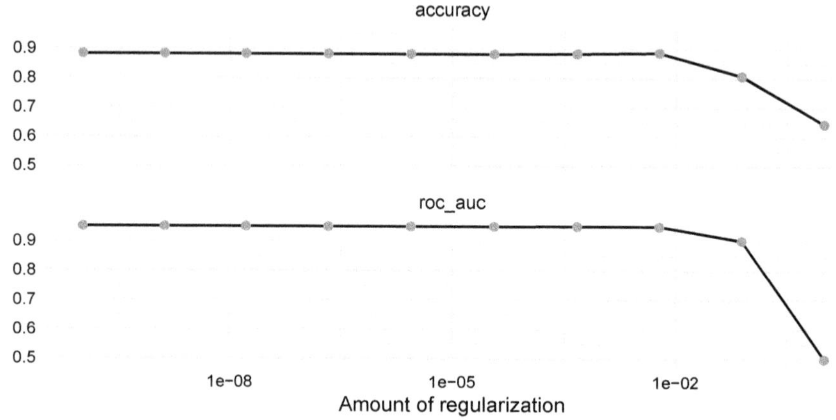

Figure 9.1: Metrics for each fold of the tuning process

In the plot of the metrics, Figure 9.1, we can see that the many of the penalty values performed similarly, with a drop-off in performance at the higher values. Conveniently, the `show_best()` function from {tune} takes a `tune_grid` object and returns the best performing hyperparameter values. The code is seen in Example 9.17.

Example 9.17.

```
# Show the best performing hyperparameter value
cls_tune |>
  show_best(metric = "roc_auc")
```

```
# A tibble: 5 x 7
        penalty .metric .estimator  mean     n std_err .config
          <dbl> <chr>   <chr>      <dbl> <int>   <dbl> <chr>
1 0.000464       roc_auc binary     0.952    10 0.00487 Preprocessor1_Model07
2 0.00599        roc_auc binary     0.952    10 0.00344 Preprocessor1_Model08
3 0.0000000001   roc_auc binary     0.951    10 0.00502 Preprocessor1_Model01
4 0.00000000129 roc_auc binary     0.951    10 0.00502 Preprocessor1_Model02
5 0.0000000167   roc_auc binary     0.951    10 0.00502 Preprocessor1_Model03
```

We can make this selection programmatically by using the `select_best()` function. This function needs a metric to select by. We will use the ROC-AUC and select the best value for the penalty hyperparameter. The code is seen in Example 9.18.

Example 9.18.

```
# Select the best performing hyperparameter value
cls_best <-
  select_best(cls_tune, metric = "roc_auc")

# Preview
cls_best
```

```
# A tibble: 1 x 2
   penalty .config
     <dbl> <chr>
1 0.000464 Preprocessor1_Model07
```

All of that to tune a hyperparameter! Now we can update the model specification and workflow with the best performing hyperparameter value using the previous `cls_wf_tune` workflow and the `finalize_workflow()` function. The `finalize_workflow()` function takes a workflow and the selected parameters and returns an updated `workflow` object, as seen in Example 9.19.

Example 9.19.

```
# Update model specification
cls_wf_lasso <-
  cls_wf |>
  finalize_workflow(cls_best)

# Preview
cls_wf_lasso
```

```
══ Workflow ════════════════════════════════════════════
Preprocessor: Recipe
Model: logistic_reg()

── Preprocessor ────────────────────────────────────────

• step_tokenize()
• step_tokenfilter()
• step_tfidf()

── Model ───────────────────────────────────────────────
Logistic Regression Model Specification (classification)

Main Arguments:
  penalty = 0.000464158883361278
  mixture = 1

Computational engine: glmnet
```

Our model specification and the workflow are updated with the tuned hyperparameter.

As a reminder, we are still working in step 5 of our workflow, interrogating the data. So far, we have selected and engineered the features, split the data into training and testing sets, and selected a classification algorithm. We have also tuned the hyperparameters of the model and updated the model specification and workflow with the best performing hyperparameter value.

The next step is to assess the performance of the model on the training set given the features we have engineered, the algorithm we have selected, and the hyperparameters we have tuned. Instead of evaluating the model on the training set directly, we will use cross-validation on the training set to gauge the variability of the model.

The reason for this is that the model's performance on the entire training set at once is not a reliable indicator of the model's performance on new data —just imagine if you were to take the same test over and over again, you would get better and better at the test, but that doesn't mean you've learned the material any better. Cross-validation is a technique that allows us to estimate the model's performance on new data by simulating the process of training and testing the model on different subsets of the training data.

Similar to what we did to tune the hyperparameters, we can use cross-validation to gauge the variability of the model. The `fit_resamples()` function takes a workflow and a resampling object and returns metrics for each fold. The code is seen in Example 9.20.

Example 9.20.

```
# Cross-validate workflow
cls_lasso_cv <-
  cls_wf_lasso |>
  fit_resamples(
    resamples = cls_vfold,
    # save predictions for confusion matrix
    control = control_resamples(save_pred = TRUE)
  )
```

We want to aggregate the metrics across the folds to get a sense of the variability of the model. The `collect_metrics()` function takes the results of a cross-validation and returns a data frame with the metrics.

Example 9.21.

```r
# Collect metrics
collect_metrics(cls_lasso_cv)
```

```
# A tibble: 3 x 6
  .metric     .estimator   mean     n std_err .config
  <chr>       <chr>       <dbl> <int>   <dbl> <chr>
1 accuracy    binary     0.884     10 0.00554 Preprocessor1_Model1
2 brier_class binary     0.0823    10 0.00385 Preprocessor1_Model1
3 roc_auc     binary     0.952     10 0.00487 Preprocessor1_Model1
```

From the accuracy and ROC-AUC metrics in Example 9.21 it appears we have a decent candidate model, but there is room for potential improvement. A good next step is to evaluate the model errors and see if there are any patterns that can be addressed before considering what approach to take to improve the model.

> **Tip**
> To provide context in terms of what is a good model performance, it is useful to compare the model's performance to a null model. A **null model** (or baseline model) is a simple model that is easy to implement and provides a benchmark for the model's performance. For classification tasks, a common null model is to predict the most frequent class. In modeling, this is the minimal benchmark we want to beat, if we are doing better than this, we are doing better than chance.

For classification tasks, a good place to start is to visualize a confusion matrix. A **confusion matrix** is a cross-tabulation of the predicted and actual outcomes. The `conf_mat_resampled()` function takes a `fit_resamples` object (with predictions saved) and returns a table (`tidy = FALSE`) with the confusion matrix for the aggregated folds. We can pass this to the `autoplot()` function to plot as in Example 9.22.

Example 9.22.

```r
# Plot confusion matrix
cls_lasso_cv |>
  conf_mat_resampled(tidy = FALSE) |>
  autoplot(type = "heatmap")
```

The top left to bottom right diagonal contains the true positives and true negatives. These are the correct predictions. The top right to bottom left diagonal contains the false positives and false negatives—our errors. The convention is to speak of one class being the positive class and the other class being the negative class. In our case, we will consider the positive class to be the 'learner' class and the negative class to be the 'natives' class.

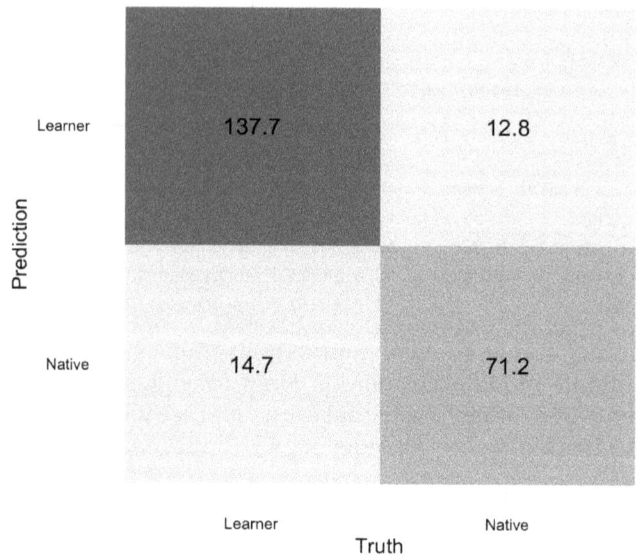

Figure 9.2: Confusion matrix for the aggregated folds of the cross-validation

We can see that there are more learners falsely predicted to be natives than the other way around. This may be due to the fact that there are simply more learners than natives in the dataset or this could signal that there are some learners that are more similar to natives than other learners. Clearly this can't be the entire explanation as the model is not perfect, even some natives are classified falsely as learners! But it may be an interesting avenue for further exploration. Perhaps these are learners that are more advanced or have a particular style of writing that is more similar to natives.

Dive deeper
Another perspective often applied to evaluate a model is the receiver operating characteristic (ROC) curve. The ROC curve is a plot of the true positive rate (TPR) against the false positive rate (FPR) for different classification thresholds. This metric, and visualization, can be useful to gauge the model's ability to distinguish between the two classes. {yardstick} provides the `roc_curve()` function to calculate the ROC curve on an `fit_resamples` object.

To improve supervised learning models, consider:

1. Engineering the features differently
2. Selecting different (or additional) features
3. Changing the algorithm
4. Tuning the hyperparameters differently

Of these options, adjusting the feature engineering process is the option that diverges least from our current workflow `cls_wf_lasso`. Recall that in our recipe specification we set a token filter to limit the number of features to 100. We can adjust this number to see if it has an effect on the model's performance.

To help select the optimal number of tokens, we again can use the tuning process we explored for the hyperparameters. This time, however, the `tune()` placeholder will be included as the argument to the `max_tokens` argument in the `step_tokenfilter()` function.

I repeat the recipe with the tuning placeholder in Example 9.23.

Example 9.23.

```
# Create a recipe with a token filter step
cls_rec <-
  recipe(
    formula = outcome ~ text,
    data = cls_train
    ) |>
  step_tokenize(text) |>
  step_tokenfilter(text, max_tokens = tune()) |>
  step_tfidf(text)
```

With the updated recipe, we can update the `cls_wf_lasso` and tune the `max_tokens` hyperparameter. The code is seen in Example 9.24.

Example 9.24.

```
# Update workflow with token filter tuning
cls_wf_lasso <-
  cls_wf_lasso |>
  update_recipe(cls_rec)
```

One thing to note is that we will want to consider what values of `max_tokens` we want to use to tune the hyperparameter. So instead of only specifying the levels in the `grid_regular()` function, we are best off to provide a range of values that we think are reasonable. Let's add a range of values between our current value 100 and 2,000 to start. And let's tell the grid to select five values from this range.

The code is seen in Example 9.25.

Example 9.25.

```r
# Create a grid of values for the max tokens hyperparameter
cls_grid <-
  grid_regular(max_tokens(range = c(100, 2000)), levels = 5)

# Preview
cls_grid
```

```
# A tibble: 5 x 1
  max_tokens
       <int>
1        100
2        575
3       1050
4       1525
5       2000
```

From here, the process is the same as before. We will use the `tune_grid()` function to tune the `max_tokens` hyperparameter, select the best value, and finalize the workflow, as seen from Example 9.15 through Example 9.19.

After tuning the `max_tokens` hyperparameter, the best performing value is 1,050. We now used the updated `cls_wf_lasso_tokens` workflow to cross-validate the model and collect the metrics. The code is seen in Example 9.26.

Example 9.26.

```r
# Cross-validate workflow
cls_lasso_tokens_cv <-
  cls_wf_lasso_tokens |>
  fit_resamples(
    resamples = cls_vfold,
    # save predictions for confusion matrix
    control = control_resamples(save_pred = TRUE)
  )

# Collect metrics
collect_metrics(cls_lasso_tokens_cv)
```

```
# A tibble: 3 x 6
  .metric     .estimator   mean     n std_err .config
  <chr>       <chr>       <dbl> <int>   <dbl> <chr>
1 accuracy    binary     0.918     10 0.00555 Preprocessor1_Model1
2 brier_class binary     0.0680    10 0.00418 Preprocessor1_Model1
3 roc_auc     binary     0.968     10 0.00289 Preprocessor1_Model1
```

The metrics from Example 9.26 show that the model's performance has improved for both the accuracy and the ROC-AUC. The confusion matrix from Example 9.27 shows that the number of false positives and false negatives has decreased. This is a good sign that the model is more robust.

Example 9.27.

```
# Plot confusion matrix
cls_lasso_tokens_cv |>
  conf_mat_resampled(tidy = FALSE) |>
  autoplot(type = "heatmap")
```

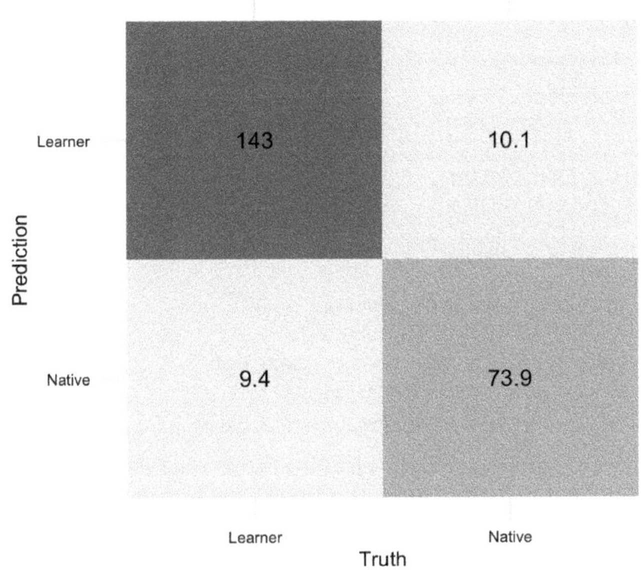

Figure 9.3: Confusion matrix for the aggregated folds of the cross-validation

From Figure 9.3, it appears that the model is more robust with the updated `max_tokens` hyperparameter. We could continue to explore other model improvement strategies, but for now we will move on to the next step in our workflow.

We are now ready to move on to step 7, evaluating the model on the test set. To do this we need to fit the tuned workflow to the training set, which is the actual training phase. We will use the `last_fit()` function from {workflows} to fit the workflow to the training set.

The `last_fit()` function takes a workflow and a split object and returns a `last_fit` object. The `last_fit` object contains the results of the model fit on the training set and the results of the model evaluation on the test set. The code is seen in Example 9.28.

We will use the `last_fit()` function to train the final model and predict the outcome on the test set. The `collect_metrics()` function takes a data frame with the actual and predicted outcomes and returns a data frame with the metrics for the model. The code is seen in Example 9.28.

Example 9.28.

```
# Fit the model to the training set and evaluate on the test set
cls_final_fit <-
  last_fit(
    cls_wf_lasso_tokens,
    split = cls_split
  )

# Evaluate model on testing set
collect_metrics(cls_final_fit)
```

```
# A tibble: 3 x 4
  .metric     .estimator .estimate .config
  <chr>       <chr>          <dbl> <chr>
1 accuracy    binary        0.909  Preprocessor1_Model1
2 roc_auc     binary        0.962  Preprocessor1_Model1
3 brier_class binary        0.0758 Preprocessor1_Model1
```

The performance metrics are very close to those we achieved on the training set in Example 9.26. This is a good sign that the model is robust as it performs well on both training and test sets. We can evaluate the confusion matrix on the test set as well. The code is seen in Example 9.29 and the visualization in Figure 9.4.

Example 9.29.

```
# Plot confusion matrix
cls_final_fit |>
  collect_predictions() |>
  conf_mat(truth = outcome, estimate = .pred_class) |>
  autoplot(type = "heatmap")
```

On the test set the false instances are balanced, which is a good sign that the model is robust. Ideally, there would be no errors, but this is not realistic. The model is not perfect, but it is useful.

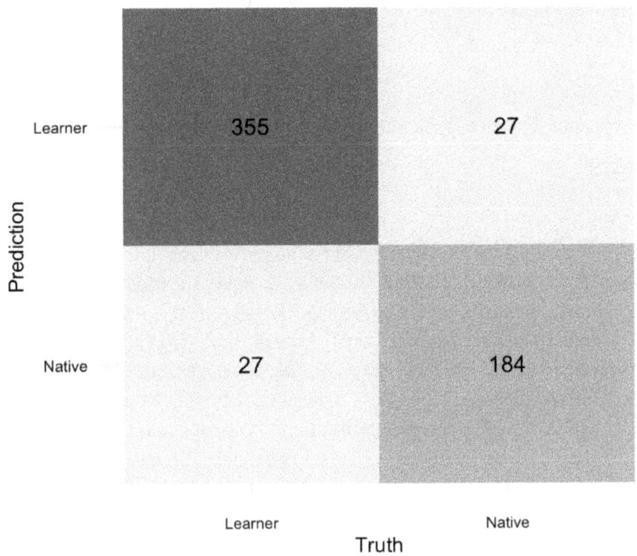

Figure 9.4: Confusion matrix for the test set

Now a model that can predict the nativeness of a writer based on their writing sample is a useful tool in itself. You could imagine that this could be a pre-processing step for a language learning application, for example. But for a study that is more interested in learning about what features are most important for predicting the native versus non-native features of a writer, we still have some work to do. We can inspect the errors on the test set to gain some insight into what writing samples, and which proficiency levels of the writers, are most difficult to predict. We can also inspect the estimates for the features in the model to gain some insight into what features are most important for predicting the outcomes.

Let's first approach this from a document-proficiency point of view. First, we will want to integrate the predictions with the test set to inspect the errors. We can use the `collect_predictions()` function to collect the predictions from the `last_fit` object and attach them with the test set `cls_test` with `bind_cols`. Note, we can drop the `outcome` variable from `cls_test` as we have this column in our fitted model. The code is seen in Example 9.30.

Example 9.30.

```
# Collect predictions from the model
cls_lasso_fit_preds_test <-
  cls_final_fit |>
```

```
  collect_predictions() |>
  bind_cols(cls_test[, -1])

# Preview
glimpse(cls_lasso_fit_preds_test)
```

```
Rows: 593
Columns: 9
$ .pred_class    <fct> Learner, Learner, Learner, Native, Learner, Learner, Lea~
$ .pred_Learner <dbl> 1.0000, 1.0000, 1.0000, 0.0996, 1.0000, 0.9928, 1.0000, ~
$ .pred_Native  <dbl> 9.59e-06, 1.13e-05, 3.16e-09, 9.00e-01, 2.83e-06, 7.17e-~
$ id            <chr> "train/test split", "train/test split", "train/test spli~
$ .row          <int> 3, 7, 15, 21, 22, 25, 36, 43, 47, 50, 53, 57, 62, 66, 68~
$ outcome       <fct> Learner, Learner, Learner, Learner, Learner, Learner, Le~
$ .config       <chr> "Preprocessor1_Model1", "Preprocessor1_Model1", "Preproc~
$ proficiency   <fct> Lower beginner, Lower beginner, Lower beginner, Lower be~
$ text          <chr> "Sanaa Lathan es muy famosa persona. Ella es en de telev~
```

I will then select the columns with the actual outcome, the predicted outcome, the proficiency level, and the text and separate the predicted outcome to inspect them separately, as seen in Example 9.31.

Example 9.31.

```
# Inspect errors
cls_lasso_fit_preds_test |>
  filter(outcome != .pred_class) |>
  select(outcome, .pred_class, proficiency, text)
```

```
# A tibble: 54 x 4
   outcome .pred_class proficiency        text
   <fct>   <fct>       <fct>              <chr>
 1 Learner Native      Lower beginner     "Un día un pequeño nino fue dado una ~
 2 Learner Native      Upper beginner     "Un dia, El niño estaba durmiendo cua~
 3 Learner Native      Upper beginner     "Yo vivo en la ciudad de Atlanta. En ~
 4 Learner Native      Upper beginner     "Hola me llamo Jason.\n Mis amigos es~
 5 Learner Native      Lower intermediate "Recientemente vi una película que es~
 6 Learner Native      Upper intermediate "Vivo en la ciudad de Richmond en Vir~
 7 Learner Native      Upper intermediate "A la semana pasada, yo vi la pelicul~
 8 Learner Native      Upper intermediate "Un día decidí llevarme a casa una ra~
 9 Learner Native      Lower advanced     "Bueno, el año pasado mi novia y yo v~
10 Learner Native      Lower advanced     "Un día Pablo, un niño de 6 años, enc~
# i 44 more rows
```

```
# Inspect learners falsely predicted to be natives
cls_lasso_fit_preds_test |>
```

```
    filter(outcome == "Learner", .pred_class == "Native") |>
    select(outcome, .pred_class, proficiency, text) |>
    count(proficiency, sort = TRUE)
```

```
# A tibble: 6 x 2
  proficiency            n
  <fct>              <int>
1 Upper advanced        10
2 Lower advanced         9
3 Upper beginner         3
4 Upper intermediate     3
5 Lower beginner         1
6 Lower intermediate     1
```

Interestingly, the majority of misclassified learners are advanced, which could be expected as they are more similar to natives. There are some beginners that are misclassified as natives, but this is not as common. Yes, it is still an open question as to why some natives are classified as learners.

We can inspect the estimates for the features in the model to gain some insight into what features are most important for predicting the outcomes. The `extract_fit_parsnip()` function takes a trained model specification `cls_final_fit` and returns a data frame with the estimated coefficients for each feature. The code is seen in Example 9.32.

Example 9.32.

```
# Extract estimates
cls_final_fit_features <-
  cls_final_fit |>
  extract_fit_parsnip() |>
  tidy()
```

The estimates are the log odds of the outcome. In a binary classification task, the log odds of the outcome is the log of the probability of the outcome divided by the probability of the other outcome. In our case, the reference outcome is "Learner", so negative log-odds indicate that the feature is associated with the "Learner" outcome and positive log-odds indicate that the feature is associated with the "Native" outcome.

The estimates are in log-odds, so we need to exponentiate them to get the odds. The odds are the probability of the outcome divided by the probability of the other outcome. The probability of the outcome is the odds divided by the odds plus one. The code is seen in Example 9.33.

Example 9.33.

```
# Calculate probability
cls_final_fit_features |>
  mutate(probability = exp(estimate) / (exp(estimate) + 1))
```

```
# A tibble: 1,051 x 4
   term                   estimate  penalty probability
   <chr>                     <dbl>    <dbl>       <dbl>
 1 (Intercept)              -13.6  0.000464  0.00000129
 2 tfidf_text_10              0    0.000464  0.5
 3 tfidf_text_2               0    0.000464  0.5
 4 tfidf_text_3               0    0.000464  0.5
 5 tfidf_text_4               0    0.000464  0.5
 6 tfidf_text_5               0    0.000464  0.5
 7 tfidf_text_a              64.9  0.000464  1
 8 tfidf_text_abandonado      7.02 0.000464  0.999
 9 tfidf_text_abuela         -8.64 0.000464  0.000176
10 tfidf_text_abuelos         2.14 0.000464  0.895
# i 1,041 more rows
```

So just looking at the snippet of the features returned from Example 9.33, we can see that the features 'a' and 'abandonado' are associated with the "Native" outcome, 'abuela' is associated with "Learners", and the other features are neutral (`probability` = 0.5).

A quick way to extract the most important features for predicting each outcome is to use the `vi()` function from {vip}. It takes a trained model specification and returns a data frame with the most important features. The code is seen in Example 9.34.

Example 9.34.

```
# Load package
library(vip)

# Avoid conflicts for function names from other packages
conflicted::conflicts_prefer(vip::vi)

# Extract important features
var_importance_tbl <-
  cls_final_fit |>
  extract_fit_parsnip() |>
  vi()

# Preview
var_importance_tbl
```

```
# A tibble: 1,050 x 3
   Variable             Importance Sign
   <chr>                     <dbl> <chr>
 1 tfidf_text_época           354. POS
 2 tfidf_text_mayoría         320. NEG
 3 tfidf_text_ésta            312. POS
 4 tfidf_text_ante            278. POS
 5 tfidf_text_proximo         274. NEG
 6 tfidf_text_esperar         245. NEG
 7 tfidf_text_mucha           244. NEG
 8 tfidf_text_seguir          242. POS
 9 tfidf_text_poder           241. POS
10 tfidf_text_ahí             235. POS
# i 1,040 more rows
```

The `Variable` column contains each feature (with the feature type and corresponding variable `tfidf_text_`), `Importance` provides the absolute log-odds value, and the `Sign` column indicates whether the feature is associated with the "NEG" ("Learner") or the "POS" ("Native") outcome. We can recode the `Variable` and `Sign` columns to make them more interpretable and then plot them using `ggplot()`, as in Example 9.35.

Example 9.35.

```
# Recode variable and sign
var_importance_tbl <-
  var_importance_tbl |>
  mutate(
    Feature = str_remove(Variable, "tfidf_text_"),
    Outcome = case_when(
      Sign == "NEG" ~ "Learner",
      Sign == "POS" ~ "Native"),
    ) |>
  select(Outcome, Feature, Importance)

# Plot
var_importance_tbl |>
  slice_max(Importance, n = 50) |>
  ggplot(aes(x = reorder(Feature, Importance), y = Importance)) +
  geom_point() +
  coord_flip() +
  facet_wrap(~ Outcome, scales = "free_y") +
  labs(x = NULL, y = "Importance", fill = NULL) +
  theme_minimal(base_size = 10)
```

We can inspect Figure 9.5, and qualitatively assess what these features may be telling us about the differences between the learners and the natives.

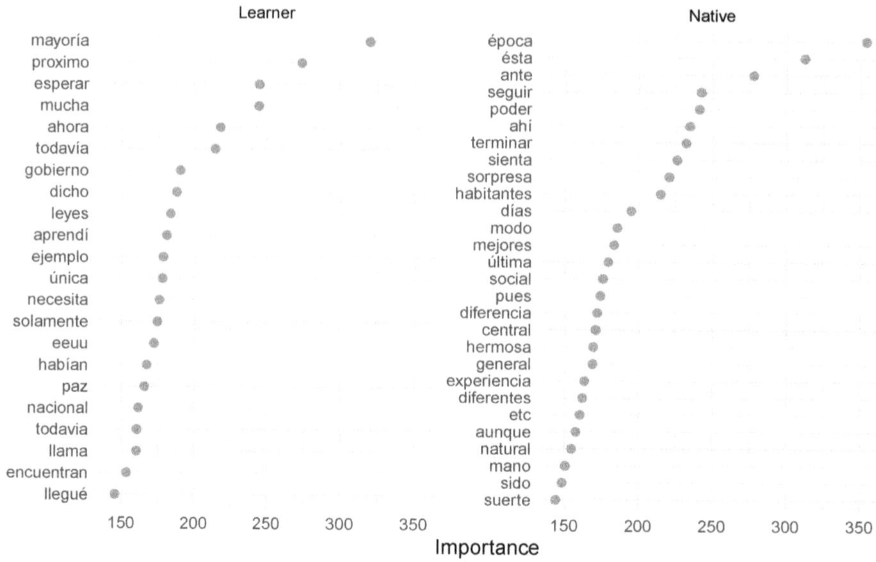

Figure 9.5: Most important features for predicting the outcome

In this section, we've build a text classifier using a regularized logistic regression model. We've tuned the hyperparameters to arrive at a robust model that performs well on both the training and test sets. We've also evaluated the model errors and inspected the most important features for predicting the outcome.

9.2.2 Text regression

We will now turn our attention to the second task in this section, text regression. In this task, we will use the same original dataset as in the classification task, but we will predict the placement score based on the learner writing samples. I will make reference to but not repeat the steps we took in the classification task, as many of the steps are the same. This is one of the benefits of using Tidymodels—the workflow is by-and-large the same for different tasks.

Let's start by extracting the observations (only learners) and the relevant variables from the original dataset. The code is seen in Example 9.36.

Example 9.36.

```
# Extract observations and relevant variables
reg_tbl <-
```

```
  cedel_tbl |>
  filter(subcorpus == "Learner") |>
  select(outcome = place_score, proficiency, text)

# Preview
glimpse(reg_tbl)
```

```
Rows: 1,906
Columns: 3
$ outcome     <dbl> 14.0, 16.3, 16.3, 18.6, 18.6, 18.6, 20.9, 20.9, 20.9, 20.9~
$ proficiency <fct> Lower beginner, Lower beginner, Lower beginner, Lower begi~
$ text        <chr> "Yo vivo es Alanta, Georgia. Atlanta es muy grande ciudad.~
```

In this task, our outcome variable is numeric and our predictor variable `text` is the same as before. It might be useful to engineer the features differently, but we will start with the same feature engineering process as before, namely the tf-idf method for the top 1,050 words.

I create a data split, `reg_split` and the training and testing sets, `reg_train` and `reg_test` and create a `reg_rec` recipe object which contains the starting recipe for the regression task. And, since we are using the same recipe as before, there is no need to validate the recipe. We can skip straight to the model building.

As before, we will want to start with a simple model and then build up to more complex models. The list in Table 9.3, includes algorithms that are commonly used in classification tasks. Interestingly, many of these same algorithms can be applied to regression. One exception is that instead of logistic regression, linear regression is used for numeric outcomes. As with logistic regression, linear regression model is one of the simpler models. And just as with logistic regression, we will want to tune the regularization hyperparameter of the linear regression model. Instead of detailing these steps again, let me summarize the process, in Table 9.4, and then we will discuss the results from the regularized linear regression model.

Table 9.4: Steps to build and tune a model

Step	Description
1	Build a model specification with a placeholder to tune the model.
2	Create a workflow with the recipe and the model specification.
3	Create a grid of values for the regularization hyperparameter.
4	Tune the model using cross-validation.
5	Select the best performing hyperparameter value (based on RMSE).
6	Update the model specification and workflow with the best performing hyperparameter value.
7	Fit the model to the training set and evaluate the performance using cross-validation.

Applying the steps 1 through 7, we have cross-validated results for our model in the `reg_lasso_cv` object. We can collect the relevant metrics, root mean squared error (RMSE) and R-squared (R^2) values. Let's aggregate these measures using the code is seen in Example 9.37.

Example 9.37.

```
# Collect metrics
collect_metrics(reg_lasso_cv)
```

```
# A tibble: 2 x 6
  .metric .estimator   mean     n std_err .config
  <chr>   <chr>       <dbl> <int>   <dbl> <chr>
1 rmse    standard   14.1      10  0.269  Preprocessor1_Model1
2 rsq     standard    0.621    10  0.0119 Preprocessor1_Model1
```

Now, the **root mean squared error** (RMSE) estimate is 14.1. RMSE is a measure of the difference between the predicted and the actual values expressed in the same units as the outcome variable. In this case, the outcome variable is the placement test score percent. So the RMSE is 14.1 percentage points. **R-squared** (R^2) is a measure of the proportion of the variance in the outcome variable that is explained by the model. The R^2 estimate is 0.621. This means that the model explains 62% of the variance in the outcome variable. Taken together, this isn't the greatest model.

But how good or bad is it? This is where we can use the null model to compare the model to. The null model is a model that predicts the mean of the outcome variable for each of the outcomes. We can use the `null_model()` function to create a null model and submit it to cross-validation, Example 9.38.

Example 9.38.

```
# Create null model
null_model <-
  null_model() |>
  set_engine("parsnip") |>
  set_mode("regression")

# Cross-validate null model
null_cv <-
  workflow() |>
  add_recipe(reg_rec) |>
  add_model(null_model) |>
  fit_resamples(
    resamples = vfold_cv(reg_train, v = 10),
    metrics = metric_set(rmse)
  )
```

```r

# Collect metrics
collect_metrics(null_cv)
```

```
# A tibble: 1 x 6
  .metric .estimator  mean     n std_err .config
  <chr>   <chr>      <dbl> <int>   <dbl> <chr>
1 rmse    standard    22.6    10   0.203 Preprocessor1_Model1
```

> **⚠ Warning**
> For model specifications in which the model can be used in a classification or regression task, the model specification must be set to the correct mode before fitting the model. We have not set the mode for the `logistic_reg()` or `linear_reg()` model specifications, as the task is inferred. However, we have set the mode for the `null_model()`, and other model specifications that can be used in both classification and regression tasks.

Our regression model performs better than the null model (22.6), which means that it is picking up on some signal in the data.

Let's visualize the distribution of the predictions and the errors from our model to see if there are any patterns of interest. We can use the `collect_predictions()` function to extract the predictions of the cross-validation and plot the true outcome against the predicted outcome using `ggplot()`, as in Example 9.39.

Example 9.39.

```r
# Visualize predictions
reg_lasso_cv |>
  collect_predictions() |>
  ggplot(aes(outcome, .pred, shape = id)) +
  geom_point(alpha = 0.5, position = position_jitter(width = 0.5)) +
  geom_smooth(method = "lm", se = FALSE, linewidth = 0.5) + # trend for each
  ↪ fold
  labs(
    x = "Truth",
    y = "Predicted score",
    shape = "Fold"
  )
```

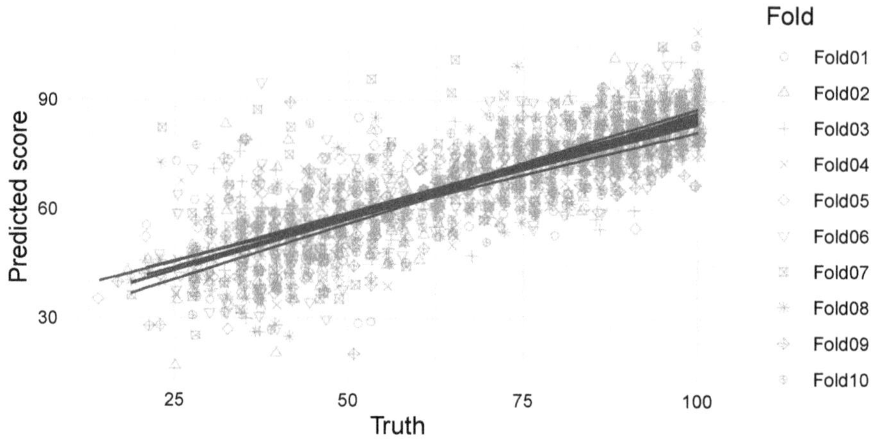

Figure 9.6: Distribution of the RMSE for the cross-validated linear regression model

From Figure 9.6, we see data points for each predicted and truth value pair for each of the ten folds. There is a trend line for each fold which shows the linear relationship between the predicted and truth values for each fold. The trend lines are more similar than different, which is a good sign that the model is not wildly overfitting the training data. Looking closer, however, we can see the errors. Some are noticeably distant from the linear trend lines, *i.e.* outliers, in particular for test scores in the lower ranges.

If the R^2 value is in the ballpark, this means that somewhere around 40% of the variation is not explained by the frequency of the top 1,050 words. This is not surprising, as there are many other factors that contribute to the proficiency level of a text.

We have a model that is performing better than the null model, but it is not performing well enough to be very useful. We will need to update the model specification and/ or the features to try to improve the model fit. Let's start with the model. There are many different model specifications we could try, but we will likely need to use a more complex model specification to capture the complexity that we observe in the errors from the current linear regression model.

Let's try a decision tree model. **Decision trees** are models that are able to model nonlinear relationships and interactions between the features and the outcome and tend to be less influenced by outliers. Furthermore, decision trees are interpretable, which is a nice feature for an exploratory-oriented analysis. These are all desirable characteristics. Decision trees, however, can be prone to overfitting. For this reason, we will tune the maximum depth of the tree to minimize overfitting.

To implement a new model in Tidymodels, we need to create a new model specification and a new workflow. We will use the `decision_tree()` function from {parsnip} to create the model specification. The `decision_tree()` function takes a `tree_depth` argument that we want to tune. We create the new model specification with the tuning placeholder in Example 9.40.

Example 9.40.

```
# Create model specification
reg_spec <-
  decision_tree(tree_depth = tune()) |>
  set_engine("rpart") |>
  set_mode("regression")

# Preview
reg_spec
```

```
Decision Tree Model Specification (regression)

Main Arguments:
  tree_depth = tune()

Computational engine: rpart
```

With the model and tuning specification in place, we can now continue through the steps outlined in Table 9.4 for this decision tree model. To create the grid of values for the tree depth hyperparameter, we will include the `grid_regular()` function with 10 levels, as seen in Example 9.41.

Example 9.41. Tuning values for the tree depth hyperparameter

```
reg_grid <-
  grid_regular(tree_depth(), levels = 10)
```

We can collect the metrics and inspect the RMSE and R^2 values. The code is seen in Example 9.42.

Example 9.42.

```
# Collect metrics
collect_metrics(reg_tree_cv)
```

```
# A tibble: 2 x 6
  .metric .estimator  mean     n std_err .config
  <chr>   <chr>      <dbl> <int>   <dbl> <chr>
1 rmse    standard   15.9     10  0.256  Preprocessor1_Model1
2 rsq     standard    0.510   10  0.0210 Preprocessor1_Model1
```

The performance for the decision tree is worse than the regularized linear regression model. The RMSE is 15.9 and the R^2 is 0.51. And, if we compare the standard error between the two models, we can see that the decision tree model has a lower standard error. This means that the decision tree model is likely overfitting, despite our efforts to tune tree depth.

Given the sensitivity of the decision tree branching process and random initialization, it is possible that the decision tree model is capturing too much nuance, and not enough generalities. Re-running the model with a different seed may result in a different model. This is a limitation with decision tree models, but it is also a feature, if we consider combining multiple decision trees to make a prediction. This is the basis of **ensemble models**. An ensemble model is a model that combines multiple models with the goal to draw out the strengths of each model and minimize the weaknesses.

A **random forest** is an ensemble model that combines multiple decision trees to make a prediction. In addition, random forests also perform random feature selection. This helps to reduce the correlation between the decision trees and thus works to reduce the overall variance of the model.

Let's try a random forest model to address our text regression task. We will use the `rand_forest()` function from {parsnip} to create the model specification. The `rand_forest()` function also takes a hyperparameter for the number of trees to be used in the model. We will select the `ranger` engine. Additionally, we will add the `importance` argument to ensure that we can extract feature importance if this model proves to be useful. We create the new model specification in Example 9.43.

Example 9.43.

```r
# Create model specification
reg_spec <-
  rand_forest(trees = tune()) |>
  set_engine("ranger", importance = "impurity") |>
  set_mode("regression")

# Preview
reg_spec
```

```
Random Forest Model Specification (regression)

Main Arguments:
  trees = tune()

Engine-Specific Arguments:
  importance = impurity

Computational engine: ranger
```

> **Consider this**
> The model building process is iterative and many of the steps are the same. This is a good indication that creating a custom function to build and tune the model would be a good idea.
> Consider the following: What would you include in the function? What would you leave out? What required and/ or optional arguments would you include? What would you hard code? What would you return?

Again, we apply the steps in Table 9.4 to build and tune the random forest model. As part of this process, I will limit the range of the number of trees from 100 to 500 in five levels in the tuning grid, as seen in Example 9.44.

Example 9.44. Tuning values for the number of trees hyperparameter

```
reg_grid <-
  grid_regular(trees(range = c(100, 500)), levels = 5)
```

Let's collect the metrics and inspect the RMSE and R^2 values. The code is seen in Example 9.45.

Example 9.45.

```
# Collect metrics
collect_metrics(reg_rf_cv)
```

```
# A tibble: 2 x 6
  .metric .estimator   mean     n std_err .config
  <chr>   <chr>       <dbl> <int>   <dbl> <chr>
1 rmse    standard   12.9      10  0.320  Preprocessor1_Model1
2 rsq     standard    0.697    10  0.0164 Preprocessor1_Model1
```

The random forest model performs better than the decision tree model and the regularized linear regression model. The RMSE is 12.9 and the R^2 is 0.697. We also see that the standard error falls between the models we have tried so far.

Before we settle on this model, let's try one more model. In this case, we will introduce a neural network model. **Neural networks** are models that are able to model nonlinear relationships and interactions between the features and the outcome. They are also able to model complex relationships between the features and the outcome. We will use the `mlp()` function from {parsnip} to create the model specification. We will choose the `brulee` engine which allows us to tune the learning rate. The learning rate is a hyperparameter that controls the size of the steps that the model takes to update the weights during training.

> **⚠ Warning**
> The `brulee` engine requires that the Torch computing resources are available on the computing environment. To facilitate the installation, {torch} provides the `install_torch()` function. This is a one-time operation. From this point on, R packages which depend on Torch will be able to take advantage of this rich machine learning framework.

We create the new model specification with the tuning placeholder in Example 9.46.

Example 9.46.

```
# Create model specification
reg_spec <-
  mlp(learn_rate = tune()) |>
  set_engine("brulee") |>
  set_mode("regression")

# Preview
reg_spec
```

```
Single Layer Neural Network Model Specification (regression)

Main Arguments:
  learn_rate = tune()

Computational engine: brulee

Model fit template:
brulee::brulee_mlp(x = missing_arg(), y = missing_arg(), learn_rate = tune())
```

And include the code in Example 9.47 to create a grid of values for the learning rate hyperparameter, as part of the model building workflow.

Example 9.47. Tuning values for the learning rate hyperparameter

```
reg_grid <-
  grid_regular(learn_rate(), levels = 10)
```

Let's collect the metrics and inspect the RMSE and R^2 values. The code is seen in Example 9.48.

Example 9.48.

```
# Collect metrics
collect_metrics(reg_mlp_cv)
```

```
# A tibble: 2 x 6
  .metric .estimator   mean     n std_err .config
  <chr>   <chr>       <dbl> <int>   <dbl> <chr>
1 rmse    standard   14.7      10  0.951  Preprocessor1_Model1
2 rsq     standard    0.627     9  0.0214 Preprocessor1_Model1
```

So in summary, we've tried four different model specifications. The regularized linear regression model, the decision tree model, the random forest model, and the neural network model. The random forest model performed the best. For each of these models, however, we have only tried word features measured by $tf\text{-}idf$. We could imagine that the performance of these models could be improved by varying the features to include bigrams, for example. We could also explore different measures of word usage. Furthermore, for some of our models, we could try different engines and/ or hyperparameters (some have more than one!).

We could continue to try to explore these possible combinations, and you likely would in your research. But at this point we have a model that is performing better than the null model and is performing better than the other models we have tried. So we will consider this model to be good enough for our purposes.

Let's take our random forest model, fit it to our training data, apply it to the testing data, and collect the metrics on the test set. The code is seen in Example 9.49.

Example 9.49.

```
# Fit the model to the training set and
# evaluate on the test set
reg_final_fit <-
  last_fit(
    reg_wf_rf,
    split = reg_split
  )

# Evaluate model on testing set
collect_metrics(reg_final_fit)
```

```
# A tibble: 2 x 4
  .metric .estimator .estimate .config
  <chr>   <chr>          <dbl> <chr>
1 rmse    standard      12.9   Preprocessor1_Model1
2 rsq     standard       0.689 Preprocessor1_Model1
```

OK. The difference between the cross-validated metrics and the metrics for the test set differ —but only slightly. This suggests that the model is robust and that we have not overfit the data from the training set.

Now, our likely goal as an academic is to understand something about the features that contribute to the performance of the model. So let's approach extracting feature importance from the random forest model we build with the `ranger` engine. Remember, we added an `importance` argument to the `set_engine()` function and set it to 'impurity'. We can now take advantage by using {vip} to extract the feature importance. The code is seen in Example 9.50.

Example 9.50.

```
# Extract feature importance
reg_vip <-
  reg_final_fit |>
  extract_fit_parsnip() |>
  vi(scale = TRUE)

# Preview
reg_vip |>
  slice_head(n = 10)
```

```
# A tibble: 10 x 2
   Variable         Importance
   <chr>                 <dbl>
 1 tfidf_text_que        100
 2 tfidf_text_es          68.8
 3 tfidf_text_una         57.4
 4 tfidf_text_por         57.2
 5 tfidf_text_pero        54.0
 6 tfidf_text_del         48.5
 7 tfidf_text_con         46.1
 8 tfidf_text_se          44.9
 9 tfidf_text_para        44.1
10 tfidf_text_muy         43.6
```

We can now visualize the feature importance of the model. The code is seen in Example 9.51.

Example 9.51.

```
# Extract predictions
reg_vip |>
  mutate(Variable = str_replace(Variable, "^tfidf_text_", "")) |>
  slice_max(Importance, n = 20) |>
  # reorder variables by importance
  ggplot(aes(reorder(Variable, Importance), Importance)) +
  geom_point() +
  coord_flip() +
  labs(
```

```
    x = "Feature",
    y = "Importance"
  )
```

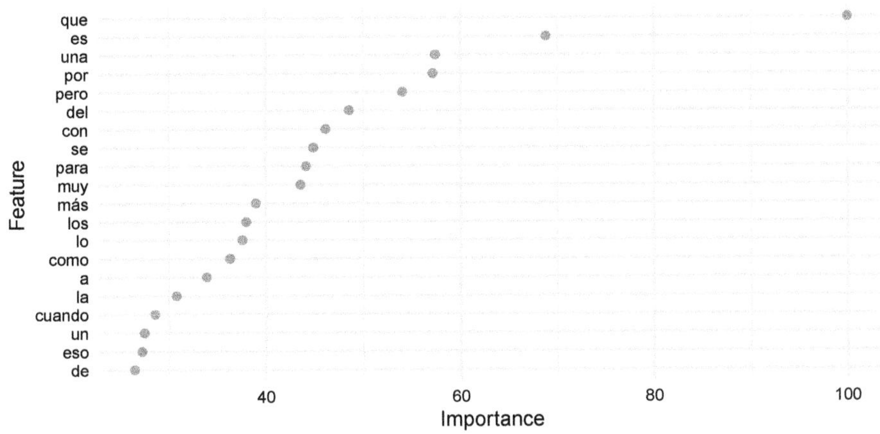

Figure 9.7: Feature importance of the random forest model

In this section, we've built text regression models focusing on the ability to change algorithms and hyperparameters. We have also seen some of the differences between evaluating model performance between classification and regression tasks. There are many more combinations of model specifications and feature selection and engineering that can be applied. In your research, you will find yourself using these tools to explore the best model for your data.

Activities

In the following activities, we will apply the concepts and techniques we have learned in this chapter. We will use the Tidymodels framework to build and evaluate supervised machine learning models for text classification and regression tasks.

> **Recipe**
> **What**: Building predictive models
> **How**: Read Recipe 9, complete comprehension check, and prepare for Lab 9.
> **Why**: To continue to build experience building predictive models with the Tidymodels framework.

Lab
What: Text classification
How: Clone, fork, and complete the steps in Lab 9.
Why: To apply your knowledge of supervised machine learning to a text classification task.

Summary

In this chapter, we outlined the workflow for approaching predictive modeling and the Tidymodels framework. We then applied the workflow to text classification and regression tasks. In the process, we gained experience identifying, selecting, and engineering features on the one hand, and building and tuning models on the other. To evaluate the models, we used cross-validation for performance and finalized our interpretation with techniques to extract feature importance.

10

Infer

> **Outcomes**
>
> - Identify the research goals of inferential data analysis
> - Describe the workflow for inferential data analysis
> - Indicate the importance of quantifying uncertainty in inferential data analysis

In this chapter, we consider approaches to deriving knowledge from information which can be generalized to the population from which the data is sampled. This process is known as statistical inference. The discussion here implements descriptive assessments, statistical tests, and evaluation procedures for a series of contexts which are common in the analysis of corpus-based data. During our treatment of these contexts, we will establish a foundational understanding of statistical inference using a simulation-based approach.

> **>_ Lessons**
> **What**: Advanced Tables
> **How**: In an R console, load {swirl}, run `swirl()`, and follow prompts to select the lesson.
> **Why**: To explore how to enhance dataset summaries using {janitor} and present them effectively with {kableExtra}'s advanced formatting options.

10.1 Orientation

In contrast to exploratory and predictive analyses, inference is not a data-driven endeavor. Rather, the goal of inferential data analysis (IDA) is to make theoretical claims about the population and assess the extent to which the data supports those claims. This implicates two key methodological restrictions which are not in play in other analysis methods.

10.4324/9781003393764.10

First, the research question and expected findings are formulated *before* the data is analyzed, in fact strictly speaking this should take place even before data collection. This helps ensure that the data is aligned with the research question, that the data is representative of the population, and that the analysis has a targeted focus and does not run the risk of becoming a 'just-so' story[1] or a 'significance-finding' mission[2], both of which violate the principles of significance testing.

Second, the data used in IDA is only used once. That is to say, the entire dataset is used a single time to statistically interrogate the relationship(s) of interest. In both exploratory and predictive data analysis the data can be approached multiple times in different ways and the results of the analysis can be used to inform the next steps in the analysis. In IDA, however, the data is used to test a specific hypothesis and the results of the analysis are interpreted in the context of that hypothesis.

The methodological approach to IDA is the most straightforward of the analysis types covered in this textbook. As the research goal is to test a claim, the steps necessary are fewer than in EDA or PDA, where the exploratory nature of these approaches includes various possible iterations. The workflow for IDA is shown in Table 10.1.

Table 10.1: Workflow for inferential data analysis

Step	Name	Description
1	Identify	Identify and map the hypothesis statement to the appropriate response and explanatory variables
2	Inspect	Assess the distribution of the variable(s) with the appropriate descriptive statistics and visualizations.
3	Interrogate	Apply the appropriate statistical procedure to the dataset.
4	Interpret	Review the statistical results and interpret them in the context of the hypothesis.

Based on the hypothesis statement, we first identify and operationalize the variables. The response variable is the variable whose variation we aim to explain. Additionally, in most statistical designs, one or more explanatory variables are included in the analysis in an attempt to gauge the extent to which these variables account for the variation in the response variable. For both response and explanatory variables, it is key to confirm that your operationalization of the variables is well-defined and that the data aligns.

[1]"Hypothesis After Result is Known" (HARKing) involves selectively analyzing data, trying different variables or combinations until a significant p-value is obtained, or stopping data collection when a significant result is found (Kerr, 1998).

[2]"p-hacking" is the practice of running multiple tests until a statistically significant result is found. This practice violates the principles of significance testing (Head, Holman, Lanfear, Kahn, & Jennions, 2015).

Consider this
What are the explanatory and/or response variables in each of these statements? How are these variables operationalized? What key sampling features are necessary for the data to test these hypotheses?

1. There will be statistically significant differences in the kinds of collocations used in English dialects spoken in urban areas compared to those spoken in rural areas.
2. French L2 learners will make more vocabulary errors in oral production than in written production.
3. The association strength between Mandarin words and their English translations will be a significant predictor of translation difficulty for novice translators.
4. The prevalence of gender-specific words in German-speaking communities on distinct online forums will significantly reflect gender roles.
5. The frequency of function words used by Spanish L2 learners will be a significant predictor of their stage in language acquisition.

Next, we determine the informational values of the variables. The informational value of each variable will condition how we approach visualization, interrogation, and ultimately interpretation of the results. Note that some informational types can be converted to other types, specifically higher-order types can be converted to lower-order types. For example, a continuous variable can be converted to a categorical variable, but not vice versa. It is preferable, however, to use the highest informational value of a variable. Simplifying data results in a loss of information —which will result in a loss of information and hence statistical power which may lead to results that obscure meaningful patterns in the data (Baayen, 2004).

With our design in place, we can now inspect the data. This involves assessing the distribution of the variables using descriptive statistics and visualizations. The goal of this step is to confirm the integrity of the data (missing data, anomalies, *etc.*), identify general patterns in the data, and identify potential outliers. As much as this is a verification step, it also serves to provide a sense of the data and the extent to which the data aligns with the hypothesis. This is particularly true when statistical designs are complex and involve multiple explanatory variables. An appropriate visualization provides context for interpreting the results of the statistical analysis.

Interrogating the data involves applying the appropriate statistical procedure to the dataset. In the **Null Hypothesis Significance Testing** (NHST) paradigm, this process includes calculating a statistic from the data, comparing it to a null hypothesis distribution, and measuring the evidence against the null hypothesis. The **null hypothesis distribution** is a distribution of statistic values that we would expect if the null hypothesis were true, *i.e.* that there is no difference or relationship between the explanatory and/or response variables. By comparing the observed statistic to the null hypothesis distribution, we can determine the likelihood of observing the observed statistic, if the null hypothesis were true. The estimate of this likelihood is a ***p*-value**. When the p-value is below a threshold, typically 0.05, the result is considered statistically significant. This means that the observed statistic is sufficiently different from the null hypothesis distribution that we can reject the null hypothesis.

Now let's consider how to approach interpreting the results from a statistical test. The p-value provides a probability that the results of our statistical test could be explained by the null hypothesis. When this probability is below the alpha level of 0.05, the result is considered statistically significant, otherwise we have a 'null result' (*i.e.* non-significant).

However, this sets up a binary distinction that can be problematic. On the one hand, what is one to do if a test returns a p-value of 0.051? According to standard practice these "marginally significant" results would not be statistically significant. On the other hand, if we get a statistically significant result, say a p-value of 0.049, do we move on —case closed? To address both of these issues, it is important to calculate a confidence interval for the test statistic. The **confidence interval** is the range of values for our test statistic that we would expect the true statistic value to fall within some level of uncertainty. Again, 95% is the most common level of uncertainty. The upper and lower bounds of this range are called the confidence limits for the test statistic.

Used in conjunction with p-values, confidence intervals can provide a more nuanced interpretation of the results of a statistical test. For example, if we get a p-value of 0.051, but the confidence interval is very narrow, we can be more confident that the results are reliable. Conversely, if we get a p-value of 0.049, but the confidence interval is very wide, we can be less confident that the results are reliable. If our confidence interval contains the null value, then even a significant p-value will require a more nuanced interpretation.

> **Dive deeper**
> Overgeneralization and undergeneralization are more formally known as Type I and Type II error, respectively. Type I error (false positive) occurs when we reject the null hypothesis when it is true. That is, we erroneously detect a significant result, when in fact the tested relationship is not borne out in the population. Type II error (false negative) occurs when we fail to reject the null hypothesis when it is false. This is a case of missing a significant result due to the limitations of the analysis which can stem from the sample size, the design of the study, or the statistical test used.

It is important to underscore that the purpose of IDA is to draw conclusions from a dataset which are generalizable to the population. These conclusions require that there are rigorous measures to ensure that the results of the analysis do not overgeneralize (suggest there is a relationship when there is not one) and balance that with the fact that we don't want to undergeneralize (miss the fact that there is a relationship in the population, but our analysis was not capable of detecting it).

10.2 Analysis

In this section, we will discuss the practical application of inferential data analysis. The discussion will be divided into two sections based on the type of response variable: categorical and numeric. We will then explore specific designs for univariate, bivariate, and multivariate tests. We will learn and implement NHST using a simulation-based workflow. In contrast to theory-based methods, simulation-based methods tend to be more intuitive, easier to implement, and provide a better conceptual understanding of the statistical designs and analyses (Morris, White, & Crowther, 2019; Rossman & Chance, 2014).

The steps for implementing a simulation-based approach to significance testing are outlined in Table 10.2.

Table 10.2: Simulation-based workflow for significance testing

Step	Name	Description
1	Specify	Specify the variables of interest and their relationship
2	Calculate	Calculate the observed statistic
3	Hypothesize	Generate the null hypothesis distribution
4	Get p-value	Calculate the p-value
5	Get confidence interval	Calculate the confidence interval

{infer} (Bray et al., 2024) provides a Tidyverse-friendly framework to implement simulation-based methods for statistical inference. Designed to be used in conjunction with {tidyverse}, {infer} provides a set of functions that can be used to specify the variables of interest, calculate the observed statistic, generate the null hypothesis distribution and calculate the p-value and the confidence interval.

Let's load the necessary packages we will use in this section, as seen in Example 10.1.

Example 10.1.

```r
# Load packages
library(infer)      # for statistical inference
library(skimr)      # for descriptive statistics
library(janitor)    # for cross-tabulation
```

10.2.1 Categorical

Here we demonstrate the application of IDA to categorical response variables. This will include various common statistical designs and analyses. In Table 10.3, we see common design scenarios, the variables involved, and the statistic used in the analysis.

Table 10.3: Statistical test designs for categorical response variables

Scenario	Explanatory Variable(s)	Statistical Test	infer
Univariate	-	Proportion	`prop`
Bivariate	Categorical	Difference in proportions	`diff in props`
Bivariate	Categorical (3+ levels)	Chi-square	`chisq`
Multivariate	Categorical or Numeric	Logistic regression	`fit()`

We will use a derived version of the `dative` dataset from {languageR} (Baayen & Shafaei-Bajestan, 2019). It contains over 3k observations describing the realization of the recipient clause in English dative constructions drawn from Switchboard corpus and the Treebank Wall Street Journal collection. To familiarize ourselves with the dataset, let's consider the data dictionary in Table 10.4.

Table 10.4: Data dictionary for the `dative_tbl` dataset.

variable	name	type	description
rcp_real	Realization of RCP	categorical	The realization of the recipient (NP/PP)
modality	Modality	categorical	The modality of the utterance (spoken/written)
rcp_len	Length of RCP	numeric	The length of the recipient (number of words)
thm_len	Length of THM	numeric	The length of the theme (number of words)

We see that this dataset has four variables, two categorical and two numeric. In our demonstrations we are going to use the `rcp_real` as the response variable, the variable whose variation we are investigating.

For a bit more context, a dative is the phrase which reflects the entity that takes the recipient role in a ditransitive clause. In English, the recipient (dative) can be realized as either a prepositional phrase (PP) as seen in Example 10.2 (1) or as a noun phrase (NP) as seen in (2).

Example 10.2. Dative examples

(1) John gave the book [to Mary $_{PP}$].
(2) John gave [Mary $_{NP}$] the book.

Together these two syntactic options are known as the Dative Alternation (Bresnan, Cueni, Nikitina, & Baayen, 2007).

Let's go ahead and load the dataset, as seen in Example 10.3.

Example 10.3.

```
# Load datasets
dative_tbl <-
  read_csv("../data/dative_ida.csv")
```

In preparation for statistical analysis, I performed a statistical overview and diagnostics of the dataset. This included checking for missing data, outliers, and anomalies. I also checked the distribution of the variables using descriptive statistics and visualizations, noting that the `rcp_len` and `thm_len` variables are right-skewed. This is something to keep in mind. The results of this overview and diagnostics are not shown here, but they are important steps in the IDA workflow. In this process, I converted the character variables to factors as most statistical tests require factors. A preview of the dataset is shown in Example 10.4.

Example 10.4.

```
# Preview
glimpse(dative_tbl)
```

```
Rows: 3,263
Columns: 4
$ rcp_real <fct> NP, NP, NP, NP, NP, NP, NP, NP, NP, NP, NP, NP, NP, NP, NP, N~
$ modality <fct> written, written, written, written, written, written, written~
$ rcp_len  <dbl> 1, 2, 1, 1, 2, 2, 2, 1, 1, 1, 2, 2, 1, 2, 1, 1, 4, 1, 2, 1, 2~
$ thm_len  <dbl> 14, 3, 13, 5, 3, 4, 4, 1, 11, 2, 3, 3, 5, 2, 8, 2, 35, 3, 4, ~
```

We can see that the dataset includes 3,263 observations. We will take a closer look at the descriptive statistics for the variables as we prepare for each analysis.

Univariate analysis

The univariate analysis is the simplest statistical design and analysis. It includes only one variable. The goal is to describe the distribution of the levels of the variable. The `rcp_real` variable has two levels: NP and PP. A potential research question for a case like this may aim to test the claim that:

- NP realizations of the recipient clause are the canonical form in English dative constructions, and therefore will be the most frequent realization of the recipient clause.

This hypothesis can be tested using a **difference in proportion test**. The null hypothesis is that there is no difference in the proportion of NP and PP realizations of the recipient clause. The alternative hypothesis is that NP realizations of the recipient clause are more frequent than PP realizations of the recipient clause.

Before we get into statistical analysis, it is always a good idea to cross-tabulate or visualize the question, depending on the complexity of the relationship. In Example 10.5, we see the code shows the distribution of the levels of the `rcp_real` variable in a contingency table.

Example 10.5.

```
# Contingency table of `rcp_real`
dative_tbl |>
  tabyl(rcp_real) |>
  adorn_pct_formatting(digits = 2) |>
  kable() |>
  kable_styling()
```

Table 10.5: Distribution of the levels of the `rcp_real` variable.

rcp_real	n	percent
NP	2414	73.98%
PP	849	26.02%

From Table 10.5, we see that the proportion of NP realizations of the recipient clause is higher than the proportion of PP realizations of the recipient clause. However, we cannot conclude that there is a difference in the proportion of NP and PP realizations of the recipient clause. We need to conduct a statistical test to determine if the difference is statistically significant.

To determine if the distribution of the levels of the `rcp_real` variable is different from what we would expect if the null hypothesis were true, we need to calculate the difference observed in the sample and compare it to the differences observed in many samples where the null hypothesis is true.

First, let's calculate the proportion of NP and PP realizations of the recipient clause in the sample. We turn to the `specify()` function from {infer} to specify the variable of interest, step 1 in the simulation-based workflow in Table 10.2. In this case, we only have the response variable. Furthermore, the argument `success` specifies the level of the response variable that we will use as the 'success'. The term 'success' is used because the `specify()` function was designed for binomial variables where the levels are 'success' and 'failure', as seen in Example 10.6.

Example 10.6.

```
# Specify the variable of interest
dative_spec <-
  dative_tbl |>
  specify(
    response = rcp_real,
    success = "NP"
  )

# Preview
dative_spec
```

```
Response: rcp_real (factor)
# A tibble: 3,263 x 1
   rcp_real
   <fct>
 1 NP
 2 NP
 3 NP
 4 NP
 5 NP
 6 NP
 7 NP
 8 NP
 9 NP
10 NP
# i 3,253 more rows
```

The `dative_spec` is a data frame with attributes which are used by {infer} to maintain information about the statistical design for the analysis. In this case, we only have information about what the response variable is.

Step 2 is to calculate the observed statistic. The `calculate()` function is used to calculate the proportion statistic setting `stat = "prop"`, as seen in Example 10.7.

Example 10.7.

```
# Calculate the proportion statistic
dative_obs <-
  dative_spec |>
  calculate(stat = "prop")

# Preview
dative_obs
```

```
Response: rcp_real (factor)
# A tibble: 1 x 1
   stat
  <dbl>
1 0.740
```

Note that the observed statistic, proportion, is the same as the proportion we calculated in Table 10.5. In such a simple example, the summary statistic and the observed statistic are the same. But this simple example shows how choosing the 'success' level of the response variable is important. If we had chosen the 'PP' level as the 'success' level, then the observed statistic would be the proportion of PP realizations of the recipient clause. There is nothing wrong with choosing the 'PP' level as the 'success' level, but it would change the direction of the observed statistic.

Now that we have the observed statistic, our goal will be to determine if the observed statistic is different from what we would expect if the null hypothesis were true. To do this, we simulate samples where the null hypothesis is true, step 3 in our workflow.

Simulation means that we will randomly sample from the `dative_tbl` data frame many times. We need to determine how the sampling takes place. Since `rcp_real` is a variable with only two levels, the null hypothesis is that both levels are equally likely. In other words, in a null hypothesis world, NP and PP we would expect the proportions to roughly be 50/50.

To formalize this hypothesis with `infer` we use the `hypothesize()` function and set the null hypothesis to "point" and the proportion to 0.5. Then we can `generate()` a number of samples, say 1,000, drawn from our 50/50 world. Finally, the `prop` (proportion) statistic is calculated for each of the 1,000 samples and returned in a data frame, as seen in Example 10.8.

Example 10.8.

```
# Generate the null hypothesis distribution
dative_null <-
  dative_spec |>
```

```
  hypothesize(null = "point", p = 0.5) |>
  generate(reps = 1000, type = "draw") |>
  calculate(stat = "prop")

# Preview
dative_null
```

```
Response: rcp_real (factor)
Null Hypothesis: point
# A tibble: 1,000 x 2
   replicate  stat
       <int> <dbl>
 1         1 0.486
 2         2 0.493
 3         3 0.497
 4         4 0.512
 5         5 0.492
 6         6 0.496
 7         7 0.498
 8         8 0.491
 9         9 0.499
10        10 0.502
# i 990 more rows
```

The result of Example 10.8 is a data frame with as many rows as there are samples. Each row contains the proportion statistic for each sample drawn from the hypothesized distribution that the proportion of NP realizations of the recipient clause is 0.5.

To appreciate the null hypothesis distribution, we can visualize it using a histogram. {infer} provides a convenient `visualize()` function for visualizing distributions, as seen in Example 10.9.

Example 10.9.

```
# Visualize the null hypothesis distribution
visualize(dative_null)
```

In Figure 10.1, we see that on the x-axis is the proportion statistic of NP realizations of the recipient clause that we would expect if the null hypothesis were true. For the 1,000 samples, the proportion statistic ranges from 0.47 to 0.53. Importantly we can appreciate that most of the proportion statistics are around 0.5. In fact, the mean is 0.5 with a standard deviation of 0.01, which is what we would expect if the null hypothesis were true. But there is variation, as we would also expect.

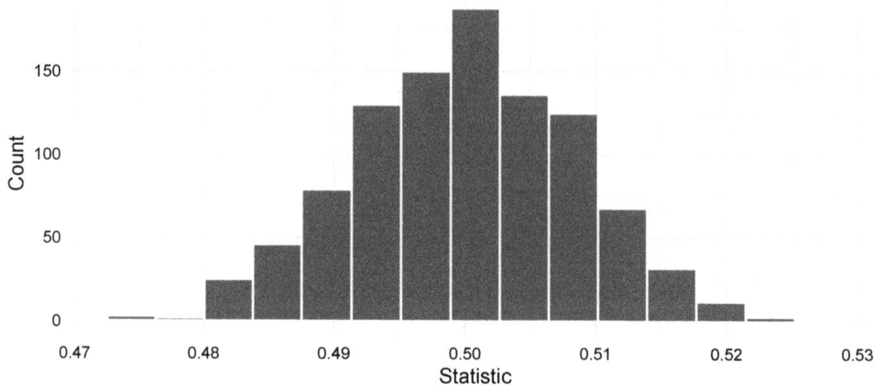

Figure 10.1: Simulation-based null distribution

Why would we expect variation? Consider the following analogy. If we were to flip a fair coin 10 times, we would expect to get 5 heads and 5 tails. But this doesn't always happen. Sometimes we get 6 heads and 4 tails. Sometimes we get 7 heads and 3 tails, and so on. As the number of flips increases, however, we would expect the proportion of heads to be closer to 0.5, but there would still be variation. The same is true for the null hypothesis distribution. As the number of samples increases, we would expect the proportion of NP realizations of the recipient clause to be closer to 0.5, but there would still be variation. The question is whether the observed statistic we obtained from our data, in Example 10.7, is within some level of variation that we would expect if the null hypothesis were true.

Let's visualize the observed statistic on the null hypothesis distribution, as seen in Figure 10.2, to gauge whether the observed statistic is within some level of variation that we would expect if the null hypothesis were true. The `shade_p_value()` function will take the null hypothesis distribution and the observed statistic and shade the sample statistics that fall within the alpha level.

Example 10.10.

```
dative_null |>
  visualize() + # note we are adding a visual layer `+`
  shade_p_value(
    obs_stat = dative_obs, # the observed statistic
    direction = "greater" # the direction of the alternative hypothesis
  )
```

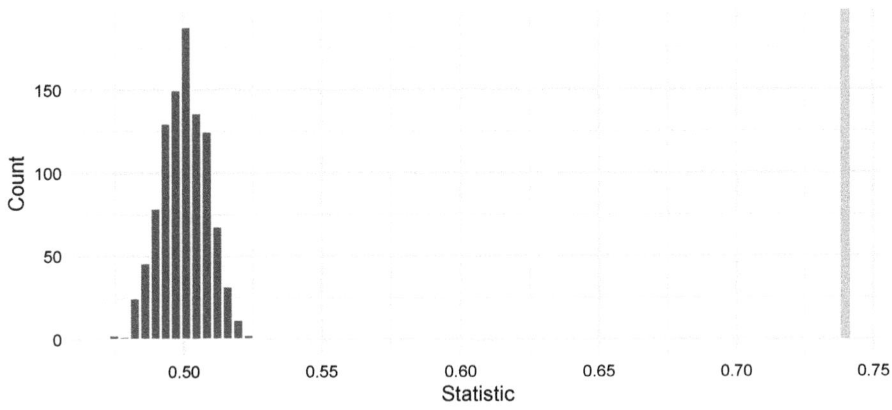

Figure 10.2: Simulation-based null distribution with the observed statistic.

Just from a visual inspection, it is obvious that the observed statistic lies far away from the null distribution, far right of the right tail. No shading appears in this case as the observed statistic is far from the expected variation. This suggests that the observed statistic is not within the level of variation that we would expect if the null hypothesis were true.

> **Tip**
> The direction of the alternative hypothesis is important because it determines the p-value range. The "two-sided" direction means that we are interested in the proportion being different from 0.5. If we were only interested in the proportion of one outcome being greater than 0.5, then we would use the "greater" direction, or "less" in the opposite scenario.

But we need to quantify this. We need to calculate the probability of observing the observed statistic or a more extreme statistic if the null hypothesis were true, the p-value. Calculating this estimate is step 4 in the workflow. The p-value is calculated by counting the number of samples in the null hypothesis distribution that are more extreme than expected within some level of uncertainty. 95% is the most common level of uncertainty, which is called the **alpha level**. The remaining 5% of the distribution is the space where the likelihood that the null hypothesis accounts for the statistic is below our given alpha level of 0.05. This means that if the p-value is less than 0.05, then we reject the null hypothesis. If the p-value is greater than 0.05, then we fail to reject the null hypothesis.

With `infer` we can calculate the p-value using the `get_p_value()` function. Let's calculate the p-value for our observed statistic, as seen in Example 10.11.

Example 10.11.

```
# Calculate the $p$-value (observed statistic)
dative_null |>
  get_p_value(
    obs_stat = dative_obs, # the observed statistic
    direction = "greater" # the direction of the alternative hypothesis
  )
```

```
# A tibble: 1 x 1
  p_value
    <dbl>
1       0
```

```
Warning message:
Please be cautious in reporting a $p$-value\index{p-value} of 0. This result
↪ is an approximation based on the number of `reps` chosen in the
`generate()` step.
```

The p-value for our observed statistic is reported as 0, with a warning that the p-value estimate is contingent on the number of samples we generate in the null distribution. 1,000 is a reasonable number of samples, so we likely have a statistically significant result at the alpha level of 0.05.

The p-value is one, traditionally very common, estimate of uncertainty. Another estimate of uncertainty is the confidence interval, our 5th and final step. The confidence interval is the range of values for our test statistic that we would expect the true statistic value to fall within some level of uncertainty. Again, 95% is the most common level of uncertainty. The upper and lower bounds of this range are called the **confidence limits** for the test statistic. The confidence interval is calculated by calculating the confidence limits for the test statistic for many samples from the observed data. But instead of generating a null hypothesis distribution, we generate a distribution based on resampling from the observed data. This is called the bootstrap distribution. The **bootstrap distribution** is generated by resampling from the observed data, with replacement, many times. This simulates the process of sampling from the population many times. Each time the test statistic is generated for each sample. The confidence limits are the 2.5th and 97.5th percentiles of the bootstrap distribution. The confidence interval is the range between the confidence limits.

In Example 10.12, we see the code for calculating the confidence interval for our observed statistic.

Example 10.12.

```
# Generate bootstrap distribution
dative_boot <-
  dative_spec |>
  generate(reps = 1000, type = "bootstrap") |>
  calculate(stat = "prop")

dative_ci <-
  dative_boot |>
  get_confidence_interval(level = 0.95) # 95% confidence interval

dative_ci
```

```
# A tibble: 1 x 2
  lower_ci upper_ci
     <dbl>    <dbl>
1    0.725    0.755
```

Let's visualize the confidence interval using the `visualize()` and `shade_confidence_interval()` function in Example 10.13 on our bootstrapped samples, as seen in Figure 10.3.

Example 10.13.

```
# Visualize the bootstrap distribution with the confidence interval
dative_boot |>
  visualize() +
  shade_confidence_interval(
    dative_ci # the confidence interval
  )
```

The confidence level is the probability that the confidence interval contains the true value. The confidence level is typically set to 0.95 in the social sciences. This means that if the confidence interval contains the null hypothesis value, then we fail to reject the null hypothesis. If the confidence interval does not contain the null hypothesis value, then we reject the null hypothesis.

Confidence intervals are often misinterpreted. Confidence intervals are not the probability that the true value is within the range. The true value is either within the range or not. The confidence interval is the probability that the range contains the true value. This is a subtle but important distinction. Interpreted correctly, confidence intervals can enhance our understanding of the uncertainty of our test statistic and reduces the interpretation of p-values

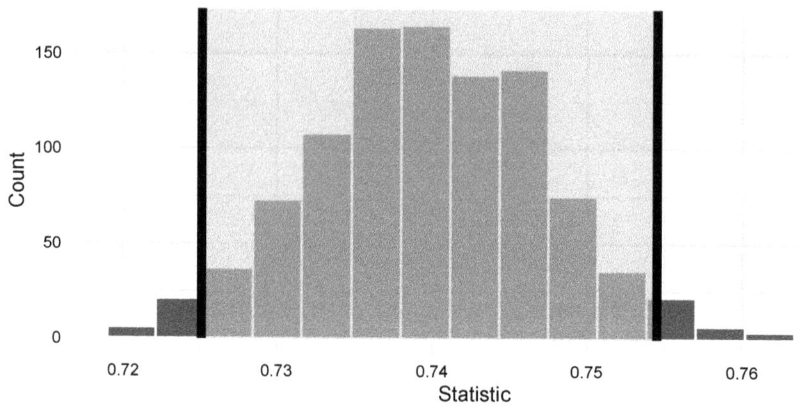

Figure 10.3: Bootstrap distribution of the proportion of NP realizations of the recipient clause with the confidence interval.

(which are based on a relatively arbitrary alpha level) as a binary decision, significant or not significant. Confidence intervals encourage us to think about the uncertainty of our test statistic, as we would expect the true value to fall somewhere within that range, with varying levels of uncertainty.

Our stat is 0.74 and the confidence interval limits are 0.725 and 0.755. The confidence interval does not contain the null hypothesis value of 0.5, which supports the evidence from the p-value that the proportion of NP realizations of the recipient clause is greater than 0.5.

Bivariate analysis

The univariate case is not very interesting or common in statistical inference, but it is a good place to start to understand the simulation-based process and the logic of statistical inference. The bivariate case, on the other hand, is much more common and interesting. The bivariate case includes two variables. The goal is to test the relationship between the two variables.

Using the `dative_tbl` dataset, we can imagine making the claim that:

- The proportion of NP and PP realizations of the recipient clause are contingent on the modality.

This hypothesis can be approached using a **difference in proportions** test, as both variables are binomial (have two levels). The null hypothesis is that there is no difference in the proportion of NP and PP realizations of the recipient clause by modality. The alternative hypothesis is that there is a difference in the proportion of NP and PP realizations of the recipient clause by modality.

We can cross-tabulate or visualize, but let's cross-tabulate this relationship as it is a basic 2-by-2 contingency table. In Example 10.14, we see the code for the cross-tabulation of the `rcp_real` and `modality` variables. Note I've made use of {janitor} to adorn this table with percentages, totals, and observation numbers.

Example 10.14.

```
dative_tbl |>
  tabyl(rcp_real, modality) |> # cross-tabulate
  adorn_totals(c("row", "col")) |> # provide row and column totals
  adorn_percentages("col") |> # add percentages to the columns
  adorn_pct_formatting(rounding = "half up", digits = 0) |> # round the
  ↪ digits
  adorn_ns() |> # add observation number
  adorn_title("combined") |> # add a header title
  kable(booktabs = TRUE) |>  # pretty table)
  kable_styling()
```

Table 10.6: Contingency table for `rcp_real` and `modality`.

rcp_real/modality	spoken	written	Total
NP	79% (1,859)	61% (555)	74% (2,414)
PP	21% (501)	39% (348)	26% (849)
Total	100% (2,360)	100% (903)	100% (3,263)

In Table 10.6, we can appreciate that the proportion of NP realizations of the recipient clause is higher in both modalities, as we might expect from our univariate analysis. However, the proportion appears to be different with the spoken modality having a higher proportion of NP realizations of the recipient clause than the written modality. But we cannot conclude that there is a difference in the proportion of NP and PP realizations of the recipient clause by modality. We need to conduct a statistical test to determine if the difference is statistically significant.

To determine if the distribution of the levels of the `rcp_real` variable by the levels of the `modality` variable is different from what we would expect if the null hypothesis were true, we need to calculate the difference observed in the sample and compare it to the differences observed in many samples where the null hypothesis is true.

{infer} provides a pipeline, steps 1 through 5, which maintains a consistent workflow for statistical inference. As such, the procedure is very similar to the univariate analysis we performed, with some adjustments. Let's focus on the adjustments. First, our `specify()` call needs to include the relationship between two variables: `rcp_real` and `modality`. The `response` argument is the response variable, which is `rcp_real`. The `explanatory` argument is the explanatory variable, which is `modality`.

There are two approaches to specifying the relationship between the response and explanatory variables. The first approach is to specify the response variable and the explanatory variable separately as values of the arguments `response` and `explanatory`. The second approach is to specify the response variable and the explanatory variable as a formula using the ~ operator. The formula approach is more flexible and allows for more complex relationships between the response and explanatory variables. In Example 10.15, we see the code for the `specify()` call using the formula approach.

Example 10.15.

```
# Specify the relationship between the response and explanatory variables
dative_spec <-
  dative_tbl |>
  specify(
    rcp_real ~ modality,
    success = "NP"
  )

# Preview
dative_spec
```

```
Response: rcp_real (factor)
Explanatory: modality (factor)
# A tibble: 3,263 x 2
   rcp_real modality
   <fct>    <fct>
 1 NP       written
 2 NP       written
 3 NP       written
 4 NP       written
 5 NP       written
 6 NP       written
 7 NP       written
 8 NP       written
 9 NP       written
10 NP       written
# i 3,253 more rows
```

The `dative_spec` now contains attributes about the response and explanatory variables encoded into the data frame.

We now calculate the observed statistic with `calculate()`, as seen in Example 10.16.

Example 10.16.

```
# Calculate the observed statistic
dative_obs <-
  dative_spec |>
  calculate(
    stat = "diff in props",
    order = c("spoken", "written")
  )

# Preview
dative_obs
```

```
Response: rcp_real (factor)
Explanatory: modality (factor)
# A tibble: 1 x 1
   stat
  <dbl>
1 0.173
```

Two differences are that our statistic is now a difference in proportions and that we are asked to specify the order of the levels of `modality`. The statistic is clear, we are investigating whether the proportion of NP realizations of the recipient clause is different between the spoken and written modalities. The order of the levels of `modality` is important because it determines the direction of the alternative hypothesis, specifically how the statistic is calculated (the order of the subtraction).

So our observed statistic 0.173 is the proportion of NP realizations of the recipient clause in the spoken modality minus the proportion of NP realizations of the recipient clause in the written modality, so the NP realization appears 17% more in the spoken modality compared to the written modality.

The question remains, is this difference statistically significant? To answer this question, we generate the null hypothesis distribution and calculate the p-value, as seen in Example 10.17.

Example 10.17.

```
# Generate the null hypothesis distribution
dative_null <-
  dative_spec |>
```

```
  hypothesize(null = "independence") |>
  generate(reps = 1000, type = "permute") |>
  calculate(stat = "diff in props", order = c("spoken", "written"))

# Calculate the $p$-value
dative_null |>
  get_p_value(
    obs_stat = dative_obs, # the observed statistic
    direction = "two-sided" # the direction of the alternative hypothesis
  )
```

```
# A tibble: 1 x 1
  p_value
    <dbl>
1       0
```

Note, when generating the null hypothesis distribution, we use the `hypothesize()` function with the `null` argument set to "independence". This is because we are interested in the relationship between the response and explanatory variables. The null hypothesis is that there is no relationship between the response and explanatory variables. When generating the samples, we use the permutation approach, which randomly shuffles the response variable values for each sample. This simulates the null hypothesis that there is no relationship between the response and explanatory variables.

The p-value is reported as 0. To provide some context, we will generate a confidence interval for our observed statistic using the bootstrap method, as seen in Example 10.18.

Example 10.18.

```
# Generate bootstrap distribution
dative_boot <-
  dative_spec |>
  generate(reps = 1000, type = "bootstrap") |>
  calculate(stat = "diff in props", order = c("spoken", "written"))

# Calculate the confidence interval
dative_ci <-
  dative_boot |>
  get_confidence_interval(level = 0.95)

# Preview
dative_ci
```

```
# A tibble: 1 x 2
  lower_ci upper_ci
     <dbl>    <dbl>
1    0.137    0.209
```

The confidence interval does not contain the null hypothesis value of 0 (no difference), which provides evidence that the proportion of NP realizations of the recipient clause is different between the spoken and written modalities.

Multivariate analysis

In many scenarios, it is common to have multiple explanatory variables that need to be considered. In such cases, logistic regression is a suitable modeling technique. Logistic regression allows for the inclusion of both categorical and continuous explanatory variables. The primary objective of using logistic regression is to assess the association between these variables and the response variable. By analyzing this relationship, we can determine how changes in the explanatory variables influence the probability of the outcome occurring.

To explore this scenario, let's posit that:

- NP and PP realizations of the recipient clause are contingent on modality and word length ratio of the recipient and theme.

The length ratio gets at the length of the recipient clause relative to the length of the theme clause. This ratio is an operationalization of a phenomenon known as 'Heavy NP' shift. There are many ways to operationalize this phenomenon, but the length ratio is a simple method to approximate the phenomenon. It attempts to capture the idea that the longer the theme clause is relative to the recipient clause, the more likely the recipient clause will be realized as an NP —in other words, when the theme is relatively longer than the recipient, the theme is ordered last in the sentence, and the recipient is ordered first in the sentence and takes the form of an NP (instead of a PP).

The hypothesis, then, is that Example 10.19 (2) would be less likely than (1) because the theme is relatively longer than the recipient.

Example 10.19.

> (1) John gave [Mary $_{\text{NP}}$] the large book that I showed you in class yesterday.
> (2) John gave the large book that I showed you in class yesterday [to Mary $_{\text{PP}}$].

Let's consider this variable `length_ratio` and `modality` together as explanatory variables for the realizations of the recipient clause `rcp_real`.

Let's create the `length_ratio` variable by dividing the `thm_len` by the `rcp_len`. This will give us values larger than 1 when the theme is longer than the recipient. And since we are working with a skewed distribution, let's log-transform the `length_ratio` variable. In Example 10.20, we see the code for creating the `length_ratio` variable.

Example 10.20.

```
# Create the `length_ratio_log` variable
dative_tbl <-
  dative_tbl |>
  mutate(
    length_ratio_log = log(thm_len / rcp_len)
  ) |>
  select(-thm_len, -rcp_len)

# Preview
glimpse(dative_tbl)
```

```
Rows: 3,263
Columns: 3
$ rcp_real         <fct> NP, NP, NP, NP, NP, NP, NP, NP, NP, NP, NP, NP, NP, N~
$ modality         <fct> written, written, written, written, written, written,~
$ length_ratio_log <dbl> 2.639, 0.405, 2.565, 1.609, 0.405, 0.693, 0.693, 0.00~
```

Let's visualize the relationship between `rcp_real` and `length_ratio_log` separately and then together with `modality`, as seen in Example 10.21.

Example 10.21.

```
# Visualize the proportion of `rcp_real` by `modality`
dative_tbl |>
  ggplot(aes(x = rcp_real, fill = modality)) +
  geom_bar(position = "fill") +
  labs(
    x = "Realization of recipient clause",
    y = "Proportion",
    fill = "Modality"
  )

# Visualize the relationship between `rcp_real` and `length_ratio_log`
dative_tbl |>
  ggplot(aes(x = rcp_real, y = length_ratio_log)) +
  geom_boxplot() +
  labs(
    x = "Realization of recipient clause",
    y = "Length ratio"
  )
```

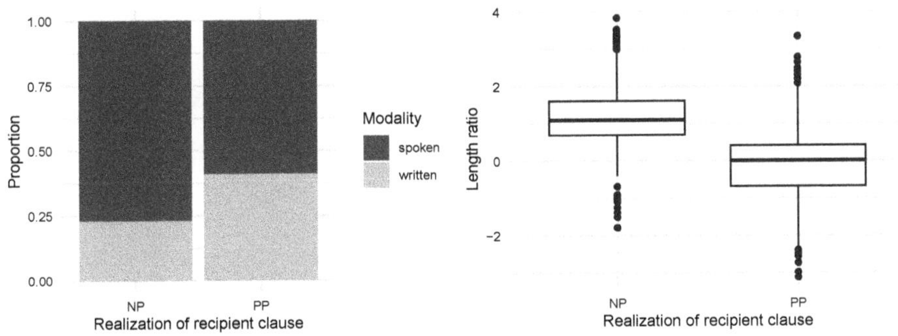

(a) RCP by modality (b) RCP by length ratio

Figure 10.4: Distribution the variables `modality` and `length_ratio_log` by the levels of the `rcp_real` variable.

To understand visualizations in Figure 10.4, remember the null hypothesis is that there is no difference in the proportion of NP and PP realizations of the recipient clause by modality or length ratio. On the flip side, the alternative hypothesis is that there is a difference in the proportion of NP and PP realizations of the recipient clause by modality and length ratio. From the visual inspection, it appears that NP realizations of the recipient clause are more common in the spoken modality and that the NP realizations have a higher overall length ratio (larger theme relative to recipient) than PP realizations of the recipient clause. This suggests that the alternative hypothesis is likely true, but we need to conduct a statistical test to determine if the differences are statistically significant.

Let's calculate the statistics (not statistic) for our logistic regression by specifying the relationship between the response and explanatory variables and then using `fit()` to fit the logistic regression model, as seen in Example 10.22.

Example 10.22.

```
# Specify the relationship
dative_spec <-
  dative_tbl |>
  specify(
    rcp_real ~ modality + length_ratio_log
  )

# Fit the logistic regression model
dative_fit <-
  dative_spec |>
```

```
  fit()

# Preview
dative_fit
```

```
# A tibble: 3 x 2
  term              estimate
  <chr>                <dbl>
1 intercept           -0.563
2 modalitywritten      1.01
3 length_ratio_log    -1.63
```

> **Tip**
> The reference level in R is assumed to be the first level alphabetically, unless otherwise specified. We can override this default by using the `fct_relevel()` function from {forcats} (Wickham, 2023a). The reason we would want to do this is to make the reference level more interpretable. In our case, we would want to make the spoken modality the reference level. This allows us to estimate the difference of the proportion of NP realizations of the recipient as a positive value. Remember that in Figure 10.4a, the proportion of NP realizations of the recipient clause is higher in the spoken modality than in the written modality. If we were to use the written modality as the reference level, the difference would be negative. Not that we couldn't interpret this, but working with positive integers is easier to interpret.

Note I pointed out statistics, not statistic. In logistic regression models, the number of statistic reported depends on the number of explanatory variables. If there are two variables there will be at least three terms, one for each variable and the intercept term. If one or more variables are categorical, however, there will be additional terms when the categorical variable has three or more levels.

In our case, the `modality` variable has two levels, so there are three terms. The first term is the intercept term, which is the log odds of the proportion of NP realizations of the recipient clause in the written modality when the `length_ratio_log` is 1. The second term is the log odds of the proportion of NP realizations of the recipient clause in the spoken modality when the `length_ratio_log` is 1. The third term is the log odds of the proportion of NP realizations of the recipient clause when the `length_ratio_log` is 1 in the written modality. Notably, the spoken modality does not explicitly appear but is implicitly represented by the `modalitywritten` term statistic. `modalityspoken` is used as the reference level for the `modality` variable. For categorical variables, one of the levels is used as the point of reference, or **reference level**, for which every other level is compared.

Now let's generate the null hypothesis distribution and calculate the p-value for each of the terms, as seen in Example 10.23.

Example 10.23.

```
# Generate the null hypothesis distribution
dative_null <-
  dative_spec |>
  hypothesize(null = "independence") |>
  generate(reps = 1000, type = "permute") |>
  fit()

# Calculate the $p$-value
dative_null |>
  get_p_value(
    dative_fit, # the observed statistics
    direction = "two-sided" # the direction of the alternative hypothesis
  )
```

```
# A tibble: 3 x 2
  term              p_value
  <chr>               <dbl>
1 intercept               0
2 length_ratio_log        0
3 modalitywritten         0
```

It appears that our main effects, `modality` and `length_ratio_log`, are statistically significant. Let's generate the confidence intervals for each of the terms, as seen in Example 10.24.

Example 10.24.

```
# Generate boostrap distribution
dative_boot <-
  dative_spec |>
  generate(reps = 1000, type = "bootstrap") |>
  fit()

# Calculate the confidence interval
dative_ci <-
  dative_boot |>
  get_confidence_interval(
    point_estimate = dative_fit,
    level = 0.95
  )

# Preview
dative_ci
```

```
# A tibble: 3 x 3
  term              lower_ci upper_ci
  <chr>                <dbl>    <dbl>
1 intercept           -0.688   -0.449
2 length_ratio_log   -1.79    -1.49
3 modalitywritten     0.799    1.20
```

The confidence intervals for the main effects, `modality` and `length_ratio_log`, do not contain the null hypothesis value of 0, which provides evidence that each of the explanatory variables is related to the proportion of NP realizations of the recipient clause.

> **Dive deeper**
> Significance tests are not the only way to evaluate the evidence for the null hypothesis. We can also quantify the effect size of each of the explanatory variables using the odds ratio to calculate the r (correlation coefficient) and R^2 (coefficient of determination) values. {effectsize} (Ben-Shachar et al., 2024) provides a function `logoddsratio_to_r()` to calculate the r and R^2 values for logistic regression models.
> It can be important to use these measures to distinguish between statistically significant and practically significant results. A statistically significant result is one that is unlikely to have occurred by chance. A practically significant result is one that has a meaningful effect.

Our logistic regression model as specified considers the explanatory variables `modality` and `length_ratio_log` independently, controlling for the other explanatory variable. This is an **additive model**, which is what we stated in our hypothesis and represented in the formula `y ~ x1 + x2`.

Not all multivariate relationships are additive. We can also hypothesize an interaction between the explanatory variables. An **interaction model** is one which hypothesizes that the effect of one explanatory variable on the response variable is dependent on the other explanatory variable(s). In our case, we could have hypothesized that the effect of `length_ratio_log` on the proportion of NP realizations of the recipient clause is dependent on `modality`. We can specify this relationship using the formula approach, as seen in Example 10.25.

Example 10.25.

```
# Specify the relationship between the response and explanatory variables
dative_inter_spec <-
  dative_tbl |>
  specify(
    rcp_real ~ modality * length_ratio_log
  )
```

Replacing the + with a * tells the model to consider the interaction between the explanatory variables. A model with an interaction changes the terms and the estimates. In Example 10.26, we see the terms for the logistic regression model with an interaction.

Example 10.26.

```
# Fit the logistic regression model
dative_inter_fit <-
  dative_inter_spec |>
  fit()

# Preview
dative_inter_fit
```

```
# A tibble: 4 x 2
  term                               estimate
  <chr>                                 <dbl>
1 intercept                            -0.549
2 modalitywritten                       0.958
3 length_ratio_log                     -1.69
4 modalitywritten:length_ratio_log      0.138
```

> **Consider this**
> As an exercise, consider the following research question:
>
> - NP and PP realizations of the recipient clause are contingent on modality and word length ratio of the recipient and theme, and the effect of the length ratio on the proportion of NP realizations of the recipient clause is dependent on the modality.
>
> Follow the simulation-based process to test this hypothesis. What are the results? What are the implications of the results?

The additional term `modalitywritten:length_ratio_log` is the interaction term. We also see the log odds estimates have changed for the previous terms. This is because this interaction draws some of the explanatory power from the other terms. Whether or not we run an interaction model depends on our research question. Again, the hypothesis precedes the model. If we hypothesize an interaction, then we should run an interaction model. If we do not, then we should not.

10.2.2 Numeric

We now turn our attention to the analysis scenarios where the response variable is numeric. Just as for categorical variables, we can have univariate, bivariate, and multivariate analysis scenarios. The statistical tests for numeric variables are summarized in Table 10.7.

Table 10.7: Statistical test design for numeric response variables

Scenario	Explanatory Variable(s)	Statistical Test	infer
Univariate	-	Mean	`mean`
Bivariate	Numeric	Correlation	`correlation`
Bivariate	Categorical (2 levels)	Difference in means	`diff in means`
Bivariate	Categorical (3+ levels)	ANOVA	`f`
Multivariate	Numeric or Categorical	Linear regression	`fit()`

The dataset we will use is drawn from the Switchboard Dialog Act Corpus (University of Colorado Boulder, 2008). The data dictionary is found in Table 10.8.

Table 10.8: Data dictionary for the transformed SWDA dataset

variable	name	type	description
speaker_id	Speaker ID	numeric	Unique identifier for each speaker
age	Age	numeric	Age of the speaker in years
sex	Sex	categorical	Gender of the speaker
education	Education	ordinal	Level of education attained by the speaker
fillers_orf	Fillers per 100	numeric	Number of filler words used per 100 utterances (observed relative frequency)
total_fillers	Total Fillers	numeric	Total number of filler words used
total_utts	Total Utterances	numeric	Total number of utterances made by the speaker

We see the dataset has seven variables. The `fillers_orf` will be used as our response variable and corresponds to the rate of filler usage per speaker, normalized by the number of utterances. The other variables we will consider as explanatory variables are `age`, `sex`, and `education`, providing us a mix of numeric and categorical variables.

The context for these analysis demonstrations comes from the socio-linguistic literature on the use of filled pauses. Filled pauses have often been associated with a type of disfluency; speech errors that occur during speech production. However, some authors have argued that filled pauses can act as sociolinguistic markers of socio-demographic characteristics of speakers, such as gender, age, and educational level (Shriberg, 1994; Tottie, 2011).

Reading the dataset and performing some basic diagnostics, a preview of the `fillers_tbl` dataset is seen in Example 10.27.

Example 10.27.

```
# Preview the dataset
fillers_tbl
```

```
# A tibble: 441 x 4
     age sex    education            fillers_orf
   <dbl> <fct>  <ord>                      <dbl>
 1    38 Female Less Than College           2.14
 2    52 Male   More Than College          25.3
 3    29 Female College                     4.13
 4    34 Female College                     2.41
 5    36 Female College                     3.79
 6    27 Female College                     0
 7    53 Female Less Than College           8.33
 8    60 Male   Less Than College           1.82
 9    28 Female College                     5.22
10    35 Female College                     6.23
# i 431 more rows
```

Our `fillers_tbl` dataset has 441 observations. Again, we will postpone more specific descriptive statistics for treatment in the upcoming scenarios.

Univariate analysis

In hypothesis testing, the analysis of a single variable is directed at determining whether or not the distribution or statistic of the variable differs from some expected distribution or statistic. In the case of a single categorical variable with two levels (as Section 10.2.1), we sampled from a binomial distribution by chance. In the case of a single numeric variable, we can sample and compare the observed distribution to a theoretical distribution. When approaching hypothesis testing from a theoretical perspective, it is often necessary to assess how well a numeric variable fits the normal distribution as many statistical tests assume that the data are normally distributed. However, we have adopted the simulation-based approach to hypothesis testing, which does not require that the data fit the normal distribution, or any other distribution for that matter.

The other approach to analyzing a single numeric variable is to compare an observed statistic to an expected statistic. This approach requires *a priori* knowledge of the expected statistic. For example, imagine we are interested in testing the hypothesis that the length of words in a medical corpus tend to be longer than the average length of words in English. We would then calculate the observed mean for the length of words in the medical corpus and then generate a null distribution of means for the length of words in English, as in Example 10.28.

Example 10.28.

```
# Observed mean
obs_mean <-
  medical_df |>
  specify(response = word_length) |>
  calculate(stat = "mean")

# Null distribution of means
null_mean <-
  medical_df |>
  specify(response = word_length) |>
  hypothesize(null = "point", mu = 5) |>
  generate(reps = 1000, type = "draw") |>
  calculate(stat = "mean")
```

Note that instead of a `p =` argument, as was used in the `hypothesize()` step to generate a null distribution of proportions, we use a `mu =` argument in Example 10.28 to specify the expected mean. The rest of the hypothesis testing workflow is the same as for the null distribution of proportions.

> **Dive deeper**
> The mean `mu` is not the only statistic we can specify for a numeric variable. We can also specify the median `med`, or the standard deviation `sigma`.

In our case, we do not have *a priori* knowledge of the expected statistic for the `fillers_orf` variable, so we will not pursue this approach. However, it is useful to take a closer look at the distribution of a numeric variable in order to detect extreme skewing and/or outliers. This is important because the presence of skewing and outliers can affect the results of statistical tests. We can visualize the distribution of the `fillers_orf` variable using a histogram and density plot as in Example 10.29 and rendered in Figure 10.5.

Example 10.29.

```
# Histogram-density plot
fillers_tbl |>
  ggplot(aes(x = fillers_orf)) +
  geom_histogram(aes(y = after_stat(density)), bins = 50) +
  geom_density() +
  labs(x = "Fillers per 100 utterances", y = "Density")
```

The distribution of `fillers_orf` is indeed skewed to the right. We might have predicted this given that we are working with ratio based on count data, perhaps not. In any case, the skewing we observe tends to compress the distribution and may make it difficult to see any patterns. To mitigate this, we

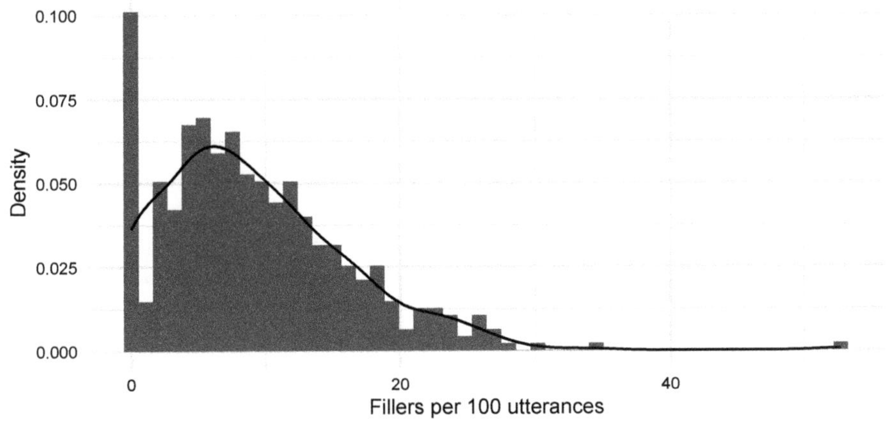

Figure 10.5: Histogram and density plot of the `fillers_orf` variable

can log transform the variable. But we will run into a problem if we have any speakers who do not use any fillers at all as these speakers will have a value of zero, as we can see in Figure 10.5. The log of zero is undefined. So we need to address this.

Eliminating the speakers who do not use any fillers at all is one option. This is quite extreme as we may lose quite a few speakers and it is not clear that removing data in this way will not cause inordinate bias in the results as these speakers may be different in some way from the rest of the speakers. Looking at the speakers with zero fillers in Example 10.30, we can see that there is some potential for bias as the speakers with zero fillers are not evenly distributed across the levels of the `education` and `sex` variables.

Example 10.30.

```
# Cross-tabulation of zero fillers by education and sex
fillers_tbl |>
  filter(fillers_orf == 0) |>
  tabyl(education, sex)
```

```
           education Female Male
   More Than College      3   14
             College     16   11
   Less Than College      2    0
 Less Than High School    1    0
             Unknown      1    0
```

Another approach is to add a small value to the `fillers_orf` variable, for all speakers. This will allow us to log transform the variable and will likely not have any (or very little) impact on the results. It also allows us to keep these speakers.

Adding values can be done in one of two ways. We can add a small constant value to all speakers, or we can add a small random value to all speakers. The former is easier to implement, but means that we will still have a spike in the distribution at the value of the constant. Since we do not expect that speakers that did not use fillers at all would never do so and that when they do we would not expect them to be at exactly the same rate as other speakers, we can add a small random value to all speakers.

In R, we can use the `jitter()` function to add a small amount of random noise to the variable. Note, however, this random noise can be positive or negative. When a negative value is added to a zero value, we are still in trouble when we go to log-transform. So we need to make sure that none of the jitter produces negative values. We can do this by simply taking the absolute value of the jittered variable with the `abs()` function. Let's see how this works in Example 10.31.

Example 10.31.

```
set.seed(1234) # for reproducibility

# Add jitter to fillers
fillers_tbl <-
  fillers_tbl |>
  mutate(fillers_orf_jitter = abs(jitter(fillers_orf)))

fillers_tbl
```

```
# A tibble: 441 x 5
     age sex    education          fillers_orf fillers_orf_jitter
   <dbl> <fct>  <ord>                    <dbl>              <dbl>
 1    38 Female Less Than College         2.14               2.14
 2    52 Male   More Than College        25.3               25.3
 3    29 Female College                   4.13               4.13
 4    34 Female College                   2.41               2.41
 5    36 Female College                   3.79               3.80
 6    27 Female College                   0                  0.000561
 7    53 Female Less Than College         8.33               8.33
 8    60 Male   Less Than College         1.82               1.82
 9    28 Female College                   5.22               5.22
10    35 Female College                   6.23               6.23
# i 431 more rows
```

The results from Example 10.31 show that the `fillers_orf_jitter` variable has been added to the `fillers_tbl` dataset and that zero values for `fillers_orf` now have a small amount of random noise added to them. Note that the other values also have a small amount of random noise added to them, but it is so small that rounding to 2 decimal places makes it look like nothing has changed.

Now let's return to log transforming the `fillers_orf_jitter` variable. We can do this with the `log()` function. Let's see how this works in Example 10.32.

Example 10.32.

```
# Log transform fillers (with jitter)
fillers_tbl <-
  fillers_tbl |>
  mutate(fillers_orf_log = log(fillers_orf_jitter))

fillers_tbl
```

```
# A tibble: 441 x 6
     age sex    education            fillers_orf fillers_orf_jitter fillers_orf_log
   <dbl> <fct>  <ord>                      <dbl>              <dbl>           <dbl>
 1    38 Female Less Than College           2.14           2.14               0.762
 2    52 Male   More Than College          25.3           25.3                3.23
 3    29 Female College                     4.13           4.13               1.42
 4    34 Female College                     2.41           2.41               0.880
 5    36 Female College                     3.79           3.80               1.33
 6    27 Female College                     0              0.000561          -7.49
 7    53 Female Less Than College           8.33           8.33               2.12
 8    60 Male   Less Than College           1.82           1.82               0.597
 9    28 Female College                     5.22           5.22               1.65
10    35 Female College                     6.23           6.23               1.83
# i 431 more rows
```

Let's now plot the log-transformed variable, as seen in Example 10.33 and visualized in Figure 10.6.

Example 10.33.

```
# Histogram-density plot
fillers_tbl |>
  ggplot(aes(x = fillers_orf_log)) +
  geom_histogram(aes(y = after_stat(density)), bins = 50) +
  geom_density() +
  labs(x = "Fillers per 100 utterances", y = "Density")
```

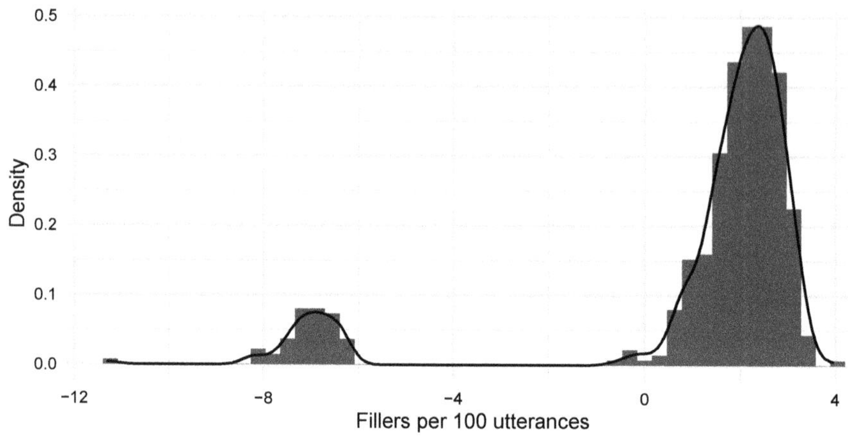

Figure 10.6: Histogram and density plot of the `fillers_orf_log` variable

The distribution of the log-transformed variable is more spread out now, but the zero-filler speakers do show a low-level spike in the left tail of the distribution. Jitter and log transformation, however, smooth over their effect to a large degree.

Bivariate analysis

When considering a numeric response variable and another variable, it is key to consider the nature of the other variable. If it is a categorical variable with two levels, then we can compare a statistic between the two groups (mean or median). If it is categorical with more than two levels, Analysis of Variance (ANOVA) is used to compare the means. Finally, if it is a numeric variable, then we can use a correlation test to see if there is an association between the two variables.

The `fillers_tbl` contains the `sex` variable which is a categorical variable with two levels. According to the literature, filled pauses are associated with differences between men and women (Shriberg, 1994; Tottie, 2011, 2014) . The findings suggest that men use fillers at a higher rate than women. Let's test to see if this holds for the SWDA data.

Let's first explore the distribution from a descriptive point of view. With a numeric response variable `fillers_orf_log` and a categorical explanatory variable `sex`, a boxplot is a natural fit, as seen in Example 10.34.

Example 10.34.

```
# boxplot
fillers_tbl |>
  ggplot(aes(x = fillers_orf_log, y = sex)) +
  geom_boxplot(notch = TRUE) +
  labs(
    x = "Filler use (log)",
    y = "Sex"
  )
```

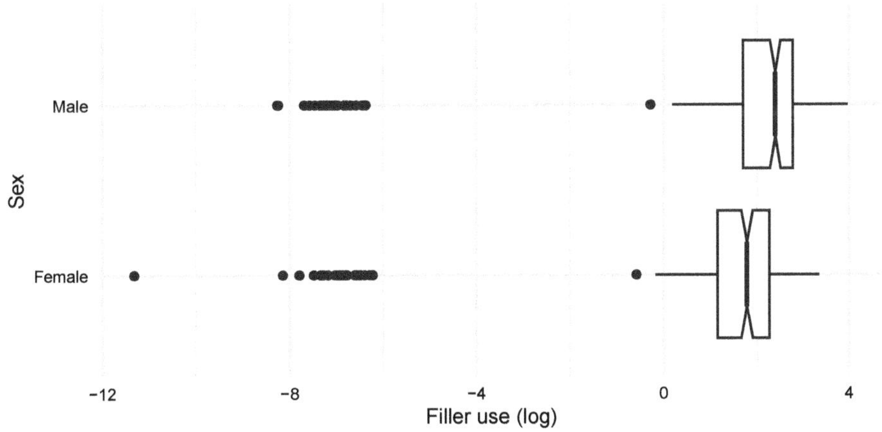

Figure 10.7: boxplot of the `fillers_orf_log` variable by `sex`

Looking at the boxplot in Figure 10.7, we see that there appears to be an overall higher rate of filler use for men, compared to women. We also can see that the random noise added to zero-rate speakers appear as outliers in the left tail. Since I added a notch to the boxplots, we can also gauge to some degree the uncertainty of the median. The notches do not overlap, which suggests that the medians are different.

To test these differences, let's follow the simulation-based hypothesis testing workflow and investigate if the apparent difference between men and women is statistically significant, or expected by chance[3]. The first steps are found in Example 10.35.

[3]Given the fact that we added jitter to accommodate the zeros, it may actually make more sense to compare medians, rather than means. But to compare these results with the results from the literature, we will compare means.

Example 10.35.

```
# Specify the relationship
fillers_spec <-
  fillers_tbl |>
  specify(fillers_orf_log ~ sex) # response ~ explanatory

# Observed statistic
fillers_obs <-
  fillers_spec |>
  # diff in means, Male - Female
  calculate(stat = "diff in means", order = c("Male", "Female"))

# Null distribution
fillers_null <-
  fillers_spec |>
  hypothesize(null = "independence") |> # independence = no relationship
  generate(reps = 1000, type = "permute") |> # permute = shuffle
  calculate(stat = "diff in means", order = c("Male", "Female"))

# Calculate the $p$-value
fillers_null |>
  get_p_value(obs_stat = fillers_obs, direction = "greater")
```

```
# A tibble: 1 x 1
  p_value
    <dbl>
1   0.033
```

From the analysis performed in Example 10.35, we can reject the null hypothesis that there is no difference between the rate of filler use between men and women, as the p-value is less than 0.05.

To further assess the uncertainty of the observed statistic, and the robustness of the difference, we calculate a confidence interval, as seen in Example 10.36.

Example 10.36.

```
# Resampling distribution
fillers_boot <-
  fillers_spec |>
  generate(reps = 1000, type = "bootstrap") |>
  calculate(stat = "diff in means", order = c("Male", "Female"))

# Calculate the confidence interval
fillers_ci <-
  fillers_boot |>
  get_confidence_interval(level = 0.95)
```

```

fillers_ci
```

```
# A tibble: 1 x 2
  lower_ci upper_ci
     <dbl>    <dbl>
1 -0.00378     1.05
```

The confidence interval includes 0, which suggests that the observed difference is questionable. It is of note, however, that the majority of the interval is above 0, which provides some evidence that the observed difference is not due to chance. This result highlights how p-values and confidence intervals together can provide a more nuanced picture of the data.

The second bivariate scenario we can consider is when the explanatory variable is categorical with more than two levels. We will use ANOVA to calculate the F statistic (f). The `education` variable in the `fillers_tbl` dataset is a categorical variable with five levels. Tottie (2011) suggests that the more educated a speaker, the more fillers they will use. Let's test this hypothesis.

First, we visualize the distribution of the `fillers_orf_log` variable by `education`, as seen in Example 10.37.

Example 10.37.

```
# boxplot
fillers_tbl |>
  ggplot(aes(y = fillers_orf_log, x = education)) +
  geom_boxplot(notch = TRUE) +
  labs(
    y = "Filler use (log)",
    x = "Education"
  )
```

The boxplot in Figure 10.8 does not point to any obvious differences between the levels of the `education` variable. There are a fair number of outliers, however, in the two most educated groups. These outliers are likely due to the random noise added to the 0-rate speakers and it is interesting that they are concentrated in the two most educated groups.

Let's now submit these variables to the simulation-based hypothesis testing workflow to quantify the uncertainty of the observed statistic and determine if the observed difference is statistically significant. Again, the first steps are found in Example 10.38.

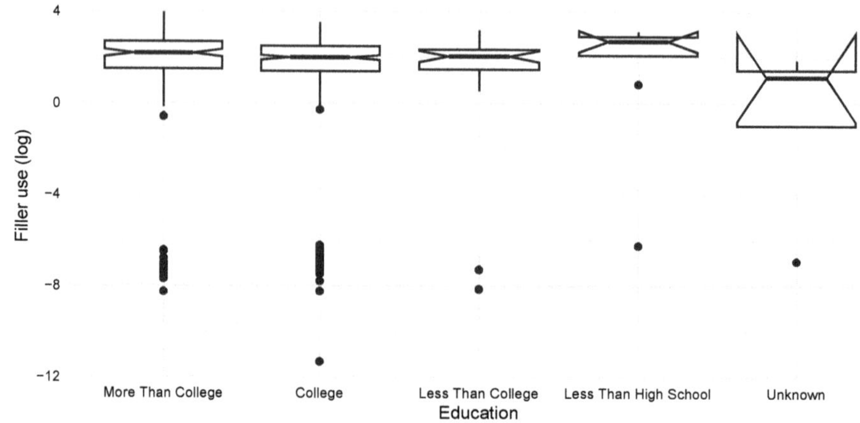

Figure 10.8: Visualizations of the `fillers_orf_log` variable by `education`

Example 10.38.

```
# Specify the relationship
fillers_spec <-
  fillers_tbl |>
  specify(fillers_orf_log ~ education) # response ~ explanatory

# Observed statistic
fillers_obs <-
  fillers_spec |>
  calculate(stat = "F") # F = variance between groups / variance within groups

# Null distribution
fillers_null <-
  fillers_spec |>
  hypothesize(null = "independence") |> # independence = no relationship
  generate(reps = 1000, type = "permute") |> # permute = shuffle
  calculate(stat = "F")

# Calculate the $p$-value
fillers_null |>
  get_p_value(obs_stat = fillers_obs, direction = "two-sided")
```

```
# A tibble: 1 x 1
  p_value
    <dbl>
1   0.426
```

The analysis in Example 10.38 suggests that the observed difference between the means of the different levels of the `education` variable are not significantly different from what we would expect by chance.

> **⚠ Warning**
> The p-value in Example 10.38 was calculated using a two-sided test, which is appropriate when the expected directionality is not known. In this case, while we do have an expected directionality, the visualizations strongly suggest that the observed difference is not in line with our expectations. To account for this uncertainty and to be conservative, we choose to use a two-sided test. This allows us to remain open to the possibility that the observed difference may actually be in the opposite direction, rather than solely focusing on our initial expectation. However, it's important to note that the decision to use a one-sided or two-sided test should also consider factors such as the specific research question and the context of the analysis.

Let's now calculate a confidence interval to assess the uncertainty of the observed statistic, as seen in Example 10.39.

Example 10.39.

```
# Resampling distribution
fillers_boot <-
  fillers_spec |>
  generate(reps = 1000, type = "bootstrap") |>
  calculate(stat = "F")

# Calculate the confidence interval
fillers_ci <-
  fillers_boot |>
  get_confidence_interval(level = 0.95)

fillers_ci
```

```
# A tibble: 1 x 2
  lower_ci upper_ci
     <dbl>    <dbl>
1    0.123     4.57
```

In Example 10.39, we see that we are in the opposite situation to the previous bivariate case—the p-value is not significant but the confidence interval does not include 0.

So how do we interpret this? Remember, the p-value is the probability of observing a statistic as extreme or more extreme than the observed statistic, given that the null hypothesis is true. The confidence interval is the range of values that we are 95% confident contains the true population parameter. We should take into consideration two aspects: (1) the confidence interval has a large range (the interval is wide) and (2) the lower limit is near 0. Taken together and in addition to the p-value, we can conclude that the observed difference is not statistically significant, and if there is a difference, it is likely to be small or negligible.

Multivariate analysis

While bivariate analysis is useful for exploring the relationship between two variables, it is often the case that we want to consider relationships between more than two variables. In this case, we can use multivariate analysis. Linear regression is a common multivariate analysis technique.

In linear regression, we are interested in predicting the value of a numeric response variable based on the values of the explanatory variablesj. The contribution of the explanatory variables can be considered individually, as an interaction, or as a combination of both.

Let's now introduce a variation of the SWDA dataset which includes a variable `filler_type` which has two levels, 'uh' and 'um', corresponding to the use of each filler. Here's a preview of the dataset in Example 10.40.

Example 10.40.

```
fillers_type_df
```

```
# A tibble: 882 x 6
   speaker_id sex    education           age filler_type fillers_orf_log
        <dbl> <fct>  <ord>             <dbl> <chr>                 <dbl>
 1       1000 Female Less Than College    38 uh                    0.561
 2       1000 Female Less Than College    38 um                   -0.941
 3       1001 Male   More Than College    52 uh                    3.22
 4       1001 Male   More Than College    52 um                   -1.64
 5       1002 Female College              29 uh                    0.956
 6       1002 Female College              29 um                    0.425
 7       1004 Female College              34 uh                    0.474
 8       1004 Female College              34 um                   -0.220
 9       1005 Female College              36 uh                    1.17
10       1005 Female College              36 um                   -0.582
# i 872 more rows
```

The `fillers_type_df` dataset has 882 observations and 6 variables. With this dataset, we will explore the hypothesis that the rate of filler use varies by the type of filler across the socio-demographic variable `sex`.

To do this we will use R formula syntax to specify the variables we want to include in the model and their relationships. The possible relationships appear in Table 10.9.

Table 10.9: Possible relationships in a multivariate analysis

Relationship	Formula	Description
Simple effects	`response ~ explanatory_1 + explanatory_2`	The response variable as a function of each explanatory variable
Interaction effects	`response ~ explanatory_1:explanatory_2`	The response variable as a function of the interaction between the two explanatory variables
Simple and interaction effects	`response ~ explanatory_1 * explanatory_2`	The response variable as a function of each explanatory variable and the interaction between the two explanatory variables

Our hypothesis is that men and women differ in the rates that they use the filler types. This describes an interaction, so we can use either the interaction or the simple and interaction effects relationships. To demonstrate the difference between simple and interaction terms, let's approach this using the third relationship (*i.e.* `fillers_orf_log ~ filler_type * sex`).

A plot will help us begin to understand the potential relationships. In Example 10.41, we use a boxplot to visualize the relationship between the `fillers_orf_log` variable and the `filler_type` variable, with a `sex` overlay.

Example 10.41.

```
# boxplot `filler_type`
fillers_type_df |>
  ggplot(aes(y = fillers_orf_log, x = filler_type)) +
  geom_boxplot(notch = TRUE) +
  labs(
    x = "Filler type",
    y = "Fillers per 100 (log)"
  )

# boxplot `filler_type` and `sex`
fillers_type_df |>
  ggplot(aes(y = fillers_orf_log, x = filler_type, fill = sex)) +
  geom_boxplot(notch = TRUE) +
  labs(
    x = "Filler type",
    y = "Fillers per 100 (log)",
    fill = "Sex"
  )
```

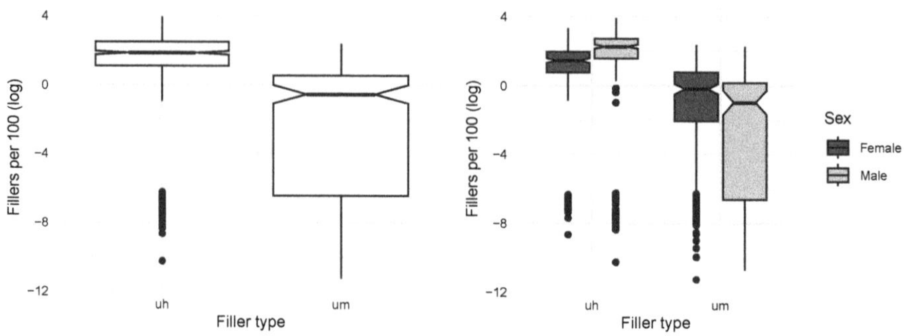

(a) Boxplot by `filler_type` (b) Boxplot by `filler_type` and `sex`

Figure 10.9: Boxplot of the `fillers_orf_log` variable by `filler_type` and `sex`

Let's interpret the boxplots in Figure 10.9. Focusing on Figure 10.9a first, we see that the filler 'uh' is more frequent than 'um' as the median is distinct and the confidence intervals do not overlap. Now, looking at Figure 10.9b, we see the same distinction between 'uh' and 'um', but we also see that the difference between the use of 'uh' and 'um' is different for males and females. This is the interaction effect we hypothesized. In this case the interaction effect goes in the same direction but the magnitude of the difference is different. The upshot, men and women both use 'uh' more than 'um' but men are even more likely to use 'uh' over 'um' than women.

Let's test this effect using the `infer` workflow. Calculating the observed statistics for the simple and interaction effects is very similar to other designs, except instead of `calculate()` to derive our statistics we will use the `fit()` function, just as we did for logistic regression. Let's go ahead and calculate the observed statistics first, as seen in Example 10.42.

Example 10.42.

```
# Specify the relationship
fillers_type_spec <-
  fillers_type_df |>
  specify(fillers_orf_log ~ filler_type * sex)

# Observed statistics
fillers_type_obs <-
  fillers_type_spec |>
  fit()

fillers_type_obs
```

```
# Specify the relationship
fillers_type_spec <-
  fillers_type_df |>
  specify(fillers_orf_log ~ filler_type * sex)

# Observed statistics
fillers_type_obs <-
  fillers_type_spec |>
  fit()

fillers_type_obs
```

```
# A tibble: 4 x 2
  term                   estimate
  <chr>                     <dbl>
1 intercept                 0.551
2 filler_typeum            -2.16
3 sexMale                   0.657
4 filler_typeum:sexMale    -1.84
```

The terms in the output from Example 10.42 provide information as to what the reference levels are. For example, `filler_typeum` tells us that the 'uh' level is the reference for `filler_type` and by the same logic, 'Female' is the reference for `sex`. These terms provide our simple effect statistics. Each can be understood as the difference between the reference level when the other variables are held constant. Our response variable is log transformed, so it is not directly interpretable beyond the fact that smaller units are lower rates of filler use and larger units are higher rates of filler use. So 'um' is used less than 'uh' and men use more fillers than women.

The interaction term `fillertypeum:sexMale` is the difference in the rate of fillers for this combination compared to the reference level combination ('uh' and 'Female'). In this case, the observed rate is lower.

We now need to generate a null distribution to compare the observed statistics to. We will again use the permutation method, but since there is an interaction effect, we need to shuffle the `filler_type` and `sex` variables together. This ensures that any relationship between the two variables is removed. Let's see how this works in Example 10.43.

Example 10.43.

```
# Null distribution
fillers_type_null <-
  fillers_type_spec |>
  hypothesize(null = "independence") |>
```

```
  generate(reps = 1000, type = "permute", variables = c("filler_type",
  ↪  "sex")) |>
  fit()

# Calculate the $p$-values
fillers_type_null |>
  get_p_value(obs_stat = fillers_type_obs, direction = "two-sided")
```

```
# A tibble: 4 x 2
  term                     p_value
  <chr>                      <dbl>
1 filler_typeum              0
2 filler_typeum:sexMale      0
3 intercept                  0
4 sexMale                    0.066
```

For the simple effects, we see that `filler_type` is significant but `sex` is not. Remember, when we only considered `sex` in isolation in the bivariate case, we found it to be significant. So why is it not significant now? It is important to remember that in every statistical design, there are other factors that are not considered. When these are not in the model, our effects may appear to account for more of the variance than they actually do. In this case, the `filler_type` variable is accounting for some of the variance that `sex` was accounting for in the bivariate case, enough, it appears, to make `sex` not significant as a simple effect.

Our interaction effect is also significant meaning the observed difference we visualized in Figure 10.9 is likely not due to chance. The upshot, both men and women use more 'uh' compared to 'um' but men's difference in use is larger than women's.

As always, let's calculate a confidence interval to assess the uncertainty of the observed statistic, as seen in Example 10.44.

Example 10.44.

```
# Resampling distribution
fillers_type_boot <-
  fillers_type_spec |>
  generate(reps = 1000, type = "bootstrap") |>
  fit()

# Calculate the confidence intervals
fillers_type_ci <-
  fillers_type_boot |>
  get_confidence_interval(level = 0.95, point_estimate = fillers_type_obs)

```

```
fillers_type_ci
```

```
# A tibble: 4 x 3
  term                  lower_ci upper_ci
  <chr>                    <dbl>    <dbl>
1 filler_typeum          -2.75     -1.54
2 filler_typeum:sexMale -2.68     -0.934
3 intercept               0.168     0.909
4 sexMale                 0.0947    1.22
```

From the confidence intervals, we see that zero is not included in any of the intervals, which suggests that the observed differences are not due to chance. Interpreting the width and the proximity to zero, however, suggests that the observed differences for `filler_type` are stronger than for `sex`, which did not result in a significant simple effect. The interaction effect is also significant, but the confidence interval is quite wide and approximates zero. This should raise some questions about the robustness of the observed effect.

Activities

The following activities aim to reinforce the concepts covered in this chapter. You'll review working with key variables, examine data distributions, and employ simulation-based statistical methods using {infer} to test hypotheses about their relationships.

> **Recipe**
> **What**: Building inference models
> **How**: Read Recipe 10, complete comprehension check, and prepare for Lab 10.
> **Why**: To review and extend your knowledge regarding the simulation-based approach to statistical inference.

> **Lab**
> **What**: Statistical inference
> **How**: Clone, fork, and complete the steps in Lab 10.
> **Why**: To apply the concepts covered in this chapter to a real-world dataset.

Summary

In sum, in this section we explored the process of null hypothesis testing using {infer}, which is a simulation-based approach to statistical inference. We considered statistical designs, such as univariate, bivariate, and multivariate analyses, and explored the process of hypothesis testing with categorical and numeric response variables. The workflow provided demonstrates that {infer} is a powerful tool for conducting statistical inference, and that it can be used to test a wide range of hypotheses with a similar workflow.

Part V

Communication

In this part, I cover the what, why, and how to communicate research findings both as research documents and as a reproducible research project. Both research documents and reproducible projects are fundamental components of modern scientific inquiry. On the one hand, a research document provides readers a detailed summary of the main import of the research study. On the other hand, making the research project available to interested readers ensures that the scientific community can gain insight into the process implemented in the research and thus enables researchers to vet and extend this research to build a more robust and verifiable research base.

11

Contribute

Outcomes

- Identify the aims of public-facing and peer-facing communication
- Understand the overlapping and distinct elements and goals of research presentations and articles
- Comprehend the importance of and recognize the aspects of well-documented and reproducible research

We have discussed the design and implementation of research that is purposive, inquisitive, informed, and methodical. In this final chapter, we turn to the task of sharing research results in a manner that is communicable. There are two primary ways to communicate the results of research: public-facing and peer-facing. We will cover both aspects of research communication, providing guidelines for effective research reporting and strategies to ensure the reproducibility of your research project.

>_ Lessons
What: Computing environment
How: In an R console, load {swirl}, run `swirl()`, and follow prompts to select the lesson.
Why: To interact with the {renv} and learn how to manage package versions in a research project.

11.1 Public-facing

Public-facing research communication is intended for audiences to become familiar with the research. Dissemination of research findings is a critical part of the research process. Whether it is through presentations, articles, blog posts, or social media, the ability to effectively communicate the results of research is essential for making a contribution to the field.

10.4324/9781003393764.11

The two most common forms of research dissemination in academics are presentations and articles. Both share a common goal: to effectively communicate the research to an audience. However, they also have distinct purposes and require different approaches to achieve their goals. These purposes complement each other, with presentations often serving as a means to engage and elicit feedback from an audience, and articles serving as a more comprehensive and permanent record of the research.

11.1.1 Structure

First, let's focus on the structural elements that appear in both research presentations and articles. The components in Table 11.1 reflect the typical structure for presenting research in the social sciences (Gries, 2016; Gries & Paquot, 2020; Sternberg & Sternberg, 2010). Their combined purpose is to trace the research narrative from the rationale and goals to connecting the findings with the research questions and aims.

Table 11.1: Common components of research presentations and articles

Component	Purpose
Introduction	Provide context and rationale based on previous research
Methods	Describe the research design and procedures
Results	Present the findings including key statistics and table and/or visual summaries
Discussion	Interpret the findings and discuss implications
Conclusion	Summarize the research and suggest future work

When research is connected to a well-designed plan, as described in Chapter 4, key elements in this structure will have already begun to take shape. The steps taken to identify an area and a problem or gap in the literature find themselves in the introduction. This section builds the case for the research and provides the context for the research question(s) and aim(s). The methods section describes the research design and procedures, including the data collection and analysis steps that are key to contextualize the findings. In the results section, the findings are presented in the appropriate manner given the research aim and the analysis performed.

The discussion and conclusions sections, however, are where the research narrative is brought together. Crafting these sections can be seen as an extension of the research process itself. Instead of elaborating on the planning steps and their implementation, the discussion focuses on the interpretation of the findings in the light of the research questions and previous literature. At this stage, the act of articulating the implications of the findings is where deeper insights are developed and refined. The conclusion, for its part, puts a finer point on the research goal and main findings, but also is an opportunity to extend suggestions to where subsequent research might go.

11.1.2 Purpose

Understanding the roles the structural elements play in contributing to the overall narrative is essential for effective research communication. Yet, presentations and articles are not the same. They have distinct goals which are reflected in the emphasis that each communication channel places on particular narrative elements and the level of detail and nuance that is included.

It is likely not a surprise that articles are more detailed and nuanced than presentations. But what is sometimes overlooked is that presentations should emphasize storytelling and relatability. A 'less is more' approach can help maintain connection with the take-home message and reduce information overload. To be sure, the research should be accurate and reliable, but the focus is on engaging the audience and connecting the research to broader themes. Even if your audience is familiar with the research area, maintaining a connection with 'why this matters' is important.

Tabular and visual summaries are key to convey complex findings, regardless of the mode of communication. However, in presentations, the use of visual aids is especially effective for engaging the audience as the visual modality does not compete with the spoken word for attention. Along these lines, limiting the amount of text on slides and increasing natural discourse with the audience is a good practice. Your presentation will be more engaging leading to more questions and feedback that you can use to refine your current or to seed future research.

The purpose of an article is to provide a comprehensive record of the research. In this record, the methods and results sections are particularly significant. The methods section should provide the reader with the necessary information to understand the research design and procedures and to evaluate the findings, as it should in presentations, but, in contrast to presentations, it should also speak to researchers, providing the details required to reproduce the research. These details summarize and, ideally, point to the data and code that are used to produce the findings in your reproducible research project (see Section 11.2).

The results section, for its part, should present the findings in a manner that is clear and concise, but also comprehensive. The research aim and the analysis performed will determine the appropriate measures and/or summaries to use. Table 11.2 outlines the statistical results, tables, and visualizations that often figure in the results section for exploratory, predictive, and inferential analyses.

Table 11.2: Key statistical results, tables, and visualizations for research results

Research Aim	Statistical Results	Summaries
Exploratory	Descriptive statistics	Extensive use of tables and/or visualizations
Predictive	Descriptive statistics, model performance metrics	Tables for model performance comparisons and/or visualizations for feature importance measures
Inferential	Descriptive statistics, hypothesis testing confidence metrics	Tables for hypothesis testing results and/or visualizations to visualize trends

By and large, the results section should be a descriptive and visual summary of the findings as they are, without interpretation. The discussion section is where the interpretation of the findings and their implications are presented. This general distinction between the results and discussion may be less pronounced in exploratory research, as the interpretation of the findings may be more intertwined with the presentation of the findings given the nature of the research.

11.1.3 Strategies

Strong research write-ups begin with well-framed and well-documented research plans. The steps outlined in Section 4.4.1 are the foundation for much of the research narrative. Furthermore, you can further prepare for the research write-up by leaving yourself a breadcrumb trail during the research process. This includes documenting the literature that you consulted, the data, processing steps, and analysis choices that you made, and saving the key statistical results, tables, and visualizations that you generated in your process script for the analysis. This will make it easier to connect the research narrative to the research process.

The introduction includes the rationale, research question, and research aim. These components are directly connected to the primary literature that you consulted. For this reason, it is a good practice to keep a record of the literature that you consulted and the notes that you took. This record will help you to trace the development of your ideas and to provide the necessary context for your research. A reference manager, such as Zotero, Mendeley, or EndNote, is a good tool for this purpose. These tools allow you to manage your ideas and keep notes, organize your references and resources, and integrate your references and resources with your writing in Quarto through BibTeX entry citation keys.

Similarly, if you are following best practices, you will have documented your data, processing steps, and analysis choices while conducting your research. The methods section stems directly from these resources. Data origin files provide the necessary context for the data that you used in your research. Data dictionary files clarify variables and values in your datasets. Literate programming, as implemented in Quarto, can further provide process and analysis documentation.

The results section can also benefit from some preparation. The key statistical results, tables, and visualizations generated in your process script for the analysis should be saved as outputs. This provides a more convenient way to include these results in your research document(s).

If you are using a project structure similar to the one outlined in Section 4.4.2, you can write statistical results as R objects using `saveRDS()`, and write tables and visualizations as files using `kableExtra::save_kable()` and `ggplot2::ggsave()`, respectively, to the corresponding *outputs/* directory. This will allow you to easily access and include these results in your research document(s) to avoid having to recreate the analysis steps from a dataset or manually copy and paste results from the console, which can be error-prone and is not reproducible.

> **Tip**
> {qtkit} provides three functions for writing general R objects, `ggplot` objects, and `knitr_kable` objects to a given directory. These functions are `write_obj()`, `write_gg()`, and `write_kbl()`, respectively. These functions also provide functionality to automatically name the output files based on the label of the code block in which they are called to make it easier to connect the output to the code that generated it. For more information, see the {qtkit} documentation.

At this point we have our ducks in a row, so to speak. We have a well-documented research plan, a record of the literature that we consulted, and a record of the data, processing steps, and analysis choices that we made. We have also saved the key statistical results, tables, and visualizations that we generated in our process script for the analysis. Now, we can begin to write our research document(s).

Although there are many tools and platforms for creating and sharing research presentations and articles, I advocate for using Quarto to create and share both. In Table 11.3, I outline the advantages of using Quarto for both presentations and articles.

Table 11.3: Advantages of using Quarto for public-facing communication

	Feature	Advantages
1	Consistency	Using Quarto for both presentations and articles allows for a seamless transition between the two
2	Fidelity	Changes in your research process will naturally be reflected in your write-ups
3	Sharing	Quarto provides a variety of output formats, including PDF, HTML, and Word, which are suitable for sharing research presentations and articles
4	Publishing	Quarto provides styles for citations and bibliographies and a variety of extensions for journal-specific formatting, which can be useful for publishing articles in specific venues

Each of the features in Table 11.3 are individually useful, but together they provide a powerful system for conducting and disseminating research. In addition, Quarto encourages modular and reproducible research practices, which connect public-facing with peer-facing communication.

11.2 Peer-facing

Peer-facing communication targets other researchers, often working in same field, and aims to make the technical aspects of research available to other researchers to reproduce and/or build upon the research. Whether for other researchers or for your future self, creating research that is well-documented and reproducible is a fundamental part of conducting modern scientific inquiry. Reproducible research projects do not replace the need to document methods and results in write-ups, but they do provide a more comprehensive and transparent record of the research that elevates transparency, encourages collaboration, and enhances the visibility and impact of research.

11.2.1 Structure

Reproducible research consists of two main components: a research compendium and a computing environment. These components are interleaved and when shared, work together to ensure that the research project is transparent, well-documented, and reproducible.

Research compendium consists of a collection of files and documentation that organize and document a research project. This includes the data, code, and documentation files. To ensure that the project is legible and easy to navigate, the research compendium content and the project scaffolding should be predictable and consistent, following best practices outlined in Chapter 4 (4.4.2) and found in more detail in Wilson et al. (2017).

In short, there should be a separation between input, output, and the code that interacts with the input to produce the output. Furthermore, documentation for data, code, and the project as a whole should be clear and comprehensive. This includes a *README* file, a data origin file, and a data dictionary file, among others. Finally, a main script should be used to execute and coordinate the processing of the project steps.

All computational projects require a computing environment. This includes the software and hardware that are used to execute the code and process the data. For a text analysis project using R, this will include R and R packages. Regardless of the language, however, there are system-level dependencies, an operating system, and hardware resources that the project relies on.

Figure 11.1 visualizes the relationship between the computing environment and the research compendium as layers of a research environment. The research compendium is the top layer, each of the subsequent layers represents elements of the computing environment.

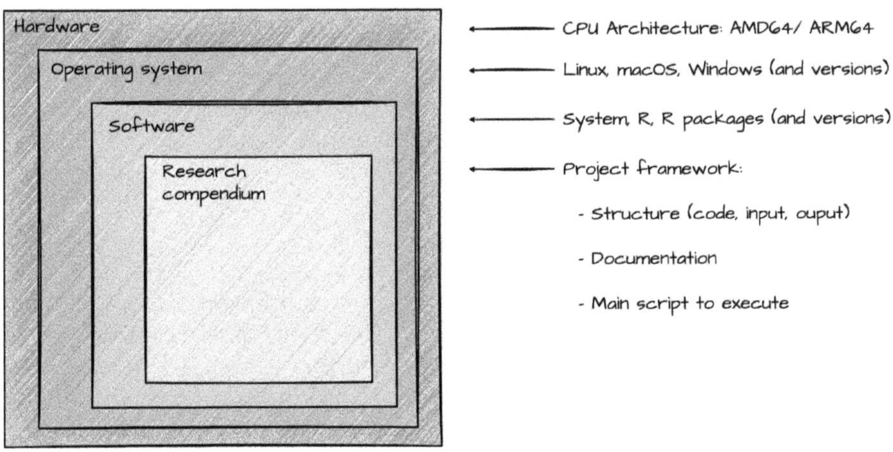

1

Figure 11.1: Layers and components of a computational research environment

The research compendium is the most visible layer, as it is the primary means of interacting with the research project. The software layer includes R, R packages, and system-level dependencies. **System-level dependencies** serve to support the software layer. Software itself, these dependencies are not directly interacted with, but they are necessary for the more 'visible' software to function. Most people are familiar with operating systems, such as Windows, macOS, and perhaps Linux, but there are many different versions of these operating systems. Furthermore, hardware resources also vary. One of the most important aspects of hardware to consider for reproducibility is the architecture of the processor (the central processing unit (CPU)).

We will consider how to create a reproducible environment which addresses each of these layers later in this chapter.

11.2.2 Purpose

The research compendium is in large part a guide book to the research process. Efforts here increase research transparency, facilitate collaboration and peer review, and enhance the visibility and impact of research. It is also the case that keeping tabs on the process in this way helps to ensure that the research is accurate and reliable by encouraging you to be more mindful of the choices that you make and the steps that you take. Any research project is bound to have its share of false starts, dead ends, or logical lapses, but leaving a breadcrumb trail during the research process can help to make these more visible and help you (and others) learn from them.

The computing environment is a means to an end. It is the infrastructure that is used to execute the code. The purpose of the computing environment is to ensure that the research can be executed and processed in the same way, producing the same results, regardless of the time or place. While a research compendium has value on its own, the ability to add a level of 'future-proofing' to the project only adds to that value. This is both true for other researchers who might want to build upon your research and for yourself, as returning to a project after some time away can highlight how much computing environments can change when errors litter the screen!

11.2.3 Strategies

The strategies for creating a reproducible research project are many and varied, although that gap is closing as reproducible research moves from a nicety to a necessity in modern scientific research. In this section, I will present an opinionated set of strategies to address each of the layers of a computational research project seen in Figure 11.1, in a way that better positions research to be accessible to more people and to be more resilient to inevitable changes in the computing environment from machine to machine and over time.

A key component to research compendiums which integrate into a reproducible workflow is the use of a project structure that modularizes the research project into predictable and consistent components. This will primarily consist of input, output, and the code that executes and documents the processing steps. But it also consists of a coordinating script, that is used to orchestrate each module in the project step sequence.

A particularly effective framework for implementing a research compendium with these features is the Quarto website. Quarto documents, as literal programming is in general, provides rich support for integrating source content, computations, and visualizations in a single document. In addition, Quarto documents are designed to be modular —each is run in a separate R session making no assumptions about inputs or previous computing states. When tied to logical processing steps, this can help to ensure that each step says what it does, and does what it says, enhancing the transparency and reproducibility of the research project.

The Quarto website treats each document as part of a set of documents that are coordinated by a *_quarto.yml* configuration file. Rendering a Quarto website will execute and compile the Quarto documents as determined in the configuration settings. In this way, the goal of easy execution of the project is satisfied in a way that is consistent and predictable and co-opts a framework with wide support in the R community.

Creating the scaffolding for a research compendium in Quarto is a matter of creating a new Quarto website through an IDE, the R Console, or the command-line interface (CLI) and adding the necessary files, directories, and documentation. In Snippet 11.1 a Quarto site structure augmented to reflect the project structure is shown.

Snippet 11.1. Quarto website structure

```
project/
├── data/
│   └── ...
├── process/
│   ├── 1_acquire.qmd
│   ├── 2_curate.qmd
│   ├── 3_transform.qmd
│   └── 4_analyze.qmd
├── reports/
│   └── ...
├── _quarto.yml
├── DESCRIPTION
├── index.qmd
└── README.md
```

Snippet 11.2 shows a snippet of the *_quarto.yml* configuration file for a Quarto project website. This file is used to coordinate the Quarto documents in the project and to specify the output format for the project as a whole and for individual documents.

Snippet 11.2. Quarto *_quarto.yml* file

```
project:
  title: "Project title"
  type: website
  render:
    - index.qmd
    - process/1_acquire.qmd
    - process/2_curate.qmd
    - process/3_transform.qmd
    - process/4_analyze.qmd
    - reports/

website:
  sidebar:
    contents:
      - index.qmd
      - section: "Process"
        contents: process/*
      - section: "Reports"
        contents: reports/*

format:
  html: default
```

In Snippet 11.2 the order in which each file is rendered can be specified to orchestrate the processing sequence. While the Quarto website as a whole will be rendered to HTML, individual documents can be rendered to other formats. This can be leveraged to create PDF versions of write-ups, for example, or use {revealjs} for Quarto to create presentations that are rendered and easily shared on the web. For ways to extend the Quarto website, visit the Quarto documentation at https://quarto.org/.

Let's now turn to layers of the computing environment, starting with the portion of the software layer which includes R and R packages. R and R packages are updated, new packages are introduced, and some packages are removed from circulation. These changes are good overall, but it means that code we write today may not work in the future. It sure would be nice if we could keep the same versions of packages that worked for a project.

{renv} is a package that helps manage R package installation by versions (Ushey & Wickham, 2024). It does this by creating a separate environment for each R project where `renv` is initialized. This environment allows us to keep snapshots of the state of the project's R environment in a **lockfile** —a file that contains the list of packages used in the project and their versions. This can be helpful for developing a project in a consistent environment and controlling what packages and package versions you use and update. More importantly, however, if the lockfile is shared with the project, it can be used to restore the project's R environment to the state it was in when the lockfile was created, yet on a different machine or at a different time.

Adding a lockfile to a project is as simple as initializing `renv` in the project directory with `renv::init()` and running `renv::snapshot()`. Added to the project, in Snippet 11.1, we see the addition of the *renv.lock* file and the *renv/* directory, in Snippet 11.3.

Snippet 11.3. Quarto website structure with {renv}

```
project/
├── data/
│   └── ...
├── process/
│   ├── 1_acquire.qmd
│   ├── 2_curate.qmd
│   ├── 3_transform.qmd
│   └── 4_analyze.qmd
├── reports/
│   └── ...
├── renv/
│   └── ...
├── _quarto.yml
├── index.qmd
├── README.md
└── renv.lock
```

The *renv.lock* file serves to document the computing environment and packages used to conduct the analysis. It therefore replaces the need for a *DESCRIPTION* file. The *renv/* directory contains the R environment for the project. This includes a separate library for the project's packages, and a cache for the packages that are installed. This directory is not shared with the project, as we will see, as the lockfile is sufficient to restore the project's R environment.

As R packages change over time, so too do other resources including R, system dependencies, and the operating system —maybe less frequently, however. These change will inevitably affect our ability to reliably execute the project ourselves over time, but it is surely more pronounced when we expect our project to run on a different machine! To address these elements of the computing environment, we need another, more computing-comprehensive tool.

A powerful and popular approach to reproducible software and operating system, as well as hardware environments, is to use Docker. Docker is software that provides a way to create and manage entire computing environments. These environments are called containers, and they are portable, consistent, and almost entirely isolated from the host system they run on. This means that a container can be run on any machine that has Docker installed, and it will run the same way regardless of the host system. Containers are widely used as they are quick to develop, easy to share, and allow for the execution of code safely separate from the host system.

Each container is based on an image —a blueprint which includes the operating system, system dependencies, and software. An images is created using a Dockerfile, which is a text file that contains a set of instructions for creating the image. We craft our own Dockerfile and build an image from it or we can take advantage of pre-built images that are available in image registries such as Docker Hub or GitHub Container Registry. Thanks to helpful R community members, there are Docker images built specifically for the R community and distributed as part of the Rocker Project. These images include a variety of R versions and R environment setups (*e.g.* R, RStudio Server, Shiny Server, *etc.*). The Rocker Project's images are built on the open source and freely available Ubuntu operating system, which is based on Linux. In line with our goal to use open and freely accessible formats and software, Ubuntu is a popular choice. Rocker images are widely used and well-maintained, and are a good choice for creating a reproducible computing environment for an R project. If you are just getting started with Docker, I recommend the Rocker Project's `rocker/rstudio` image. This image includes R, RStudio Server, which can be accessed through a web browser, and other key software. It also provides support for multiple computing architectures (*e.g.* AMD, ARM, *etc.*).

Once the research compendium is prepared and a strategy for the computing environment identified, the project can be published. If you are using a version control system, such as Git, to manage your project, you will likely want to publish the project to a remote repository. This makes your project accessible to others and provides a means to collaborate with other researchers. GitHub is a popular platform for publishing coding projects and it provides a number of services in addition to version control that are useful for research projects, including issue tracking, website hosting, and continuous integration (CI). CI is a technology which allows for the automatic building, testing, and/or deployment of code changes when they are added to a repository.

There are a few steps to take before publishing a project to a remote repository. First, you will want to ensure that the strategies for reproducing the project are well-documented. This includes describing where to find the Docker image for the project and how to run the project, including how to restore R packages from the *renv.lock* file. Second, you will want to ensure that you are publishing only the files that are necessary to reproduce the project and for which you have permissions to share.

I want to stress that adding your project to a publicly visible code repository is a form of publication. And when we work with data and datasets we need to consider the ethical implications of sharing data. As part of our project preparation we will have considered the data sources we used and the data we collected, including the licensing and privacy considerations. The steps outlined in Chapter 5 to 7 will either gather data from other sources or modify these sources which we add to our *data/* directory. If we do not have permissions to share the data included in this directory, or sub-directories, we should not share it on our remote repository. To avoid sharing sensitive data, we can use a *.gitignore* file to exclude the data from the repository. This file is a text file that contains a list of paths to files and directories that should be ignored by Git. This file can be added to the project directory and committed to the repository.

Since we have explicitly built in mechanisms in our project structure to ensure that the processing code is modular and that it does not depend on input or previous states, a researcher can easily recreate this data by executing our project. In this way, we do not share the data, but rather we share the means to recreate the data. This is a good practice for sharing data and is a form of reproducibility.

With your project published to a remote repository, you can connect it to other venues that list research projects, such as Open Science Framework, Zenodo, and Figshare. These platforms enhance the visibility of your project and provide a means to collaborate with other researchers. A Digital Object Identifier (DOI) will be assigned to the project which can be used to cite the project in articles and other research outputs.

Website hosting can also be enable with GitHub through GitHub Pages. GitHub Pages is a static site hosting service that takes HTML, CSS, and JavaScript files from a GitHub repository on a given branch and publishes a website. This can be useful for sharing the research project with others, as it provides a means to navigate the project in a web-based environment.

Dive deeper

There are a few ways to publish a Quarto website on GitHub. One way is to modify the *_quarto.yml* configuration file to include an output directory for the rendered site and then modify the GitHub repository configuration under 'Pages' to publish the site based on this directory. When you push your rendered site to the repository, it will be published to the web.

Another way is to set up a separate branch in GitHub `gh-pages` to use to store and serve your website. The `quarto` command line interface provides a command to render the site and publish it to the web. `quarto publish gh-pages` will render the site and push it to the `gh-pages` branch. In this scenario, you will not need to modify the *_quarto.yml* file but you will have to manually call `quarto publish gh-pages` to render and publish the site.

Yet another way is to use GitHub Actions to render the site and publish it to the web. This is a more advanced approach, but it provides a way to automate the rendering and publishing of the site. For more information, see the Quarto documentation.

The project structure, computing environment, and publication strategies outlined here are opinionated, but they are also flexible and can be adapted to suit the needs of your research project. The goal, however, should always be the same: to ensure that the computational research project is transparent, well-documented, and reproducible, and that it is accessible to others.

Now, as we wrap up this chapter, and the book, it is an opportune moment to consider the big picture of a reproducible research project. In Figure 11.2, we see the relationship between each stage of the research process, from planning to publication, and their interconnectivity. These efforts reflect our goal to generate insight from data and to communicate that insight to others.

I represent the four main stages in reproducible research: frame, prepare, analyze, and communicate. Each of these stages, and sub-stages are represented as parts and chapters in this book. In Table 11.4, I summarize the stages and sub-stages of a reproducible research project, including the purpose of each stage and sub-stage, the code that is used to execute the stage and sub-stage, and the input and output of each stage and sub-stage.

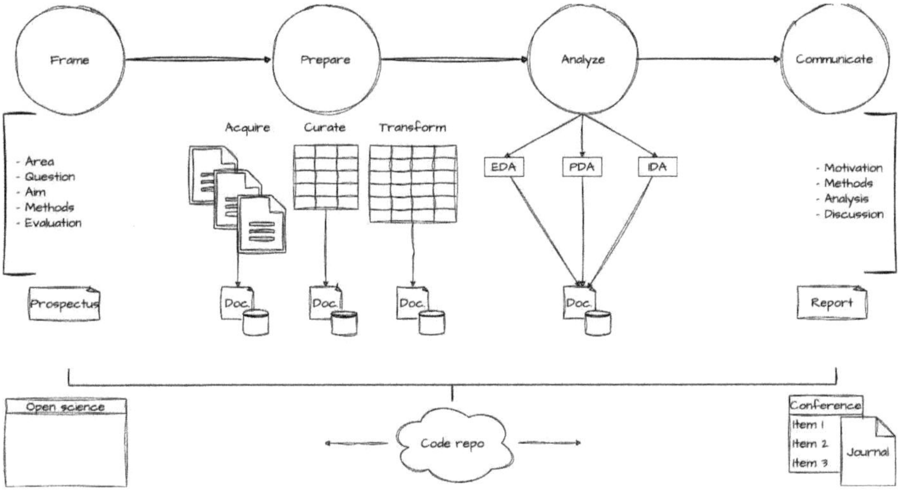

Figure 11.2: Big picture of a reproducible research project

Table 11.4: Stages and sub-stages of a reproducible research project

Stage	Sub-stage	Purpose	Input	Code	Output
Frame	Plan	Develop a research plan	Primary literature	-	Prospectus
Prepare	Acquire	Gather data	-	Collects data	Original data, data origin file
Prepare	Curate	Tidy data	Original data	Create rectangular dataset	Curated dataset, data dictionary file
Prepare	Transform	Augment and adjust dataset	Curated dataset	Prepare and/or enrich dataset	Research-aligned data, data dictionary file
Analyze	Explore, predict, or infer	Analyze data	Transformed dataset	Apply statistical methods	Key statistical results, tables, visualizations
Communicate	Public- and/or Peer-facing	Share research	Analyzed data artifacts	Write-up, publish	Research document(s), computing environment, website

In conclusion, the goal of research is to develop and refine ideas and hypotheses, sharing them with others, and to build on the work of others. The research process outlined here aims to improve the transparency, reliability, and accessibility of research, and to enhance the visibility and impact of research. These goals are not exclusive to text analysis, nor linguistics, nor any other field for that matter, but are fundamental to conducting modern scientific inquiry. I hope that the strategies and tools outlined in this book will help you to achieve these goals in your research projects.

Activities

The following activities are designed to dive deeper into the process of managing a research project and computing environment to ensure that your research project is reproducible.

Recipe
What: Manage project and computing environments
How: Read Recipe 11, complete comprehension check, and prepare for Lab 11.
Why: To follow the steps for managing a research project and computing environment for effective communication and reproducibility.

Lab
What: Future-proofing research
How: Clone, fork, and complete the steps in Lab 11.
Why: To apply the strategies for ensuring that your research project is reproducible.

Summary

In this chapter, we have discussed the importance of clear and effective communication in research reporting, and the strategies for ensuring that your research project is reproducible. We have discussed the role of public-facing research including presentations and articles. We also emphasized the importance of well-documented and reproducible research in modern scientific inquiry and outlined strategies for ensuring your research project is reproducible. As modern research practice continues to evolve, the details may change, but the principles of transparency, reliability, and accessibility will remain fundamental to conducting modern scientific inquiry.

References

Ackoff, R. L. (1989). From data to wisdom. *Journal of Applied Systems Analysis, 16*(1), 3–9.

Ädel, A. (2020). Corpus compilation. In M. Paquot & S. Th. Gries (Eds.), *A Practical Handbook of Corpus Linguistics* (pp. 3–24). Switzerland: Springer.

Albert, S., de Ruiter, L. E., & de Ruiter, J. P. (2015). CABNC: The Jeffersonian transcription of the spoken British National Corpus. TalkBank. Retrieved from https://saulalbert.github.io/CABNC/

Baayen, R. H. (2004). Statistics in psycholinguistics: A critique of some current gold standards. *Mental Lexicon Working Papers, 1*(1), 1–47.

Baayen, R. H. (2008). *Analyzing linguistic data: A practical introduction to statistics using R.* Cambridge University Press.

Baayen, R. H. (2010). A real experiment is a factorial experiment? *The Mental Lexicon, 5*(1), 149–157. doi:10.1075/ml.5.1.06baa

Baayen, R. H. (2011). Corpus linguistics and naive discriminative learning. *Revista Brasileira de Linguística Aplicada, 11*(2), 295–328.

Baayen, R. H., Feldman, L., & Schreuder, R. (2006). Morphological influences on the recognition of monosyllabic monomorphemic words. *Journal of Memory and Language, 55*, 290–313. doi:10.1016/j.jml.2006.03.008

Baayen, R. H., & Shafaei-Bajestan, E. (2019). *languageR: Analyzing linguistic data: A practical introduction to statistics*. Retrieved from https://CRAN.R-project.org/package=languageR

Baker, M. (2016). 1,500 scientists lift the lid on reproducibility. *Nature, 533*(7604), 452–454. doi:10.1038/533452a

Bao, W., Lianju, N., & Yue, K. (2019). Integration of unsupervised and supervised machine learning algorithms for credit risk assessment. *Expert Systems with Applications, 128*, 301–315. doi:10.1016/j.eswa.2019.02.033

Bengtsson, H. (2024). *future: Unified parallel and distributed processing in R for everyone*. Retrieved from https://future.futureverse.org

Benoit, K., & Obeng, A. (2024). *readtext: Import and handling for plain and formatted text files*. Retrieved from https://CRAN.R-project.org/package=readtext

Ben-Shachar, M. S., Makowski, D., Lüdecke, D., Patil, I., Wiernik, B. M., Thériault, R., & Waggoner, P. (2024). *effectsize: Indices of effect size*. Retrieved from https://easystats.github.io/effectsize/

Blischak, J. D., Carbonetto, P., & Stephens, M. (2019). Creating and sharing reproducible research code the workflowr way. *F1000Research, 8*(1749). doi:10.12688/f1000research.20843.1

Braginsky, M. (2024). *wordbankr: Accessing the wordbank database*. Retrieved from https://CRAN.R-project.org/package=wordbankr

Bray, A., Ismay, C., Chasnovski, E., Couch, S., Baumer, B., & Cetinkaya-Rundel, M. (2024). *infer: Tidy statistical inference*. Retrieved from https://github.com/tidymodels/infer

Bresnan, J. (2007). A few lessons from typology. *Linguistic Typology, 11*(1), 297–306.

Bresnan, J., Cueni, A., Nikitina, T., & Baayen, R. H. (2007). Predicting the dative alternation. In G. Bouma, I. Kraemer, & J.-W. C. Zwart (Eds.), *Cognitive Foundations of Interpretation* (pp. 1–33). Amsterdam: KNAW.

Brown, K. (2005). *Encyclopedia of language and linguistics* (Vol. 1). Elsevier.

Bryan, J., Hester, J., Robinson, D., Wickham, H., & Dervieux, C. (2024). *reprex: Prepare reproducible example code via the clipboard*. Retrieved from https://reprex.tidyverse.org

Buckheit, J. B., & Donoho, D. L. (1995). Wavelab and reproducible research. In *Wavelets and statistics* (pp. 55–81). Springer.

Bychkovska, T., & Lee, J. J. (2017). At the same time: Lexical bundles in L1 and L2 university student argumentative writing. *Journal of English for Academic Purposes, 30*, 38–52. doi:10.1016/j.jeap.2017.10.008

Campbell, L. (2001). The history of linguistics. In M. Aronoff & J. Rees-Miller (Eds.), *The Handbook of Linguistics* (pp. 81–104). Blackwell Publishers.

Carmi, E., Yates, S. J., Lockley, E., & Pawluczuk, A. (2020). Data citizenship: Rethinking data literacy in the age of disinformation, misinformation, and malinformation. *Internet Policy Review, 9*(2). Retrieved from https://policyreview.info/articles/analysis/data-citizenship-rethinking-data-literacy-age-disinformation-misinformation-and

Chambers, J. M. (2020). S, R, and data science. *Proceedings of the ACM on Programming Languages, 4*(HOPL), 1–17. doi:10.1145/3386334

Chan, S. (2014). *Routledge encyclopedia of translation technology*. Routledge.

Conway, D. (2010, September). The data science Venn diagram. *drewconway.com*. Retrieved from http://drewconway.com/zia/2013/3/26/the-data-science-venn-diagram

Conway, L. G., Gornick, L. J., Burfeind, C., Mandella, P., Kuenzli, A., Houck, S. C., & Fullerton, D. T. (2012). Does complex or simple rhetoric win elections? An integrative complexity analysis of U.S. Presidential campaigns. *Political Psychology, 33*(5), 599–618. doi:10.1111/j.1467-9221.2012.00910.x

Cross, N. (2006). Design as a discipline. *Designerly Ways of Knowing*, 95–103.

Csárdi, G., Nepusz, T., Traag, V., Horvát, S., Zanini, F., Noom, D., & Müller, K. (2024). *igraph: Network analysis and visualization*. Retrieved from https://r.igraph.org/

Data never sleeps 7.0. (2019). *Data Never Sleeps 7.0*. Infographic. Retrieved from https://www.domo.com/learn/infographic/data-never-sleeps-7

de Marneffe, M.-C., Manning, C. D., Nivre, J., & Zeman, D. (2021). Universal dependencies. *Computational Linguistics, 47*(2), 255–308. doi:10.1162/coli_a_00402

Deshors, S. C., & Gries, S. Th. (2016). Profiling verb complementation constructions across new Englishes. *International Journal of Corpus Linguistics., 21*(2), 192–218.

Desjardins, J. (2019, April). How much data is generated each day? *Visual Capitalist*. Retrieved from https://www.visualcapitalist.com/how-much-data-is-generated-each-day/

Donoho, D. (2017). 50 years of data science. *Journal of Computational and Graphical Statistics, 26*(4), 745–766. doi:10.1080/10618600.2017.1384734

Du Bois, J. W., Chafe, W. L., Meyer, C., Thompson, S. A., Englebretson, R., & Martey, N. (2005). Santa Barbara Corpus of Spoken American English, parts 1-4. Philadelphia: Linguistic Data Consortium. Retrieved from https://www.linguistics.ucsb.edu/research/santa-barbara-corpus

Dubnjakovic, A., & Tomlin, P. (2010). *A practical guide to electronic resources in the humanities*. Elsevier.

Duran, P. (2004). Developmental trends in lexical diversity. *Applied Linguistics, 25*(2), 220–242. doi:10.1093/applin/25.2.220

Eisenstein, J., O'Connor, B., Smith, N. A., & Xing, E. P. (2012). Mapping the geographical diffusion of new words. *Computation and Language*, 1–13. doi:10.1371/journal.pone.0113114

Firth, J. R. (1957). *Papers in linguistics*. Oxford University Press.

Francom, J. (2022). Corpus studies of syntax. In G. Goodall (Ed.), *The Cambridge Handbook of Experimental Syntax* (pp. 687–713). Cambridge University Press.

Francom, J. (2024). *qtkit: Quantitative text kit*. Retrieved from https://CRAN.R-project.org/package=qtkit

Gandrud, C. (2015). *Reproducible research with R and R studio* (second edition.). CRC Press.

Garg, N., Schiebinger, L., Jurafsky, D., & Zou, J. (2018). Word embeddings quantify 100 years of gender and ethnic stereotypes. *Proceedings of the National Academy of Sciences, 115*(16), E3635–E3644. doi:10.1073/pnas.1720347115

Gentleman, R., & Temple Lang, D. (2007). Statistical analyses and reproducible research. *Journal of Computational and Graphical Statistics, 16*(1), 1–23.

Gilquin, G., & Gries, S. Th. (2009). Corpora and experimental methods: A state-of-the-art review. *Corpus Linguistics and Linguistic Theory, 5*(1), 1–26. doi:10.1515/CLLT.2009.001

GitHub. (2024). GitHub. *Let's build from here*. Code Repository. Retrieved from https://github.com

Gomez-Uribe, C. A., & Hunt, N. (2015). The Netflix recommender system: Algorithms, business value, and innovation. *ACM Transactions on Management Information Systems (TMIS), 6*(4), 1–19.

Gries, S. Th. (2013). *Statistics for linguistics with R. A practical introduction* (2nd revise.).

Gries, S. Th. (2016). *Quantitative corpus linguistics with R: A practical introduction* (2nd ed.). New York: Routledge. doi:10.4324/9781315746210

Gries, S. Th. (2021). *Statistics for linguistics with R*. De Gruyter Mouton.

Gries, S. Th. (2023). New technologies and advances in statistical analysis in recent decades. In M. Díaz-Campos & S. Balasch (Eds.), *The Handbook of Usage-Based Linguistics* (first edition.). John Wiley & Sons Inc.

Gries, S. Th., & Deshors, S. C. (2014). Using regressions to explore deviations between corpus data and a standard/ target: Two suggestions. *Corpora, 9*(1), 109–136. doi:10.3366/cor.2014.0053

Gries, S. Th., & Paquot, M. (2020). Writing up a corpus-linguistic paper. In M. Paquot & S. Th. Gries (Eds.), *A Practical Handbook of Corpus Linguistics* (pp. 647–659). Springer International Publishing. doi:10.1007/978-3-030-46216-1_26

Grieve, J., Nini, A., & Guo, D. (2018). Mapping lexical innovation on American social media. *Journal of English Linguistics, 46*(4), 293–319.

Harris, Z. S. (1954). Distributional structure. *Word, 10*(2-3), 146–162. doi:10.1080/00437956.1954.11659520

Hay, J. (2002). From speech perception to morphology: Affix ordering revisited. *Language, 78*(3), 527–555.

Head, M. L., Holman, L., Lanfear, R., Kahn, A. T., & Jennions, M. D. (2015). The extent and consequences of p-hacking in science. *PLoS Biology, 13*(3), e1002106. doi:10.1371/journal.pbio.1002106

Hester, J., Wickham, H., & Csárdi, G. (2024). *fs: Cross-platform file system operations based on libuv*. Retrieved from https://fs.r-lib.org

Hicks, S. C., & Peng, R. D. (2019). Elements and principles for characterizing variation between data analyses. *arXiv*. doi:10.48550/arXiv.1903.07639

Hvitfeldt, E. (2023). *textrecipes: Extra recipes for text processing*. Retrieved from https://github.com/tidymodels/textrecipes

Ide, N., Baker, C., Fellbaum, C., Fillmore, C., & Passonneau, R. (2008). MASC: The Manually Annotated Sub-Corpus of American English. In *Sixth International Conference on Language Resources and Evaluation, LREC 2008* (pp. 2455–2460). European Language Resources Association (ELRA).

Ide, N., & Macleod, C. (2001). The American National Corpus: A standardized resource for American English. In *Proceedings of Corpus Linguistics*. Lancaster, UK.

Ignatow, G., & Mihalcea, R. (2017). *An introduction to text mining: Research design, data collection, and analysis*. Sage Publications.

Jaeger, T. F., & Snider, N. (2007). Implicit learning and syntactic persistence: Surprisal and cumulativity. *University of Rochester Working Papers in the Language Sciences, 3*(1).

Johnson, K. (2008). *Quantitative methods in linguistics*. Blackwell Pub.

Kato, A., Ichinose, S., & Kudo, T. (2024). *gibasa: An alternative Rcpp wrapper of MeCab*. Retrieved from https://CRAN.R-project.org/package=gibasa

Kerr, N. L. (1998). HARKing: Hypothesizing after the results are known. *Personality and social psychology review*, 2(3), 196–217.

Kloumann, I., Danforth, C., Harris, K., & Bliss, C. (2012). Positivity of the English language. *PLoS ONE*. doi:10.1371/journal.pone.0029484

Koehn, P. (2005). Europarl: A parallel corpus for statistical machine translation. *MT Summit X*, 12–16.

Kostić, A., Marković, T., & Baucal, A. (2003). Inflectional morphology and word meaning: Orthogonal or co-implicative cognitive domains? In R. H. Baayen & R. Schreuder (Eds.), *Morphological Structure in Language Processing* (pp. 1–44). De Gruyter Mouton. doi:10.1515/9783110910186.1

Kowalski, J., & Cavanaugh, R. (2024). *TBDBr: Easy access to TalkBankDB via R API*. Retrieved from https://github.com/TalkBank/TalkBankDB-R

Krathwohl, D. R. (2002). A revision of Bloom's Taxonomy: An overview. *Theory into Practice*, *41*(4), 212–218.

Kross, S., Carchedi, N., Bauer, B., & Grdina, G. (2020). *swirl: Learn R, in R*. Retrieved from https://CRAN.R-project.org/package=swirl

Kucera, H., & Francis, W. N. (1967). *Computational analysis of present day American English*. Brown University Press Providence.

Landau, W. M. (2021). The targets R package: A dynamic make-like function-oriented pipeline toolkit for reproducibility and high-performance computing. *Journal of Open Source Software*, *6*(57), 2959. doi:10.21105/joss.02959

Larsson, T., & Biber, D. (2024). On the perils of linguistically opaque measures and methods: Toward increased transparency and linguistic interpretability. In P. Crosthwaite (Ed.), *Corpora for language learning: Bridging the research-practice divide* (pp. 131–141). Taylor & Francis.

Leech, G. (1992). 100 million words of English: The British National Corpus (BNC), (1991), 1–13.

Lewis, M. (2004). *Moneyball: The art of winning an unfair game*. WW Norton & Company.

Liu, K., & Afzaal, M. (2021). Syntactic complexity in translated and non-translated texts: A corpus-based study of simplification. *PLoS ONE*, *16*(6), e0253454. doi:10.1371/journal.pone.0253454

Lozano, C. (2022). CEDEL2: Design, compilation and web interface of an online corpus for L2 Spanish acquisition research. *Second Language Research*, *38*(4), 965–983. doi:10.1177/02676583211050522

Macwhinney, B. (2024). TalkBank. *The TalkBank system*. Repository. Retrieved from https://talkbank.org/

Manning, C. (2003). Probabilistic syntax. In Bod, J. Hay, & Jannedy (Eds.), *Probabilistic Linguistics* (pp. 289–341). Cambridge, MA: MIT Press.

Marwick, B., Boettiger, C., & Mullen, L. (2018). Packaging data analytical work reproducibly using R (and friends). *The American Statistician*, *72*(1), 80–88.

Microsoft. (2024). Visual Studio Code. *Code Editing. Redefined.* Software. Retrieved from https://code.visualstudio.com/

Mikolov, T., Sutskever, I., Chen, K., Corrado, G., & Dean, J. (2013). Distributed representations of words and phrases and their compositionality. In *Advances in neural information processing systems* (pp. 3111–3119).

Moroz, G. (2017). *lingtypology: Easy mapping for linguistic typology*. Retrieved from https://CRAN.R-project.org/package=lingtypology

Morris, T. P., White, I. R., & Crowther, M. J. (2019). Using simulation studies to evaluate statistical methods. *Statistics in Medicine*, *38*(11), 2074–2102. doi:10.1002/sim.8086

Mosteller, F., & Wallace, D. L. (1963). Inference in an authorship problem. *Journal of the American Statistical Association*, *58*(302), 275–309. Retrieved from https://www.jstor.org/stable/2283270

Mullen, L. (2022). *tokenizers: Fast, consistent tokenization of natural language text*. Retrieved from https://docs.ropensci.org/tokenizers/

Muñoz, C. (Ed.). (2006). *Age and the rate of foreign language learning* (1st ed., Vol. 19). Clevedon: Multilingual Matters.

Nisioi, S., Rabinovich, E., Dinu, L. P., & Wintner, S. (2016). A corpus of native, non-native and translated texts. In *Proceedings of the tenth international conference on language resources and evaluation (LREC 2016)*. Portorož, Slovenia: European Language Resources Association (ELRA).

Nivre, J., De Marneffe, M.-C., Ginter, F., Hajič, J., Manning, C. D., Pyysalo, S., … Zeman, D. (2020). Universal dependencies v2: An evergrowing multilingual treebank collection. *arXiv arXiv:2004.10643*. Retrieved from https://arxiv.org/abs/2004.10643

Olohan, M. (2008). Leave it out! Using a comparable corpus to investigate aspects of explicitation in translation. *Cadernos de Tradução*, 153–169.

Ooms, J. (2023). *jsonlite: A simple and robust JSON parser and generator for R*. Retrieved from https://jeroen.r-universe.dev/jsonlite

Paquot, M., & Gries, S. Th. (Eds.). (2020). *A practical handbook of corpus linguistics*. Switzerland: Springer.

Pedersen, T. L. (2024). *ggraph: An implementation of grammar of graphics for graphs and networks*. Retrieved from https://ggraph.data-imaginist.com

Petrenz, P., & Webber, B. (2011). Stable classification of text genres. *Computational Linguistics*, *37*(2), 385–393. doi:10.1162/COLI_a_00052

Posit. (2024). RStudio. *RStudio*. Software. Retrieved from https://posit.co

R Community. (2024). The comprehensive R archive network. *The Comprehensive R Archive Network*. Repository. Retrieved from https://cran.r-project.org/

R Special Interest Group on Databases (R-SIG-DB), Wickham, H., & Müller, K. (2024). *DBI: R database interface*. Retrieved from https://dbi.r-dbi.org

Riehemann, S. Z. (2001). *A constructional approach to idioms and word formation* (PhD thesis). Stanford.

Rinker, T. (2019). *lexicon: Lexicons for text analysis*. Retrieved from https://github.com/trinker/lexicon

Robinson, D., & Silge, J. (2024). *tidytext: Text mining using dplyr, ggplot2, and other tidy tools*. Retrieved from https://juliasilge.github.io/tidytext/

ROpenSci. (2024). The R-Universe System. *The R-Universe System*. Repository. Retrieved from https://ropensci.org/r-universe/

Rossman, A. J., & Chance, B. L. (2014). Using simulation-based inference for learning introductory statistics. *WIREs Computational Statistics*, *6*(4), 211–221. doi:10.1002/wics.1302

Rowley, J. (2007). The wisdom hierarchy: Representations of the DIKW hierarchy. *Journal of Information Science*, *33*(2), 163–180. doi:10.1177/0165551506070706

Saxena, S., & Gyanchandani, M. (2020). Machine learning methods for computer-aided breast cancer diagnosis using histopathology: A narrative review. *Journal of medical imaging and radiation sciences*, *51*(1), 182–193.

Sedgwick, P. (2015). Units of sampling, observation, and analysis. *BMJ (online)*, *351*, h5396. doi:10.1136/bmj.h5396

Serigos, J. (2020). Using automated methods to explore the social stratification of anglicisms in Spanish. *Corpus Linguistics and Linguistic Theory*, *0*(0), 000010151520190052. doi:10.1515/cllt-2019-0052

Shriberg, E. E. (1994). *Preliminaries to a theory of speech disfluencies* (PhD thesis). University of California at Berkeley.

Silge, J. (2022). *janeaustenr: Jane Austen's complete novels*. Retrieved from https://github.com/juliasilge/janeaustenr

Silveira, N., Dozat, T., de Marneffe, M.-C., Bowman, S., Connor, M., Bauer, J., & Manning, C. D. (2014). A gold standard dependency corpus for English. In *Proceedings of the ninth international conference on language resources and evaluation (LREC-2014)*.

Sternberg, R. J., & Sternberg, K. (2010). *The psychologist's companion: A guide to writing scientific papers for students and researchers* (5th ed.). Cambridge University Press. doi:10.1017/CBO9780511762024

Szmrecsanyi, B. (2004). On operationalizing syntactic complexity. In *Le poids des mots. Proceedings of the seventh international conference on textual data statistical analysis. Louvain-la-Neuve* (Vol. 2, pp. 1032–1039).

The R Foundation. (2024). The R project for statistical computing. *R: The R Project for Statistical Computing*. Software. Retrieved from https://www.r-project.org/

Tottie, G. (2011). Uh and um as sociolinguistic markers in British English. *International Journal of Corpus Linguistics*, *16*(2), 173–197.

Tottie, G. (2014). On the use of uh and um in American English. *Functions of Language*, *21*(1), 6–29. doi:10.1075/fol.21.1.02tot

University of Colorado Boulder. (2008). Switchboard Dialog Act Corpus. Web download. Linguistic Data Consortium. Retrieved from https://catalog.ldc.upenn.edu/docs/LDC97S62/

Uryu, S. (2024). *washoku: Extra 'recipes' for Japanese text, date and address processing*. Retrieved from https://github.com/uribo/washoku

Ushey, K., & Wickham, H. (2024). *renv: Project environments*. Retrieved from https://rstudio.github.io/renv/

Voigt, R., Camp, N. P., Prabhakaran, V., Hamilton, W. L., Hetey, R. C., Griffiths, C. M., … Eberhardt, J. L. (2017). Language from police body camera footage shows racial disparities in officer respect. *Proceedings of the National Academy of Sciences, 114*(25), 6521–6526.

Waring, E., Quinn, M., McNamara, A., Arino de la Rubia, E., Zhu, H., & Ellis, S. (2022). *skimr: Compact and flexible summaries of data*. Retrieved from https://docs.ropensci.org/skimr/

Welbers, K., & van Atteveldt, W. (2022). *rsyntax: Extract semantic relations from text by querying and reshaping syntax*. Retrieved from https://CRAN.R-project.org/package=rsyntax

Wenfeng, Q., & Yanyi, W. (2019). *jiebaR: Chinese text segmentation*. Retrieved from https://CRAN.R-project.org/package=jiebaR

White, J. M. (2023). *ProjectTemplate: Automates the creation of new statistical analysis projects*. Retrieved from https://CRAN.R-project.org/package=ProjectTemplate

Wickham, H. (2014a). *Advanced R*. CRC Press.

Wickham, H. (2014b). Tidy data. *Journal of Statistical Software, 59*(10). doi:10.18637/jss.v059.i10

Wickham, H. (2023a). *forcats: Tools for working with categorical variables (factors)*. Retrieved from https://forcats.tidyverse.org/

Wickham, H. (2023b). *stringr: Simple, consistent wrappers for common string operations*. Retrieved from https://stringr.tidyverse.org

Wickham, H. (2023c). *tidyverse: Easily install and load the Tidyverse*. Retrieved from https://tidyverse.tidyverse.org

Wickham, H. (2024). *rvest: Easily harvest (scrape) web pages*. Retrieved from https://rvest.tidyverse.org/

Wickham, H., & Bryan, J. (2023). *R packages: Organize, test, document, and share your code* (second edition.). Beijing: O'Reilly.

Wickham, H., Chang, W., Henry, L., Pedersen, T. L., Takahashi, K., Wilke, C., … van den Brand, T. (2024). *ggplot2: Create elegant data visualisations using the grammar of graphics*. Retrieved from https://ggplot2.tidyverse.org

Wickham, H., François, R., Henry, L., Müller, K., & Vaughan, D. (2023). *dplyr: A grammar of data manipulation*. Retrieved from https://dplyr.tidyverse.org

Wickham, H., Girlich, M., & Ruiz, E. (2024). *dbplyr: A dplyr back end for databases*. Retrieved from https://dbplyr.tidyverse.org/

Wickham, H., & Grolemund, G. (2017). *R for data science* (First edit.). O'Reilly Media. Retrieved from http://r4ds.had.co.nz/

Wickham, H., & Henry, L. (2023). *purrr: Functional programming tools*. Retrieved from https://purrr.tidyverse.org/

Wickham, H., Hester, J., & Bryan, J. (2024). *readr: Read rectangular text data*. Retrieved from https://readr.tidyverse.org

Wickham, H., Miller, E., & Smith, D. (2023). *haven: Import and export SPSS, Stata and SAS files*. Retrieved from https://haven.tidyverse.org

Wickham, H., Vaughan, D., & Girlich, M. (2024). *tidyr: Tidy messy data*. Retrieved from https://tidyr.tidyverse.org

Wijffels, J. (2023). *udpipe: Tokenization, parts of speech tagging, lemmatization and dependency parsing with the UDPipe 'NLP' toolkit*. Retrieved from https://bnosac.github.io/udpipe/en/index.html

Wijffels, J., & Watanabe, K. (2023). *word2vec: Distributed representations of words*. Retrieved from https://github.com/bnosac/word2vec

Wilson, G., Bryan, J., Cranston, K., Kitzes, J., Nederbragt, L., & Teal, T. K. (2017). Good enough practices in scientific computing. *PLoS Computational Biology, 13*(6), 1–20. doi:10.1371/journal.pcbi.1005510

Wulff, S., Stefanowitsch, A., & Gries, S. Th. (2007). Brutal Brits and persuasive Americans. *Aspects of Meaning*.

Xie, Y. (2024). *tinytex: Helper functions to install and maintain TeX Live, and compile LaTeX documents*. Retrieved from https://github.com/rstudio/tinytex

Zipf, G. K. (1949). *Human behavior and the principle of least effort*. Oxford, England: Addison-Wesley Press.

Index

D

G

H

I

J

K

L

M

N

V

W

Y

Z